"And He has made from one blood every nation of men to dwell on all the face of the earth, and has determined their preappointed times and the boundaries of their habitation, so that they should seek the Lord." Acts 17:26–27

▶ Special Thanks to:

- Kathy Follette, Grace Balloch Memorial Library, who never said, "Impossible";

- Melissa Schneider of Rainbow Resources, for her diligent work of searching out the best in-print titles for this book;

- Paul Hawkins, international educator with Youth With A Mission, for his wise advice and counsel in issues of Biblical education;

- Janet Blomberg, interim international director of Asia Education Resource Consortium, for her kind encouragement and helpful suggestions;

- Rosalie Pedder, late friend, mentor, and international teacher in the areas of learning issues, for her invaluable ministry and encouragement;

- Ruth Beechick, author of numerous books, for her encouraging comments about the original version of this curriculum, and for her ongoing work;

- Rod White Eagle Wilson, Doctor of Divinity and international educator with Youth With A Mission, for his thoughtful Scriptural insights;

- my children, Isaac, Michael, and Melody, for all of their insight, input, and support;

- my beloved husband, Bill, without whom this would be literally impossible.

▶ TABLE OF CONTENTS

Introduction

▶ Welcome…

You are about to embark on a journey. For some of you, it is a continuation of what you began in *Ancient Civilizations & The Bible*. For others, it is a brand new journey, beginning with the birth of the Church during the early years of the Roman Empire. Regardless of where you personally start this journey, you will have the amazing, arm-chair opportunity to explore and discover panoramic events, interview some of the most fascinating people, and soar to the highest heights with God's perspective. As you are introduced to Medieval and Early Modern history from a biblical view—the time when Christianity begins to permeate the world—you will be given the opportunity in each chronological period to probe the aspects that you find interesting; to discover, through a variety of hands-on activities, the connecting points between those historic time periods and your own; and to present your understanding, not through a test, but through the creative expression you find most appropriate.

This book was constructed with two objectives in mind:

1. to discover history from a biblical worldview;

2. to explore history through a curriculum that honors your God-given design.

What does it mean, "to discover history from a biblical worldview"?

» Noah Webster's 1828 dictionary defines history: "An account of facts respecting nations or states; a narrative of events in the order in which they happened with their causes and effects."

» James W. Sire, author of *The Universe Next Door*, defines *worldview*: "A set of presuppositions which we hold about the basic makeup of our world." This includes such questions as:

- What is the nature of God and the universe?

- Where did I come from?

- What value do I possess?

- What is the meaning of human history?

We will attempt to discover the biblical framework undergirding the chronological flow of people and events, so that we can understand *what* happened and *why* it happened. Once we have this insight, we can move from head knowledge to heart knowledge, from *academics* to *application*.

This might sound overwhelming, stuffy, or boring to you. And it would be, if not for the second objective, "to explore history through a curriculum that honors your God-given design."

What does it mean "to explore history through a curriculum that honors your God-given design"?

» First, for *explore*: "to travel to a place that is not well known to find out more about it."

» For *honor,* The Oxford American Dictionary says: "great respect, high public regard."

» And for your *God-given design* we are referring to the way you were intricately formed by your Creator, and includes the ways you most *enjoy* and *retain* learning.

The way this curriculum has been formatted will open the doors for you to pursue your own explorations into regions of history that look interesting, so you can see why things are the way they are. And then, because we have great respect for the fact that you are created in the image and likeness of God, and are *uniquely designed* by Him, we offer you the choice of how to express what you are learning. Options include a chance to sing, dance, cook, sketch, write, act, map, read, discuss, move, design . . . to interact with what you are learning and to express it in the way that best fits who you are and how God made you.

Putting an emphasis on "you" and focusing on learning activities tuned to the way you are designed is not to employ the recent "you/my" trend in marketing. In fact, we are very aware that self-centeredness is not a reflection of our Creator, nor honoring to Him; we have no desire to impart that to you through this curriculum. It is, instead, our concern that you excel; that you be enabled to learn thoroughly and deeply; and most of all, that your faith be increased as God reveals to you His faithfulness throughout history. This causes us to design opportunities for you to learn in the way you are most responsive, rather than in a one-size-fits-all approach.

Ravi Zacharias, an internationally renowned Christian apologist, said in an interview in the *Washington Times*, "The first thing Christianity does is raise the level of every individual. There's an essential dignity. Every human being is of essential worth." We believe this. Therefore, we have labored to create a history curriculum, which allows you the dignity of learning the wonders of HisStory in your own way.

Diana Waring
September, 2007

▶ Structural Overview

The Course of Study

The Scope

- » Unit One: The Rise of the Church & the Fall of Rome
- » Unit Two: Missionaries & Barbarians
- » Unit Three: The Byzantines & the Muslims
- » Unit Four: The Holy Roman Empire & the Vikings
- » Unit Five: The Crusades & the Mongols
- » Unit Six: Seeds of Reformation & the Late Middle Ages
- » Unit Seven: The Renaissance & the Reformation
- » Unit Eight: Puritans, Pietists, & the Divine Right of Kings
- » Unit Nine: Revivals & Revolutions

The Structure of Each Unit

The Structure

WEEK ONE: INTRODUCTION
- » Discuss the Key Concepts
- » Read the Unit article
- » Listen to the appropriate audio recordings
- » Consider and discuss opinions
- » Choose interesting books or Internet search

WEEK TWO: EXPLORATION & DISCOVERY
- » Research a topic of your choice
- » Learn the Words to Watch
- » Construct the timeline
- » Report findings on your research

WEEK THREE: HANDS-ON
- » Geography mapping
- » View art & architecture
- » Design art projects
- » Conduct science experiments
- » Music suggestions
- » Cook the recipe

WEEK FOUR: EXPRESSION
- » Linguistics: journalism, prose, poetry, playing with words
- » Art: painting/drawing, graphic design, sculpting, cartooning
- » Music: compose, practice performance
- » Drama: comedy, tragedy, reality, reader's theater, puppetry
- » Movement: pantomime, dance, action
- » Conceptual design

The Foundation Beneath the Structure

There are three foundational building blocks undergirding this curriculum—three approaches to learning, which help explain some of the differences in the ways people learn:

> » Four Learning Styles

> » Three Learning Modalities

> » Eight Intelligences

Four Learning Styles

Learning Styles refers to the categorization of how a particular personality style best learns. The method we refer to was developed by Myers-Briggs. Here is a brief description of each of the four learning styles:

These three foundational building blocks are integrally woven into the curriculum—they are already written into the lessons for you. This means that you do not have to figure out which learning style, modality, or intelligences you have, you can simply learn in the way that is most interesting and enjoyable to you.

THE FEELER	THE INTUITOR
This is the "people person" learning style. A Feeler wants to know the people perspective, i.e. how this subject affects people; how does this impact our lives now; who were the people of history, as opposed to the events or things. These learners need to be in good relationship with the people around them—their teacher, siblings, friends, etc. They love to be with other people in one-on-one conversations and in group activities, especially when they are part of a "team effort."	"Wait! I have an idea!" The Intuitor is the one brimming over with ideas about how this might have happened, or about how you might put on a play for the whole city portraying an historic event, or about what it must have been like to live in ancient times, and on and on. This learner is very good at coming up with suggestions, but is not as strong at seeing things through to completion. The Intuitor needs a lot of flexibility in schedule, and a "safe haven" for suggesting and trying out ideas.
THE THINKER	**THE SENSOR**
"Give me the facts, ma'am, just the facts." The Thinker has a black & white approach to knowledge, wanting authoritative input, not just someone's opinions. This learner truly enjoys using textbooks, encyclopedias, charts, and diagrams. There is a need to know exactly what the rules are in the class, when assignments or projects are due, what is required for good grades. Thinkers are organized and expect organization.	The "hands-on," get-it-done-now person. The Sensor is the one who can make projects happen—taking them beyond the blueprint stage and into production. This learner does NOT enjoy sitting for long periods of time, looking through books for information, or discussing things for hours on end. Instead, the Sensor prefers to be involved with things that can be efficiently accomplished with physical effort.

Three Learning Modalities

Learning Modalities refers to the approach learners use to take in new information—how they best concentrate, process, and retain. Here is a brief description of each of the three modalities:

VISUAL	AUDITORY	TACTILE/KINESTHETIC
learn best by seeing, whether through reading, looking at pictures, watching a documentary, observing.	learn best by hearing, whether through audio recordings, conversations, lectures, or reading out loud.	learn best by touching objects or moving, whether through hands-on projects or physical action, such as jumping, running, dancing, even wiggling.

Eight Intelligences

Eight Intelligences refers to natural potential and areas of talent. Howard Gardner of Harvard University theorized that intelligence is made up of more than verbal and mathematical skills, and that people can strengthen their natural giftings and improve their weaknesses. Here is a brief description of each of the eight intelligences:

INTRAPERSONAL	NATURALIST
This could be described as Self-Smart. It is the ability to enjoy being alone, working independently, and relying on self-motivation. This person needs solitary time in order to think.	This could be described as Nature Smart. It is the ability to observe, investigate, experiment, and discover the natural world, including weather, animals, plants, and geologic structures. This person needs to go outside!
BODILY-KINESTHETIC	**SPATIAL**
This could be described as Body Smart. It is the ability to use one's body through touch and movement to accomplish what is desired. It includes being able to process knowledge through bodily movement or through sensation, enjoying physical activity, and being constantly in motion even while sitting down. This person needs to move!	This could be described as Picture Smart. It is the ability to see in pictures rather than words, and includes drawing and design, three-dimensional constructing (such as LEGO® bricks), and other visual arts, such as photography, sculpting, and painting. This person needs pictures, maps, diagrams, charts, photos, and other visual/spatial material.
MUSICAL	**INTERPERSONAL**
This could be described as Music Smart. It is the ability to learn through rhythm and melody, sing or play musical instruments, enjoy listening to music, remember songs, and study more effectively when music is played. This person needs music, whether it is music lessons or musical recordings.	This could be described as People Smart. It is the ability to understand and enjoy people. A person who is interpersonal learns best when other people are involved, whether through games, team work, or cooperative learning sessions. This person needs people.

MATH/LOGICAL	LINGUISTIC
This could be described as Number Smart. It is the ability to reason mathematically, discover abstract patterns, classify and organize, enjoy mathematical computations, and think logically. This person needs to see the logic and organization in what is being learned.	This could be described as Word Smart. It is the ability to enjoy and use language through word games, books, recordings, trivia, poetry, papers, discussion, and other forms of using words. This person needs words in order to communicate.

▶ New Research on How People Learn

Traditionally, academic subjects have been taught in this manner: 1. Lecture (delivered by the expert) 2. Study (student studies textbook and memorizes material for test) 3. Test (True/False,Multiple Choice, Essay) 4. Grade (largely based on how well student regurgitated memorized facts)	Research on the brain and how people best learn has provided a new scenario: 1. Listen (read something new, hear something new, discuss something new) 2. Explore (ask your own questions and then search for answers) 3. Discover (find the answers to your questions, the "Aha!" moment) 4. Practice (interact with what you are learning through various, interesting activities) 5. Use (able to teach others, use it on a regular basis, mastery)

The emphasis has changed from the teacher being the provider of the necessary information, which the student memorizes, to the student being exposed to new information, and then actively engaging it. This shift, which we have incorporated into the curriculum, has profound implications for you: you are now an active participant in the sport of learning. Instead of passively taking in what a teacher or textbook tells you, you will have the opportunity to question, discuss, do teamwork projects, etc. What you actively put into this will be what you get out of it. There are few assignments to simply memorize, but there are many opportunities to actively participate in learning. This means getting a good grade (for students in settings that give grades) is no longer a matter of memorizing material for a test.

You will be evaluated on how actively you participate:

» in class discussions,

» in exploration activities,

» in reporting your discoveries,

» in hands-on activities,

» in creative expressions.

The Difference Between Passive & Active Learning

You can choose to go passive:	or	You can choose to go active:
• do as little as possible • avoid participating in discussions • halfheartedly work on projects		• find what interests you and do it • share with others in discussion times and in other appropriate moments • give your best effort at the projects you choose
Result: • hate history • resist learning • not comprehend history or your place in it		**Result:** • meaningful learning • greater comprehension & retention • vastly more interesting!

Enjoy

"The works of the Lord are great, studied by all who have pleasure in them." Psalm 111:2

Did you know that it is biblical to enjoy learning? In fact, we were meant to actually find pleasure in studying the amazing things God has done!

The good news is that learning improves when it is enjoyable. Your brain actually imprints and retrieves new information better when you enjoy what you are learning. This means that not only is it permissible to enjoy what you are doing, enjoyment is a critical part of learning.

In this curriculum we have brought together several disciplines, including science, fine arts, writing, speaking, even cooking, to help you enjoy the process of learning history. You have the option of creating your own project (even beyond the ones suggested in the curriculum) so that you can find what will give you joy as you do the work.

Interaction and discussion, with other students, teachers, family members, etc., are vital parts of this curriculum, because they will help you better sharpen your own ideas and expand your horizons as you hear others' ideas. Interaction is often the most enjoyable part of learning, as well.

Choose

History courses are most often sets of names, dates, and places to be memorized. Success in the course, then, is directly related to how proficiently you are able to recall these names, dates, and places.

However, history is far richer, far deeper, far more extensive than that. You can learn about a moment in time by studying a specific person, or the type of weaponry used in battle, or the form of government, or the kind of artwork, or the scientific developments, or the method of recording information, or the architectural style, or the means of transportation. And, beyond these few studies, there are thousands more.

We believe that what you personally find interesting will be what you will enjoy studying. Since history incorporates all subject areas and all time periods, you ought to be able to find something interesting! So, we give you a choice. If you can choose something that you find fascinating, you will work harder, learn more, and retain it longer than if you are compelled to simply memorize names, dates, and places. Therefore, your success in this course will be directly related to your actively choosing and pursuing what interests you.

At Your Own Level

The object is to learn, to enjoy learning, and to understand what you are learning. Therefore, use the materials that you find interesting and accessible. It will not greatly contribute to your success if you try to read materials that are beyond your grasp, or are boring in the extreme.

I suggest looking for as many books as possible on the people or events you find interesting, and as many appropriate web sites as possible, then choose which ones will work the best for you. I have often found that children's books on history are more concise, more story-filled, and more memorable than ponderous tomes written for adults (though I have read my share of these, as well). So, if you find a fantastic book on King Cyrus of Persia, for instance, but you recognize it was obviously written for a much younger (OR much older) reader than yourself, don't worry about what other people will think! Read the book.

Academics to Application

Though it is impressive to know a lot of facts about history, it might change your life to learn from history. What we are learning will reflect in our actions:

"Knowledge puffs up, but love edifies." 1 Corinthians 8:1

As you learn more about God and His ways in history; as you discover time and time again that He seeks the restoration of relationship; and as you see that our relationship with Him changes our relationship with others, I pray that you will grow in love that edifies.

Personal Evaluation

Just as you are making choices about what you study, what projects you do, and what creative expressions you use to convey what you have learned—in other words, becoming an active learner— you need to evaluate yourself. Are you learning anything about history? Are you exerting yourself in your projects? Are you seeking to do your best on the creative expressions?

These personal evaluative questions will help you stay on track as an active learner. If you ask yourself, "Am I learning anything in this unit?" and the answer is, "No," then you need to figure out why not. One suggestion is to ask your parents and teachers for ideas, since they are as concerned about your success as you are (if not more so.)

If you ask yourself, "Am I exerting myself?" and the answer is "No," then discover what is wrong. Did you choose a project that you are not really interested in, or one that is too hard? Then perhaps you should change to a different project that is more promising. Are you tired? Then consider doing a project with a friend, as it helps to share the load.

If you ask yourself, "Am I doing my best?" and the answer is, "No," then it is time to consider what your goals are for this course. If it is to just put in the time required to get a grade and move on, then you are cheating yourself of a rich opportunity to discover what you love doing best. You may find that you love sculpting, or pantomime, or writing, or journalism, or designing . . . but if you never really try, you will probably never know. Be honest with yourself. After all, this is your education and your life. If you don't like what you see, seek to change something. If you do like what you are doing and what you are learning, be sure to tell someone, especially your teacher. Enthusiasm begets enthusiasm, and you might end up finding out things you didn't know about things you never knew.

The Rise of the Church & the Fall of Rome

Saint Peter's Basilica, Vatican City

Key Concepts

- The gospel to the Jews & Gentiles

- The Roman emperors

- The growth of the persecuted Church

- Dividing & defending the Empire

- Reasons for the fall of Rome

The gospel to the Jews and Gentiles . . .

In the distant Roman province of Judea, the Roman procurator authorized the execution of a man whom local rulers had accused of treason, saying that He called Himself "King"—against the authority of the Emperor, Tiberius Caesar. Rebellions in the Roman Empire were swiftly put down, as indeed they needed to be, if the far-flung empire was to function as the controlling government. Thus, the execution of one man was, to the Romans, both the accepted fate of a rebel and far more efficient than the destruction of an entire nation—which might have been necessary had He not been silenced.

It caused no stir in the center of the empire—at least, not in the very beginning. The small band of disciples in Judea was a mere drop of water in the vast Roman ocean, and they were now leaderless. All their hopes for a restored and mighty Kingdom of Israel were as ashes; all their courage had fled with the arrival of the mob. They had believed Jesus was the Messiah, the long-awaited One who would right all wrongs. To their horror, He had been killed—mocked by the crowd and crucified as a common criminal. It was hardly the future they had envisioned while following Him down the dusty road toward Jerusalem. All that remained for them was to wearily and mournfully go back to their old lives.

If we could step back into that moment, not knowing anything of the next two thousand years, we would be as bereft as were the disciples. The might of Rome was in place to serve, not the needs of conquered people, but the interests of Rome, especially those of the emperor. Power, fame, and the accumulation of great wealth were as motivating to human beings of the Roman Empire as they are to people of today. People served various gods through assorted religious rituals, hoping that they might incur the favor of those gods and deflect their anger, much as people do today. Poverty, hunger, disease, and oppression were rampant among the majority of people, without any hope of change. Life was bleak. And for the few who had heard and believed Jesus, hope for something new had died with Him on the cross. Do you see it? Do you grasp the utter hopelessness and despair? It lasted for three agonizingly long days.

Suddenly, in a moment, an event rocked the cosmos. It turned the disciples' utter mourning into rejoicing and set their hearts on fire. The One who had been executed had broken the chains of death. He was *alive* again. But this life was altogether new and fresh. Jesus appeared, not as a mere revived human who would die again in a few years, but as the resurrected, glorified

The One that had been executed had broken the chains of death.

Messiah alive forevermore. What that means is beyond the rational comprehension of any of us, since it is not a common occurrence. In fact, it only happened once. For those who do not believe that the Resurrection occurred, it seems foolishness: an unverifiable, inconceivable, impossible-to-prove event. But for those disciples who not only saw the risen Jesus, but talked with Him, ate with Him, touched Him, and even observed Him walk into a room with locked doors, the reality of His Resurrection was incontestable.

Their lives, though, were not merely changed by seeing the risen Jesus. There was something even more earthshaking yet to come, something that would literally transform them into fearless, death-defying witnesses of their Messiah. Jesus had told them, in Acts 1:8, "You shall receive power when the Holy Spirit has come upon you; and you shall be witnesses to Me in Jerusalem, and in all Judea and Samaria, and to the end of the earth." So they obediently went back to Jerusalem, after His ascension into the heavens, and waited. What they were waiting for was, again, beyond their comprehension, because it had never happened before; but it had been prophesied. Several hundred years earlier, Joel had written: "And it shall come to pass afterward that I will pour out My Spirit on all flesh" (Joel 2:28).

And on the Day of Pentecost, that is exactly what happened. Suddenly, the words of Scripture came to life:

> I will give you a new heart and put a new spirit within you;
> I will take the heart of stone out of your flesh and
> give you a heart of flesh. I will put My Spirit within
> you and cause you to walk in My statutes, and
> you will keep My judgments and do them." Ezekiel
> 36:26–27

The power of God dwelling in human beings is not something to be taken lightly.

What did it look like when these first human beings were filled by the Spirit of God, when He took up residence within them? They began to speak of the wondrous works of God in joyous exuberance (it looked like drunkenness to scoffers), and residents of many nations miraculously understood them *in their own language.* And then, Peter—the very one who, just a short time earlier, had three times denied even knowing Jesus—powerfully explained to the gathered throng in the street what they were seeing and hearing. He finished his extemporary sermon with the words, "Therefore let all the house of Israel know assuredly that God has made this Jesus, whom you crucified, both Lord and Christ" (Acts 2:36). The writer of Acts tells us that the people, when they heard those words, were cut to the heart, and wanted to know what they should do. When Peter told them to repent, about three thousand people gladly did so.

That's earthshaking. The power of God dwelling in human beings is not something to be taken lightly. That is why Paul wrote:

> Or do you not know that your body is the temple of the Holy
> Spirit who is in you, whom you have from God, and you are
> not your own? For you were bought at a price; therefore glo-
> rify God in your body and in your spirit, which are God's. 1
> Corinthians 6:19–20

Now, when this amazing new era dawned—when God actually dwelt *in* His people—it caused a reaction. Some people gratefully received the good news and were transformed into new creatures in Christ, while others stormed violently against it. As persecution against the fledgling Church broke out in Jerusalem, many believers fled to other lands, taking their witness for Jesus to new places and people.

At this unique moment in time, all the lands bordering the Mediterranean Sea belonged to the same empire. It was the first and last time in history for such a political unity in the Mediterranean region, and it allowed unprecedented freedom to take the gospel throughout the world. Think about it: if a country closes its borders to foreigners, then it is very difficult for them to penetrate that country. But when all belong to the same unit—the same empire or federation—then travel throughout that unit is simplified considerably, especially when political peace is maintained by a formidable army.

And when you consider that most of the urban areas of the first century AD (hence the greatest population base during that time) were situated close to the Mediterranean, you realize that God's timing was, indeed, perfect.

Apostolic Age

> In a startlingly short time, Christianity could no longer be confined to the outlying Roman provinces but penetrated to the very heart of the Empire, to the city of Rome itself.

The first major church outside of Judea was located at Antioch, in the Roman province of Syria. It was comprised of both Jewish and Gentile believers, and was the first place where followers of Jesus were called *Christians* (or, "Christ-followers"). This was during the **Apostolic Age** of the early Church, the time period after Pentecost, when the disciples who had walked with Jesus were still alive. It lasted from c. AD 35–70 (though the Apostle John is believed to have lived until shortly after the end of Domitian's persecution of the Church).

It was from this church in Antioch that Paul and his co-laborers were sent out as missionaries to the world. And that world was much bigger than just Asia Minor and the nearby Middle East. On Paul's second missionary journey, he left these familiar areas and, in obedience to God's direction, took the gospel to Europe. In a startlingly short time, Christianity was no longer confined to the outlying Roman provinces but penetrated to the very heart of the Empire, to the city of Rome itself.

We know this because as early as AD 64, the Roman Emperor Nero was blaming the Christians of Rome for the huge fire that had left much of the city in ashes. The Roman historian Tacitus wrote:

> To kill the rumors [that he had started the fire] Nero charged and tortured some people hated for their evil practices—the group popularly known as Christians. The founder of this sect, Christ, had been put to death by the governor of Judea, Pontius Pilate, when Tiberius was emperor. Their deadly superstition had been suppressed temporarily, but was beginning to spring up again—not now just in Judea, but even in Rome itself, where all kinds of sordid and shameful activities are attracted and catch on. First, the authorities arrested those who confessed to being Christians. Then, on information obtained from them, the courts convicted hundreds more, not so much for starting the fire as for their antisocial beliefs. In their deaths they were made a mockery. They were covered in the skins of wild animals, torn to death by dogs, crucified, or set on fire, so that when darkness fell they burned like torches in the night. Nero opened up his own gardens for this spectacle and gave a show in the arena, where he mixed with the crowd, or stood dressed as a chari-

oteer on a chariot. As a result, although they were guilty of being Christians and deserved to die, people began to feel sorry for them. For they realized that they were being killed, not for the public good, but to satisfy one man's madness.

This was the first official persecution of Christians by the Roman government, and it was limited to the immediate vicinity of Rome. From some of the early Christian writings, this seems to have been the time when both Peter and Paul were executed by the Roman authorities for being Christians. We can tell from Tacitus's description of Nero's persecution that the message of Christianity was creating a strong response among the people who heard it, whether they embraced it or were repelled by it.

> *For they realized that they were being killed, not for the public good, but to satisfy one man's madness.*

The Roman Empire had been governed, up to this point, by one dynasty, from Augustus to Nero, known as the **Julio-Claudian Dynasty.** When Nero died in AD 68, civil war broke out when various soldiers proclaimed first one man, and then another, to be emperor. Stability was only regained when a man was chosen to rule who had the respect of everyone. Vespasian, the military commander sent by Nero to quell the Jewish Revolt in Judea, was proclaimed emperor in AD 69. In order to fulfill his responsibilities in Rome, Vespasian left his son to complete the job in Judea. Thus, it was under the command of Titus that Roman legions devastated Jerusalem, leveling the Temple itself, as Jesus had foretold in Matthew 24:2, "Assuredly, I say to you, not one stone shall be left here upon another, that shall not be thrown down." This first Jewish War against Rome ended in AD 74, with the destruction of the fortress of Masada.

Apostolic Fathers

This period, from the reign of the emperors Vespasian to Hadrian, corresponds in Church history to the **Age of the Apostolic Fathers** (from c. AD 70–140). This age is named for the first generation of Christian leaders whose writings inform us of the situation facing the Church after the apostles. It was a time for consolidating and preserving the teachings and traditions of those who had literally walked with Jesus. Ignatius of Antioch, Clement of Rome, and Polycarp of Smyrna are three of those named the Apostolic Fathers.

In Rome, Titus reigned as emperor for two years after the death of his father in AD 79. His younger brother, Domitian, the last of the **Flavian Dynasty,** then became emperor. Domitian, after several years as emperor, launched the second great persecution of the Church in the AD 90s. We need to ask, "Why?" since there was no great fire in Rome this time, and no need for Nero's scapegoat. The answer is found when we discover that Domitian had added the words, "Lord and God" to his official title. Think about what that means. This man who ruled an empire was no longer content with the honor, respect, and admiration his position held. It was not enough. So, he desired to gain for himself the type of worship that was reserved to gods, not mortals. And, because there were those more than willing to satisfy the ego of a megalomaniac, an imperial cult of emperor worship developed around him.

In an age of multiple temples devoted to numerous gods, in a time when each conquest of lands and people meant welcoming their religious systems to the other religions of the empire, bringing one more god to worship was not as heinous as it would be today. And, in fact, emperor worship was one means of instilling and verifying loyalty among a religiously and culturally diverse empire. For most people it wasn't a great difficulty, since it was common to offer worship to many gods, just to make sure one had all the bases covered in the spirit realm. It was an entirely different case, however, for Christians. They worshipped one God. Domitian didn't see it that way. In fact, he decreed that Christianity was *atheism.* And, because Christians refused to do their civic duty—offering incense as worship to Domitian—he persecuted them. Eventually, he himself was killed, assassinated by his own staff.

After the brief reign of an elderly politician, Nerva, the Roman Empire crowned one of its most renowned rulers, the Emperor Trajan. From AD 98 until AD 117, Trajan marshaled his legions to war, conquering Dacia (in modern day Romania), as well as Armenia and Mesopotamia. Although this far-eastern boundary began to collapse even before he died, Trajan had extended the Roman Empire to what would be its furthest region.

> It was a time for consolidating and preserving the teachings and traditions of those who had literally walked with Jesus.

He also made the first official government ruling concerning Christians and how to deal with them. When the governor of the Roman province of Bithynia wrote to Trajan about this issue, Trajan responded that Christians should not be actively hunted down, and that anonymous accusations against people should not be accepted. If someone was accused of being a Christian, the person should be given the opportunity to disprove it by offering worship to other gods. However, if someone was found guilty of being a Christian, he or she must be put to death. This became the standard policy of the Roman Empire for the next two hundred years, with exceptions during periods of persecution, when Christians *were* actively hunted down.

Trajan's successor, Hadrian, quickly abandoned the hard-won territories of Armenia and Mesopotamia by withdrawing his legions to the border of the Euphrates river. Hadrian did not portray himself as a military leader like Trajan, and preferred to utilize the more easily defended natural geographic borders like the Euphrates. Hadrian was also the emperor who visited the vast realms of the empire in person, in three long journeys, which lasted more than a decade. One of the results of this was his decision to build a wall in Britain, Hadrian's Wall, to serve as the northernmost boundary in the Roman Empire. Another scheme, less well-received by the local population, was to rebuild Jerusalem as a Roman city, renaming it Aelia Capitolina.

His plan was to build a temple for the worship of Jupiter on the site of the Jewish Temple. When the Jews heard this, and heard the decree to abolish circumcision, a violent reaction occurred. In AD 132 they rose in revolt against Rome in the *Second Jewish War.* It took three years for Hadrian to end the rebellion, but end it he did. Despite the Jewish efforts under the warrior Bar Kochba, the new city of Aelia Capitolina was built on the ruins of Jerusalem,

Trajan had extended the Roman Empire to what would be its furthest point.

the pagan temple occupied the site of the old sanctuary, and the name of the Roman province was changed from Judea to Syria Palestina. Jews were forbidden on pain of death to ever set foot again in Jerusalem, except on the anniversary of the destruction of the Temple. On that day, once a year, they were allowed to *pay* for the right to weep at the site of the Temple. Can you imagine how painful and tragic this was for the descendants of Abraham? How much they must have longed for their Messiah to come in power to establish justice!

Patristic Period

Christianity and Judaism had become, by this time, very distinct from one another, even though Judaism was the tree into which Christianity had been grafted. This separateness came from both sides: Judean Christians had not joined the Jews in either the First or Second Jewish War, so were seen as traitors by the remaining Jewish community; while gentile Christians increasingly distanced themselves from Judaism as they sought to explain Christianity to the culture of the Roman Empire in terms of Greco-Roman philosophy. This time period in early Church history is known as the **Patristic Period,** or the **Period of the Ante-Nicene Fathers** (*ante* meaning "before," *nicene* referring to the Council of Nicaea), and lasted from c. AD 140–325. It was a time of increasing persecutions and martyrdoms, and it was also a time when the focus turned to combating heresies and dissensions in the Church. Some of the best known figures from this time are Justin Martyr, Tertullian, Irenaeus, Clement of Alexandria, Origen, and Cyprian of Rome.

In the Empire, the first half of the second century was truly the high point in its history. It was a period of prosperity for many, a time of great building projects and acquisitions, with a confidence for the future. Emperor Antoninus Pius reigned from AD 138–161 during this golden age of the Roman Empire. His family's rule is known as the **Antonine Dynasty**, which lasted until AD 192. His adopted son, the future emperor Marcus Aurelius, wrote this concerning his father:

He was always equal to any occasion; cheerful, yet long-sighted enough to have all his dispositions unobtrusively perfected down to the last detail. He had an ever-watchful eye to the needs of the Empire, prudently conserving its resources and putting up with the criticisms that resulted. Before his gods he was not superstitious; before his fellowmen he never stooped to bid for popularity or woo the masses, but pursued his own calm and steady way.

Unfortunately, although there was no major war during his reign, there seems to have been a constant state of unrest and fighting along many of the borders of the empire: Mauretania, Germany, Egypt, Greece, Palestina, Dacia. The Golden Age began to lose its luster in light of these rumblings on the frontier.

When Marcus Aurelius came to power (AD 161–180), he faced almost continuous warfare during his reign, first on the eastern frontier and then the northern, which he sometimes faced in person. Though he was emperor, concerned with all the day-to-day business of government, he also managed to go campaigning alongside his troops on the northern borders. However, the most devastating issue of the time for the people of the Roman Empire was an outbreak of the plague, which lasted for more than ten years.

On that day, once a year, they were allowed to pay for the right to weep at the site of the Temple.

It was during this plague (called the *Antonine Plague*) that Christians had an unprecedented opportunity to serve the people around them, both Christian and non-Christian. Since belief in the resurrected Jesus gave hope for life after death to His followers, it was not unusual for them to care for the dying and afflicted, even though it put them at risk. Since the pagan priests and their followers fled the areas touched by the plague, as did the local government officials, along with anyone rich enough to do so, it left an opportunity for the Christians to be the unexpected caregivers. And, with their care, many of the non-Christians whose families abandoned them to die actually *lived* through the plague. As you might imagine, this made a deep impression on these people, with many of them converting to Christianity because they had seen the reality of God's love displayed in His people.

From the death of Marcus Aurelius, things became increasingly bleak for the people of the Empire. His successor Commodus (AD 180–192) was not interested in governing the empire, but in playing gladiator. With this lack of governing on the part of the emperor, a whole series of intrigues and power-plays began to play out behind the scenes, resulting in his assassination and in civil war.

A new dynasty, the **Severan Dynasty,** was begun by Septimius Severus, who reigned from AD 193–211. After killing off all rivals to the throne, he went to war against both Parthia and Scotland. Though he made enemies of the political leaders in Rome, the army loved him for his pay raises and for his official change of policy giving soldiers permission to marry wives and live at home. One Roman historian wrote of him, "For eighteen years he ruled, before making way for his young sons to succeed, bequeathing to them greater wealth than any previous emperor and an invincible army."

For his sons, Septimius Severus had provided his formula for success: "Agree with each other, give money to the soldiers, and scorn all other men." The first part of the formula was rejected when his son Caracalla murdered his other son Geta, after less than a year of co-rule. That was just the beginning of a reign of terror, as Caracalla—in order to feel safe—executed 20,000 people who had supported his brother. However, he did follow the rest of his father's advice, and the Roman soldiers were enthusiastic supporters of this well-paying emperor. It was all for naught when, five years later, one of his own officers assassinated Caracalla.

> The most devastating issue of the time for the people of the Roman Empire was an outbreak of the plague.

It went downhill from there, with one short respite during the reign of Alexander Severus (AD 222–235), as the Roman Empire erupted into chaos. During this time many emperors came and went after just a short time of ruling, often dying violent deaths. The Goths, a barbarian people, invaded the empire in this chaotic period, leaving death and destruction in their wake. Since the Roman legions were unsuccessful in their struggle to keep the Goths outside the borders of the empire, in many regions this led, as you might imagine, to **destabilization**—disorder and chaos that affected all of the normal affairs of life for most people: trade, business, the economy, security, and families, among others.

Christians faced increasing difficulties during this time period, as well. In AD 249 Emperor Decius made the declaration that all citizens *must* sacrifice to Roman gods. Along with many others, the bishops of Rome, Antioch, and Jerusalem were arrested—three of the leading Churchmen in the empire—and two died as a result. Under the Emperor Valerian, Christians were not allowed to assemble for worship, and offending believers had their property confiscated. Those serving in government who were known to be Christians were made slaves under the Edict of Valerian in AD 258. It is worth noting that Valerian died the next year while battling the Persians. Having their emperor killed by a foreign army was a shocking event for the citizens of Rome, but it was also, perhaps, an example of God's promise to avenge His people.

Dividing The Empire

Things were not stabilized in the Empire until the reign of Diocletian (AD 284–305), who ruled with a firm hand. He recognized that the chaos of the past was caused, in part, by too few rulers for too much territory, so Diocletian worked to reorganize the entire empire, both the political and economic structures. He divided the empire into East and West, and gave each part an Augustus (senior position) and a Caesar (junior position). Significantly, he increased the size of the army to better defend the borders and increased the number of governmental workers to better control the people of the empire. A larger army and more bureaucrats meant a larger budget. Budgets meant more money, greater taxes. Are you getting the idea? More control, larger armies, more government involvement, more financial coercion—these were all part of Diocletian's plan to keep the empire functioning. Perhaps the most oppressive part of this plan was limiting the people to their various occupations. For instance, if your father was a shipbuilder, then you became a shipbuilder. If your father was a peasant farmer, you became a peasant farmer. No exceptions.

Diocletian also launched the last and greatest persecution of the Church. Many Christians died throughout the empire in this final Roman attempt to eliminate all traces of Christianity. Churches were burned, along with copies of the Scriptures. Bishops and church leaders were arrested and forced to sacrifice to Roman gods or face martyrdom. Eventually, any Christian, whether a leader or not, could be subject to arrest and martyrdom.

One of the issues facing the Church in North Africa during and after this persecution was dealing with those who had *lapsed* (or, in some form denied Jesus). There, a bishop who was believed to have handed over copies of Scripture during the Diocletian persecution, ordained another to be bishop of Carthage. This caused a huge controversy. If the one ordaining had lapsed, was this new bishop a *true* bishop? Those who said, "No!" were called Donatists, while those who said, "Yes!" were the mainstream Catholics (the word *catholic* means "universal"). It not only caused a violent disagreement among believers for a hundred years, it also provided an opportunity for the government of the empire to interfere with the governing of the Church. This happened during the pivotal reign of Constantine.

> The Roman Empire erupted into a time of chaos.

Though Diocletian had reorganized the empire, it was not until Constantine's rule that the empire was fully revitalized. In between these two emperors, civil war spread over the entire empire as the various Augustii and Caesars vied for power. In fact, though Constantine was made Augustus of the West by the Roman legions in Britain in AD 306 (which act was officially recognized in 307), he did not gain control of the entire empire until 324. Meanwhile, in 313 Constantine issued the *Edict of Milan,* which gave legal status to Christianity—meaning that Christians were no longer to be persecuted for their faith. However, as mentioned above, the government began to involve itself with the issue of who were the *right* Christians. When Constantine became Augustus of the West, he had all church property that had been confiscated by the State returned to the Church. In North Africa the authorities returned the church property to the non-Donatist group. That action inflamed the Donatists, who appealed to Constantine to recognize those who had held to the faith during times of persecution as the real Christians. When the first Council of Arles, which had been convened by Constantine to investigate the matter, decided against the Donatists, violence erupted. At this point, in 316, Constantine sought to quell the violence by exiling the Donatists and confiscating their church property. In essence, this was the first attempt of a *Christian* ruler (though Constantine's Christianity is hotly debated) to coerce non-conforming Christians back into fellowship with the mainstream of believers. Though Constantine eventually revoked his order and instituted a policy of toleration towards the Donatists, his state-sponsored coercion would bear bitter fruit both in this instance and in the future.

Having their emperor killed by a foreign army was a shocking event for the citizens of Rome, but it was also, perhaps, an example of God's promise to avenge His people.

When Constantine reunited the empire in 324, thereby becoming sole emperor, he quickly turned his attention to another controversy dividing the Church. In 325 he called the Council of Nicaea to meet and decide whether a priest from Alexandria, Arius, was correct in his assertion that Jesus was not equal to God. In this council, Arius's beliefs were condemned as heresy (though they continued to take root throughout the empire), and the orthodox doctrine of the divinity of Jesus was victorious.

Post-Nicene Fathers

This brings us to the next period of Church history, which is known as the **Post-Nicene Fathers** (AD 326–460). With the accession of Constantine, the Church's focus shifts from issues of persecution, martyrdom, and apologetics to defining specific details of Christian doctrine. It is also the time when monasteries become a normal feature of the Church, though the practice of monasticism differs from East to West. The key figures for this historical time are Jerome, Ambrose, Augustine, Athanasius, Basil of Caesarea, and Chrysostom.

In the empire, another act of Constantine would bear significant fruit in the future: moving the capital city of the empire from Rome in the West to Constantinople, the newly-built city in the East. The declining importance of this Western city foreshadowed the imminent fall of the Western half of the empire, while the Eastern empire continued to glitter, at least in this city, for another thousand years.

Constantine's reign gave the Roman Empire one of its high points. When he died, however, the stability gained through the strength of his rule dissipated among his sons. When Julian, the last of his surviving male relatives, came to power, he sought to undo what Constantine had done in legalizing Christianity. Known in history as "The Apostate," Julian was the last to try to reinstate worship of the old Roman gods. He died in battle against the Persians (or, as some suppose, was murdered) after a reign of only a few years.

The **Valentinian Dynasty** ruled a divided and increasingly fragile empire until Emperor Theodosius I, known as Theodosius the Great, came to power. He was the ruler who outlawed paganism, making Christianity the official religion of the empire. However, his championing of Christianity did not exempt him from the correction of the Church. When he ordered the massacre of the people of Thessalonica as punishment for their murder of his army commander, Ambrose (the Bishop of Milan) excommunicated him from the Church. The emperor of the Roman Empire was not allowed to enter the church and receive communion until he had done penance for his misdeeds. This is just one example of the struggle that will be ongoing between the power of the State and the power of the Church. At this moment, the emperor (head of the State) submitted to the Bishop (a representative of the Church). But things would soon change.

> *The government began to involve itself with the issue of who were the right Christians.*

Theodosius was also a military leader, and it was his decision to end a four-year war in the East between Rome and the Visigoths with a peace treaty in AD 382 making them *foederati*, or allies, of Rome. This allowed the Visigoths to settle inside Roman territory under their own king (rather than merging into the empire as others had done), and to fight under their own leaders as allies rather than as regular legionary soldiers. It was a dangerous move for the empire, and the doors which were opened to the barbarian tribes were never to close again.

Trajan's Column, Rome, Italy

In AD 410 the city of Rome, known as the Eternal City, was sacked and burned by these same Visigoths whom Theodosius had permitted into the empire. It was the first time the city had fallen to invaders in eight hundred years, and when it violently collapsed in flames, the entire empire was shaken to its core. In far away Bethlehem, Jerome (translator of the Latin Vulgate version of the Bible) said, "My voice is choked, and sobs break my voice as I dictate this letter. The city which has conquered the whole world is itself conquered."

The fall of Rome was not the fall of the Church, however. Christianity, which had survived persecutions, martyrdoms, heresies, and divisions under the Roman Empire, would continue to grow and thrive despite this unsettled political climate. Jesus had said, "On this rock I will build My church, and the gates of Hades shall not prevail against it" (Matthew 16:18). And His Word continues.◄

Phase 1

▶ Listen to This

What in the World? VOL. 2

DISC ONE:

- » Welcome to Medieval History (track 1)
- » First-Century Church & Emperors (track 2)
- » Life in the Second Century (track 3)
- » The Plague and Restructuring (track 4)
- » Constantine & the End of the Empire (track 5)

True Tales VOL. 2

DISC ONE:

- » Introduction (track 1)
- » The Canon of Scripture (track 2)

Digging Deeper VOL. 2

DISC ONE: THE EXPLODING CHURCH

- » Introduction through Sack of Rome (tracks 1–8)

▶ Read For Your Life

The Holy Bible

- » **The Main Story:** The book of Acts (suggested reading plan: one chapter per day for twenty-eight days)

Key People (Church)

Polycarp
Disciple of Apostle John

Justin Martyr
Greatest 2nd century apologist

Irenaeus
First great theologian since Apostle Paul

Eusebius
"Father of Church history"

Athanasius
Defender of Orthodoxy

Jerome
Translated Bible into Latin

Augustine
Influential theologian

Key People (World)

Nero
Infamous emperor

Vespasian
Built the Colosseum

Titus
Captured Jerusalem

Trajan
Extended the empire

Hadrian
Strengthened Roman frontiers

Diocletian
Divided the empire

Constantine
First Christian emperor

▶ # Talk Together

Opinion Column

» What did you find to be the most interesting aspect, or the most fascinating person, you encountered in your introduction to the rise of the Church and the fall of Rome?

» Why do you suppose people used the picture of a fish (an ICHTHUS) to identify themselves to others as Christians? What would have been the possible results had they told anyone they met, "Oh, yes, I am a Christian?"

» The fire that destroyed much of Rome during Nero's reign caused Nero to need a *scapegoat* (an innocent substitute to take the blame). Why do you think he picked on the Christians? Would you want someone like Nero to be the ruler in your country? Why or why not?

» Would you have wanted to be a Roman emperor? Why or why not? What do you think would be some of the difficulties of ruling such a large empire as Rome?

» What do you think this phrase means: "The blood of the martyrs is the seed of the Church"? What impact do you think it would have had on nonbelievers to see Christians go victoriously and unashamedly to their deaths?

» Mt. Vesuvius erupted in AD 79, just nine years after the destruction of Jerusalem. Why do you think the Jews and Christians of the time believed this disaster was a judgment of God on the Romans? Can you think of any time in Scripture where God brought judgment on a culture? What do you think the Romans thought?

» If you had been a non-Roman citizen in a country under the control of Rome, do you think you would have supported the Romans? What reason would you present to your neighbors for your opinion?

Critical Puzzling

» Read Acts 6–8, and also Acts 11. From your reading, why do you think many Christians left Jerusalem? What were some of the consequences of their leaving?

» Early in the history of the Church, false teachings or heresies arose. In the audio-recording *Digging Deeper: The Exploding Church* several heresies are mentioned, including marcionism (which took away from the Word), montanism (which added to the Word), and arianism (which reduced Jesus to a super-hero rather than a member of the triune God). Are you aware of similar heresies today? What do you think are the best tools Christians (of any time period) have for combatting heresy?

» Monasticism began during this time period. Some people left the cities and traveled to the desert and desolate wilderness to be alone with God. As others joined them, they grouped together into the earliest monasteries. What would motivate people during the Roman Empire to leave their homes, friends, and activities to become monks and nuns?

» Jesus told His disciples that, after the Holy Spirit had come upon them, they would be His witnesses in Jerusalem, Judea, Samaria, and unto the uttermost parts of the earth. How far had the disciples and early converts to Christianity traveled by the end of the Book of Acts? (Hint: For a start, look in your Bible for maps showing Paul's missionary journeys.)

» If you had lived in the time of the Roman Empire, would you have preferred to live close to Rome or far from Rome? Would you have preferred to live in a city or in a rural area? Would you have wanted to be involved in government or not? List your reasons.

CODE:

AA All ages

RA Read aloud

E+ Elem & up

UE+ Upper elem & up

MS+ Middle school & up

HS High school

▶ Resources for Digging Deeper

Choose a few books that look interesting, or find your own.

CHURCH HISTORY

The Story of Christianity

Michael Collins & Matthew A. Price • A wonderful introduction to the history of Christianity (with information on Protestant, Catholic, and Orthodox faiths), this DK book is the best I've seen for a basic overview of the Church through the ages. **UE+**

From Jerusalem to Irian Jaya

Ruth A. Tucker • This book is "a biographical history of missions" beginning with the Apostle Paul. Though the biographies pertinent to Romans, Reformers, Revolutionaries represent only the first hundred pages, I heartily endorse it for your family bookshelf! It includes a wonderful timeline of missionaries through the ages. **UE+**

2000 Years of Christ's Power PART ONE: THE AGE OF THE EARLY CHURCH FATHERS

N. R. Needham • If you want to dig into Church history, this British author provides an amazingly clear, in-depth look at the people and events that make up our Christian heritage. He has taken a complex subject and made it understandable for those of us who are not professional theologians or church historians! (400 pages.) **HS+**

EARLY CHURCH

Against the World: The Odyssey of Athanasius

Henry W. Coray • A biography of "the Father of Orthodoxy," this book describes the life and work of the man who defended the doctrine of the Trinity. It includes bits and pieces of his writings. **MS+**

Early Christian Writings

Translated by Maxwell Staniforth • In these writings of the Apostolic Fathers, you will read accounts of and letters from Clement of Rome, Ignatius of Antioch, and Polycarp. It also includes an eyewitness description of the martyrdom of Polycarp. **HS+**

Augustine, The Farmer's Boy of Tagaste

P. De Zeeuw • This is a children's biography of one of the most influential Christians in history. Worth the search. **UE+**

The Fathers of the Western Church

Robert Payne • A series of short biographies about several of the most significant men in the early Church through the time of the Middle Ages. Though it is out-of-print, you may be able to find it through interlibrary loan. **HS+**

City of God

Augustine • Written in the AD 300s, this book impacted people during the Middle Ages more than any other book except for the Bible. Look for it in your library. **HS+**

Augustine and His World

Andrew Knowles and Pachomios Penkett • InterVarsity Press has a series of books on Christian history, including this excellent book on Augustine. **MS+**

ROMAN EMPIRE

The World of the Roman Emperor

Peter Chrisp • Looking specifically at the time of the Roman Empire, this beautifully illustrated children's book gives a simple overview of the most famous emperors and an understanding of what life was like during the time of the Roman Empire. **UE+**

Cultural Atlas for Young People: Ancient Rome

Mike Corbishley • For an overview of Rome, from its beginnings until the latter part of the Empire, this is a wonderful resource. It also includes a geographic look at the various parts of the Roman Empire, including Africa, Britain, Spain, Gaul, Germany, and the Middle East. **UE+**

Life of a Roman Soldier

Don Nardo • In this thorough book, a student will have the opportunity to discover the realities of life for a Roman soldier. **UE+**

Famous Men of Rome

John H. Haaren & A. B. Poland • A wonderful collection of short biographies about the most important Romans. A very helpful and worthwhile book to have. **E+**

Galen and the Gateway to Medicine

Jeanne Bendick • Galen was the preeminent medical researcher of the Roman Empire, whose work influenced the medical profession for the next 1,300 years. **E+**

The Romans and Their Empire

Trevor Cairns • One in the series *The Cambridge Introduction to History*, this is an excellent resource describing the Roman Republic, the Roman Empire, the Roman invasion of Britain, and the fall of the Roman Empire. Highly recommended! **UE+**

The Annals of Imperial Rome: Tacitus

Translated by Michael Grant • Written by the Roman historian, Tacitus, this amazing book tells the story of the Julio-Claudian emperors from just before the death of Augustus through the reigns of Tiberius, Caligula, Claudius, and Nero. If you like to know the details, you'll love this book! **HS+**

Beric the Briton A STORY OF
THE ROMAN INVASION

G. A. Henty • Another page-turning suspenseful story by the master of historical fiction for children, this book concerns the impact of the Romans upon what we call England. (It begins slowly, but it really gets exciting!) **UE+**

The Roman Colosseum

Elizabeth Mann • This well-illustrated book tells the story of the building of the Colosseum, built by Vespasian on the site of Nero's hated Golden Palace. It describes not only how the Colosseum was built, but also the conditions of Rome that gave life to this place of contested death. Fascinating. **UE+**

Make It Work!: The Roman Empire

Peter Chrisp • An absolutely delightful book to show how to create a hands-on experience when you study Rome. Highly recommended. **AA**

Lives of Famous Romans

Olivia Coolidge • Let's face it. These Romans are not pretty! To read about their lives is helpful but not nice. If you want to know more details than are given in the books listed above, this is a good choice. **MS+**

The Robe

Lloyd C. Douglas • A classic of fictional literature, this is an excellent way to better understand the conflict between Rome and Christianity. MS+

The Eagle of the Ninth

Rosemary Sutcliff • This is a fascinating fictional account of a young man's search for the truth about what happened to his father—the commander of the Ninth Roman Legion who disappeared without a trace in the wilds of Britain. It will provide students with a "you were there" experience of ancient Britain and of the Romans who were stationed there. **UE+**

The Silver Branch

Rosemary Sutcliff • Picking up the threads of the last story, this tale illustrates how quickly Roman Emperors were made and unmade, and the circumstances that led Caesar Constantius (the father of Constantine) to first come to Britain. Fascinating! **UE+**

DESTRUCTION OF JERUSALEM

Josephus, the Essential Writings

Translated by Paul L. Maier • Josephus was an eyewitness of the destruction of Jerusalem in AD 70. He wrote about the devastation he had witnessed as well as the history of the Jews in this original source document commissioned by the Roman Emperor. **HS+**

For the Temple A TALE OF
THE FALL OF JERUSALEM

G. A. Henty • This is a riveting, can't-put-it-down fiction book describing the Fall of Jerusalem in AD 70. One of my son's favorites! Back in print. **UE+**

VIDEO

How Should We Then Live?

Dr. Francis Schaeffer · The first video in this series vividly portrays the early Church and what it faced. Excellent! **UE+**

The Robe

I prefer the book, but some people prefer movies. **UE+**

For more books, use these Dewey Decimal numbers in your library:

Church History: #270

Persecution in Church History: #272

Early Church: #281

Roman Empire: #937

What books did you like best?

_____

_____

_____

_____

The Internet also contains a wealth of information about the rise of the Church and the fall of Rome.

What sites were the most helpful?

_____

_____

_____

_____

► # Student Self-Evaluation UNIT 1, PHASE 1

Dates and hours:_____

Key Concepts

Rephrase the five Key Concepts of this Unit and confirm your understanding of each:

• The gospel to the Jews and Gentiles:

_____

• The Roman Emperors:

_____

• The growth of the persecuted Church:

_____

• Dividing and defending the Empire:

_____

• Reasons for the fall of Rome:

_____

Tools for Self-Evaluation

Evaluate your personal participation in the discussions of this Phase. Bearing in mind that a good partici-pant in a discussion is not always the most vocal participant, ask yourself these questions: Were you an active participant? Did you ask perceptive questions? Were you willing to listen to other participants of the discussion and draw out their opinions? Record your observations and how you would like to im-prove your participation in the future:

_____

Every time period is too complex to be understood in one Phase of study. Evaluate your current knowl-edge of the Rise of the Church and the Fall of Rome. What have you focused on so far? What are your weakest areas of knowledge?

_____

Based on the evaluation of this introduction, project ahead what you would like to study more of in the following Phases:

_____

Phase 2

▶ Research & Reporting

Explore one or more of these areas to discover something significant!

Sharing the Gospel

Using the Book of Acts as your source, research and report on the expansion of the gospel in the first days of the Church, from the day of Pentecost through Paul's imprisonment in Rome. Show how this began the fulfillment of Jesus's words that His disciples would bear witness to Him in Jerusalem, Judea, Samaria and to the ends of the earth.

Roman Emperors

Research and report on the Roman Emperors. Since this is a long list—given the short duration of some of the emperors!—you may want to categorize them and then report on some of the main emperors and the various eras of the Roman Empire. Include such details as when they lived, what they accomplished, the length of their reign, and how they died.

Roman Empire

Find one of the books listed, or a book of your choice, for basic information on the Roman Empire. Summarize the factors that led to the *Pax Romana* and the factors leading to Rome's fall. Report your findings.

The Early Church

Find one of the books listed, or a book of your choice, for a basic introduction to early Church history. Report what you discover about the growth of Christianity from a small Jewish sect in Judea to the dominant religion of the Roman Empire.

Pompeii

Look up information on Pompeii and Mt. Vesuvius, the volcano whose eruption buried the Roman city. When did Mt. Vesuvius erupt? What were the results? What have archaeologists discovered about Pompeii, and, correspondingly, about Ro-man times? What historic accounts exist about the destruction of Pompeii and what do they tell us?

Countries of the Empire

What regions beyond the country of Italy were under the control of the Roman empire? Investigate when and how these other countries were brought under the dominion of Rome, and when and how they regained their freedom.

East and West

Investigate the results of Diocletian's division of the Empire into East and West. Delineate the flow of authority in this new division. Describe how Constantine utilized this delineation to declare himself emperor, and how he came to power.

Ptolemy

Investigate Ptolemy's life and work in astronomy, geography, and math. How were his maps used in the late Middle Ages?

Constantine & Constantinople

Research and report on this first Christian emperor of Rome. What were the factors leading to his championing Christianity? How did Constantine impact the Church? What led to his creating the new capital city of Constantinople and how was this city different than all the other cities of the Empire? Why was this such a geographically important city?

The Catacombs

Find out more about the catacombs of Rome. When were they used, and who used them? What was their purpose? What kind of information has been found in catacombs for archaeologists to study? How has this helped us better understand the conditions of the early Church? Report your findings.

Invasion of Britain

Explore and discover the Roman invasion of Britain in AD 43. What did Emperor Claudius accomplish? (Hint: Look up the city of Colchester.) Who was Boudicca (or Boudicea)? Why did her tribe revolt against the Romans? When and why did the Roman troops eventually leave? What was the result of their departure?

Martyrdom

Research and report on martyrdom in the early Church. Describe the various times of persecution under the various emperors: Was it localized in one area? What triggered the persecution? What was the attitude of the Church toward those who denied their faith?

Christianity as the Official Religion

Research and report on Emperor Theodosius, who, as emperor in the East, issued an edict announcing that all citizens in his domain were to become Christians. As emperor of both East and West, he also made paganism illegal. Describe the impact of these decisions on the Church and on the Empire.

Roman Soldiers

Investigate what life was like for a Roman soldier during the Roman Empire. What type of equipment did they use? How did they live on campaign? What were the typical conditions of life in a Roman fort? What were the typical possessions of a soldier? What is the difference between a legionary and an auxiliary soldier?

Early Church Fathers

Investigate the lives of the Western and/or Eastern Church Fathers. Describe where they lived, the region they served, the era of their lives during the Roman Empire, and what was most distinguishing about them within the Church. You may want to go through the list of Key People within the Church to get an idea of where to start.

▶ Brain Stretchers

The High Point of the Empire

The 2nd century is considered by many to be the best time of the Roman Empire. Research and report on the factors that made this time period the high point: emperors, provinces, trade, succession (after the death of an emperor), stability, etc.

Christianity in Britain

What are some of the theories of how Christianity first came to Britain? To get you started, consider the story of Joseph of Arimathea in Britain, and the similarities between Celtic Christianity and Eastern Orthodox Christianity.

Early Monasticism

Research and report on the desert monks of the early Church. What were some of the similarities as well as differences among them? Be sure to include a description of the life of Jerome.

Arianism versus Orthodoxy

Investigate the claims of Arius concerning the nature and person of Jesus. What made Arianism appealing to the masses? Who championed orthodoxy? At what Church Council was Arianism declared a heresy? Report your findings.

Apologetics

Many of the early Christians were "apologists." They defended Christianity to the Romans through the use of brilliant arguments and insightful writings. Research and report on Athenagoras, Mark Felix, Justin Martyr, Lactantius, or Tertullian.

Christianity in India

The apostle Thomas is believed to have been the first to bring the gospel to the people of India. Research and report on the evidence for his ministry and the development of Christianity in India.

Create Your Own Research Topic

_____

_____

_____

► **Timeline**

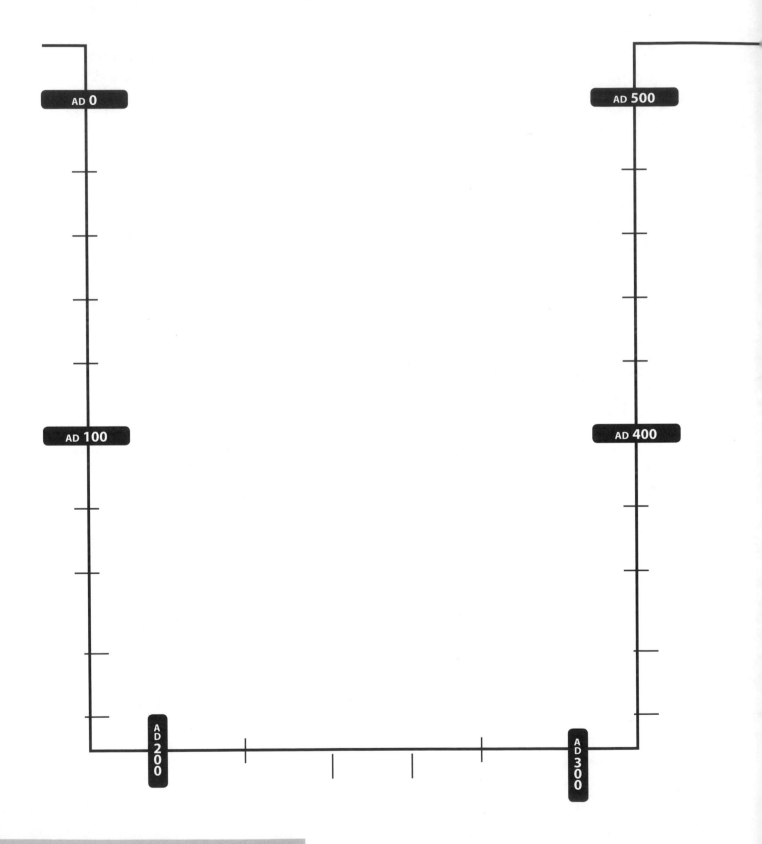

AD 0

AD 100

A D 2 0 0

AD 500

AD 400

A D 3 0 0

Consider this for your timeline

The growth of the early Church was affected by the persecution of the Church. On your timeline, you might want to color in the main years of the persecutions under Roman emperors, ending with the year that Constantine became ruler over the Empire. As you enter the major emperors and the major Christian figures during this time of persecution, the connection between the rise of te Church and the fall of Rome should become more vivid. Also consider the expansion and recession of the Roman Empire, and shade your timeline appropriately to show this.

Key Events

Roman Invasion of Britain

Destruction of Jerusalem

Hadrian's Wall built

Antonine Plague

Invasion by the Goths

Roman Empire Divided into Two

Constantinople built

Edict of Milan

City of Rome sacked

Key People in the Church list

Key People in the World list

▶ # Words to Watch

Remember—the easiest way to learn a subject is to master its terms:

colosseum	heresy	aqueduct	centurion
legion	hymns	sack	persecution
edict	dispersion	conversion	Pax Romana
ichthus	martyrdom	apostolic	apologetics
consecrate	monasticism		

Other words you need to look up:

_____

_____

_____

_____

To boost your vocabulary, try this

Locate a book of Latin root words in the library, or "Rummy Roots" (a Greek-Latin root word card game), and learn twenty Latin roots.

Extra Credit: Learn forty Latin roots.

Abundant Credit: Learn sixty Latin roots.

If you have enjoyed learning roots, you might want to go ahead and study Latin itself!

▶ # Student Self-Evaluation UNIT 1, PHASE 2

Dates and hours:_____

Research Project

Summarize your research question:

_____

_____

List your most useful sources by author, title, and page number or URL where applicable (continue list in margin if necessary):

_____

_____

Now take a moment to evaluate the sources you just listed. Do they provide a balanced view of your research question? Should you have sought an additional opinion? Are your sources credible (if you found them on your own)? Record your observations:

_____

_____

_____

Evaluate your research project in its final presentation. What are its strengths? If you had time to revisit this project, what would you change? Consider giving yourself a letter grade based on your project's merits and weaknesses.

_____

_____

_____

Letter grade: _____

You have just completed an area of specific research in the time of the Rise of the Church and the Fall of Rome. Now what would you like to explore in the upcoming Phases? Set some objectives for yourself:

_____

_____

_____

Phase 3

▶ Maps and Mapping

Physical Terrain

» Label and color the land of Palestine, which was the scene of Titus's triumph in AD 70 at the destruction of Jerusalem.

» Label and color the land of Egypt, which contained one of most important cities of the Roman Empire and the early Church.

» Label and color the "boot" of Italy, which was the center of the Roman Empire.

» Label and color the land of Asia Minor and Syria, which contained many important cities in the Roman Empire, and one of the most important of the early Church.

Geopolitical

» Draw the boundaries of the Roman Empire under Trajan.

» Label the location of the five most important cities in the early Church: Jerusalem, Rome, Alexandria, Antioch, and Constantinople.

» Draw the travels of Emperor Hadrian to Gaul, Britain, Dacia, Egypt, Sicily, Spain, and North Africa.

» Draw the missionary journeys of the Apostle Paul.

Explore

» *Christian Outreach:* What is the status of evangelical outreach today to Egypt, Asia Minor, and Israel (the sites of the four eastern metropolitan cities of the early Church)? What opportunities and what difficulties face those who share the gospel in these areas?

» *Trade in the Empire:* What products did Rome import from its outlying regions? Are these products still being exported from these regions? Investigate the sea routes and land routes for trade in the empire.

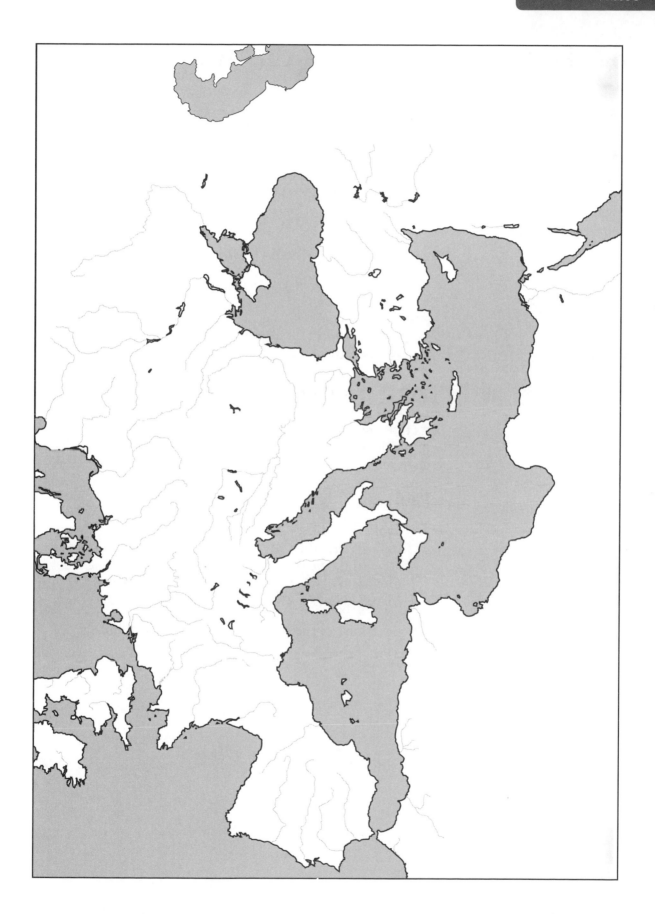

CONSIDER:

Mosaics were used by the Roman people to decorate floors and walls in their homes. Many different scenes were created in mosaics, including a mosaic from Pompeii of a snarling dog, with the inscription *cave canem* —"beware of the dog."

▶ Art Appreciation

Mosaics from Pompeii

This art dates from the first century and reflects the style of the early Roman Empire.

> » What are the subjects of the mosaics? What does this show about the Roman people of the time?

> » What words could you use to describe the mosaic style of art?

Catacomb of St. Calixtus in Rome—*Jonah and the Whale*

> » How would you describe the style of painting used by the catacomb artist?

> » Why do you think the catacomb painters painted biblical scenes?

▶ Architecture

This is the time of the Christian basilica style of architecture. The basilica was derived from Imperial Roman architecture, which was itself a development from the covered markets of the Roman Republic.

St. Paul's Outside-The-Walls Basilica

> » Look for images of St. Paul's Outside-The-Walls. This is a basilica built over the site of St. Paul's tomb in Rome. It was built about the time of Constantine, and is Roman-style architecture borrowed for use by the Church. How would you describe this building?

Don't forget to look for pictures of the mosaics inside the building.

▶ Arts in Action

Select one or more, and let your artistic juices flow!

Catacomb Painting

Start by setting up an easel with blank paper (or secure the paper to a hard surface on the wall). Work in a dark room, with someone holding a flashlight to illuminate your painting. Using earth-tone paints, crayons, or markers, try to create a scene that tells a Bible story.

Mosaics

Make a small mosaic using white poster board as the base and colored card stock cut into small squares for the tesserae. Draw a design on the poster board, and then fill it in by gluing the card stock squares in the design.

▶ Science

Ptolemy, who lived in Alexandria in the second century AD, was an amazing astronomer, geographer, and mathematician. It was his Ptolemaic System which proclaimed the theory that the earth was the center of the universe. This was believed until Copernicus showed, in the sixteenth century, that the sun—not the earth—is the center of the solar system.

Ptolemy also made a map showing everything that was known about the geography of the world at that time. He made errors, but that was fortunate for us all, since his estimate of the distance going west from Europe to China was what encouraged Columbus to make his historic voyage!

Flat to Round

» How do you make a flat map of a round world? That is the difficulty all map makers face. Try this activity to get a sample of their plight. Blow up a balloon. With markers, make a face on the balloon. Next, have a brave child pop the balloon with a pin. Then, using scissors, cut off a tiny piece at the top and the bottom so that it leaves a rectangle. What does the face look like now?

Create a Globe

» Do the same project listed above, except draw the continents as found on a globe instead of a face. When it is in the shape of a rectangle, how distorted are the continents? Now, looking at a map of the world and observing how the map makers deal with the distortions caused by putting a curved shape on flat paper, draw the continents again, but on a flat surface. *Activity ideas courtesy of Cindy Wiggers, Geography Matters.*

▶ Music

One of the most fascinating and least studied aspects of Church history is the story of music within the Church. It shouldn't surprise us to discover that, in addition to singing the Psalms, there were also wonderful songs of worship to God that were written by some of the earliest Christians. Now they didn't have recording equipment, and the melodies were not written down, so we are not sure of what the melodies sounded like. And writers didn't speak English in the first hymn. The result is that we have translations of songs from Latin and Greek, put to melodies from later centuries. However, it is eminently satisfying to sing a song of praise and worship that was conceived in someone's heart nearly two thousand years ago!

Discover

O Splendor of God's Glory Bright

Ambrose of Milan (AD 340–397) • "Ambrose for bishop" was the cry of the people of Milan, though Ambrose was not yet ordained. He was the greatest churchman of his day, and was largely responsible for winning over Augustine to Christianity. He introduced congregational singing to the Western Church, and his own hymns became very popular throughout western Europe.

Lord Jesus, Think on Me

Synesius of Cyrene (AD 375–430) • Synesius was one of the last great citizens of this ancient city. He was descended from Spartan kings, as well as being an educated, wealthy man. A friend of St. Augustine of Hippo, Synesius became bishop of Cyrene about AD 410.

Listen

All Glory, Laud, & Honor music CD:

Lord Jesus, Think On Me

Try This

Gather a group and have a "Hymn Sing" with as many hymns or Scripture songs as you can find. But, to imitate the style of the early Church, you must sing these songs unaccompanied AND you must stand the whole time!

Until the 1300s, church services in the West did not include pews—everyone stood throughout the entire service. Church pews were NEVER introduced into the Eastern Church.

CONSIDER:

No musical instruments were used in the early Church, as believers associated musical instruments with pagan worship and with Jewish worship, but not with the apostolic traditions or teachings.

► Cooking

Challah Bread

1¾ cups flour	3 tbsp sugar
1½ tsp salt	1 pkg dry active yeast
½ cup butter, softened	1 cup warm water
4 eggs (room temperature)	up to 5 cups more flour
1 tsp cold water	½ tsp poppy or sesame seeds

Combine flour, sugar, salt, and yeast in a large bowl. Mix in the softened butter. Slowly add warm water to the flour mixture and blend thoroughly. Beat for two minutes with mixer at medium speed, scraping the bowl occasionally. Separate the yolk and white of one egg. Blend the single egg white and the other three whole eggs into the batter. Reserve the single egg yolk. Stir ½ cup of the flour into the batter and beat at high speed for two minutes, scraping bowl occasionally. Blend in enough additional flour to make a soft dough. Knead the dough on a lightly floured board about 8 to 10 minutes, or until it is smooth and elastic. Place the dough in a greased bowl, turning it once to grease the top. Cover and allow the dough to rise in a warm, draft-free place until double in bulk (approximately one hour).

On a lightly floured surface, divide the dough into two equal portions. Divide each of those portions into two unequal pieces, so that you have one third of the dough for one piece and two-thirds of the dough for the other. Divide one of the larger pieces into three equal portions. Roll each of these into 12-inch ropes. Braid the lengths together tightly, using the fingers to press the dough together at the ends. Divide the smaller piece into three equal portions. Roll each of these into 10-inch lengths and braid tightly. Place the smaller braid on top of the larger one and seal the ends. Repeat this process to form the second loaf.

Place both braided loaves on a greased baking sheet. Mix the reserved single egg yolk with one tsp. cold water and brush the tops of the loaves with this mixture. Sprinkle with the poppy or sesame seeds, and let the loaves rise until double in bulk in a warm, draft-free place (approximately one hour). Bake in a preheated 400-degree oven for 20 to 25 minutes. Remove from the oven and cool on racks.

▶ **Student Self-Evaluation** UNIT 1, PHASE 3

Dates and hours:_____

Evaluate your projects

- List which of the activities listed in this Phase you did:

  _____

  _____

- Rate your enthusiasm: _____

  Explain: _____

  _____

- Rate the precision of your approach:_____

  Explain: _____

  _____

- Rate your effort toward the completion of the project: _____

  Explain: _____

  _____

- Ask yourself what worked and what did not. What would you do differently in the future, and what would you repeat?

  _____

  _____

- How specifically did these hands-on activities enhance your knowledge of the Rise of the Church and the Fall of Rome? What made them worthwhile?

  _____

  _____

- In the first three Phases of this Unit, what aspect of the time period has most captured your imagination? What would you like to creatively pursue to conclude your study?

  _____

  _____

Phase 4

▶ In Your Own Way…

We have seen the supernatural power of God displayed as Christianity has grown from a backwater Jewish sect to the favored religion of the Roman Emperor, Constantine. This has been a time of dynamic growth for the early Church, despite fearful persecution, and it has also been a time of gradual decline in the formidable Roman Empire. Now, choose a selection of these activities, or create your own, which will best express what you have learned from this Unit.

LINGUISTICS

Journalism

Write an article for the *Christian Insider*, a magazine specially devoted to up-to-the-minute reports on the Church in the Roman Empire. Your editor has assigned you to cover the events of Constantine's battle at the Milvian Bridge.

You are a Roman television reporter from the *All Around the Empire* news show. Interview Polycarp in order to discover why on earth this elderly, seemingly respectable man, won't recant his "atheistic" religion.

Poetry

Write an ode to Rome's Emperors, including: Augustus, who said he found Rome a city of sun-dried bricks and left her clothed in marble; Caligula, who threatened to give his favorite horse the political position of consul; Nero, who won a chariot race at the Olympic games; Hadrian, who traveled with his own team of architects; Diocletian, who styled himself as a Persian king—with people kneeling before him and kissing the hem of his robe; and Constantine, who oversaw the Church Council of Nicaea just a few short years after the worst Empire-wide persecution of Christians.

Prose

You have recently been assigned to a legion of soldiers stationed in Britain. Write a letter home to describe this island, and the people who live here. Be sure to include descriptions of the unpredictable voyage.

Playing with Words

Finish this limerick:

There once was a bad guy named Nero,
Who ended his life as a zero . . .

ART

Illustration

Romans used storytelling reliefs to describe their mighty triumphs in battle. Emperor Trajan had a massive column created (almost 100 feet tall), which depicted his victory over the Dacians.

Using Trajan's Column as a model, create a comic-strip showing one of the Roman emperor's lives, whether his battles, his noteworthy accomplishments, or his struggle to keep the throne.

Mosaics

Create a mosaic with a Bible story as the subject, which would be similar to mosaics created by early Christians.

Political Cartooning

Emperor Hadrian had a huge wall built in England to protect the Empire from barbarians. Draw a political cartoon showing how effective Hadrian's Wall was when it came to keeping out the Picts and Scots!

Sculpting

Create a statue (head and shoulders) in the manner of the Romans, who did not create flawless-looking individuals, but actually enjoyed showing the characteristics (imperfections included) of the person being sculpted.

MUSIC

Performance Practice

With your teacher's help, select an appropriate piece of music which expresses some element of the early Church: the love feasts, the secrecy, the persecution, or the joyful courage of these believers. Prepare and perform the piece for an audience. Communicate with your audience the reason for your selection either in the program notes or in a short speech.

Compose

Write a song based on the Nicene Creed, to be used in worship. The emphasis, remember, is on who Jesus is—of the same substance as the Father, begotten not made, very God of very God.

DRAMA

Comedy

Enact the real-life difficulties of one who lived close to the Roman baths—especially if trying to take a nap. Use this quote from Seneca, writing in Rome in the first century, to get you started:

"I live over the public baths—you know what that means. Ugh! It's sickening. First there are the strongmen doing their exercises and swinging heavy lead weights about with grunts and groans. Next the lazy ones having a cheap massage—I can hear someone being slapped on the shoulders. Then there's the man who always likes the sound of his own voice in the bath. And what about the ones who leap into the pool making a huge splash!"

Reality

Pick several scenes from the book of Acts and weave them together into a play about the beginning days of the Church.

Puppetry

Put on a puppet show of Constantine at the Milvian Bridge. Be sure to include his vision on the night before this famous battle.

Prop Needs

_____

_____

Costume Ideas

_____

_____

Role/Player

_____

_____

Set Suggestions

_____

_____

MOVEMENT

Pantomime

Pantomime the Emperor Claudius successfully invading the country of Britain, and then riding in triumph on an elephant to the city of Camulodunum (now known as Colchester). His stay in Britain was only sixteen days, so do the whole thing quickly.

Dance

Choreograph a dance which shows the strong yet graceful aqueducts built by the Romans, and their role in conveying clean water from the high hills to the cities.

For inspiration, look for a photo of the Pont du Gard at Nîmes, France.

Action

Demonstrate with movement the elements of a Church service during the time of the early Church. Show what activities were open to non-baptized people, and at what point only those who had received baptism were allowed to remain. It will be more appealing visually if you are able to find and use appropriate props.

CONCEPTUAL DESIGN

Create-a-Game

Demonstrate to younger children the explosion of the early Church from a small group of disciples waiting in Jerusalem for the outpouring of the Holy Spirit to a widespread, influential gathering of believers who, by AD 64, had "turned the world upside down"—to the point that there are even believers in the Roman Emperor's household—by creating a game which shows the progression of these miraculous events.

CREATE YOUR OWN EXPRESSION

_____

_____

_____

_____

▶ # Student Self-Evaluation UNIT 1, PHASE 4

Dates and hours:_____

Evaluate your projects

- What creative project did you choose:

  _____

- What did you expect from your project, and how does the final project compare to your initial expectations?

  _____

  _____

- What do you like about your project? What would you change?

  _____

  _____

In Conclusion

Revisit the five Key Concepts from the beginning of this Unit. Explain how your understanding of and appreciation for each has grown over the course of your study.

- _____

  _____

- _____

  _____

- _____

  _____

- _____

  _____

- _____

  _____

Record your concluding thoughts on the Rise of the Church and the Fall of Rome:

_____

Missionaries & Barbarians

Key Concepts

- Motivations for invasion

- Barbarians' impact on the West

- The Church's response

- Celtic missionaries

- Celtic Christianity

Celtic Cross, Ireland

Into the Tumult . . .

During the supremacy of the Roman Empire, two extensive rivers formed a boundary line 2,600 miles long between her imperial citizens and their German neighbors to the north. These two formidable rivers were the Rhine and the Danube, which obstructed the southward movements of Germanic tribes all the way from the North Sea to the Black Sea. However, obstacles are eventually overcome if one persists. In this case, many persisted.

By the fourth century, the Germanic tribes, who were eagerly looking for opportunities to cross the border into the wealthy Roman empire, had spread all the way across Europe to the Russian steppes. It would be helpful to open an atlas at this point to understand what is being described. In the west, just across the Rhine river, the Franks and the Alemanni faced the

> *It was an interesting and potentially dangerous situation: hiring barbarian tribes to fight barbarian tribes.*

Roman-held province of Gaul. Behind them, in northwest Germany and on the peninsula of Jutland (in modern day Denmark) were the Saxons, Angles, and Jutes. East of the Saxons, in northwest Germany, were the Lombards and other members of the Suevi tribes. In Eastern Europe, the Marcomanni held what is known as Bohemia, while the Vandals lived on the plains of Hungary. East, beyond the Vandals, were the Goths, who were separated into the western Visigoths and the eastern Ostrogoths. The Visigoths lived as farmers in Dacia (known today as Romania) while the Ostrogoths had a huge empire in present day Ukraine.

Motivations for Invasion

Owing to their proximity to the Roman Empire, many of these tribes had been influenced by its culture and civilization. They were acculturated, meaning their cultures had been modified by borrowing or adapting aspects of the Roman way of life. This impacted their economies, as they traded with the Romans; their lifestyles, as they had more Roman luxuries; their languages, as they learned the trade languages; and their cultures, depending on their receptivity to Roman civilization.

One particular opportunity that sometimes developed from this close connection with the Empire was having a tribe accept the status of *foederati* (allies or mercenaries subsidized by the Romans in exchange for military service). This allowed barbarian tribes to live within the boundaries of the Empire, with their warriors pledged to fight invading tribes on behalf of Rome. An unusual facet of this agreement provided that these warriors were to go to battle under their own war chiefs. It was an interesting and potentially dangerous situation: hiring barbarian tribes to fight barbarian tribes.

In northern Gaul, a group of Franks entered the Empire and became foederati during the reign of Julian the Apostate. In the pay of Rome, they held the border against others of their own tribe. The Visigoths entered the Empire as foederati in AD 376, when they crossed the Danube river. The Emperor Valens, who allowed the Visigoths into the Empire, probably saw them as the first line of defense against the newest menace—the ferocious Huns. Valens subsequently died during the Battle of Adrianople in 378 against these same Visigoths who had been battered and betrayed by Roman officials.

Many individuals from various barbarian tribes also joined the Roman army directly, which was desperately in need of fighting men by this time. Since they were from warrior-based cultures, these hardy volunteers often rose to positions of prominence—one of the most famous of these being Stilicho. Though he was half Vandal, Stilicho rose quickly through the ranks to become *Master of the Horse* (commander of the cavalry) in the Roman army. Emperor Theodosius was so impressed with his work that he gave his favorite niece in marriage to Stilicho as well as making him guardian of his son, Honorius. When Theodosius died, the young Honorius became Emperor of the West, which made Stilicho the effective ruler of the West from 395–408. It was his responsibility to keep the barbarians out of the West, which was becoming far easier said than done.

Visigoths

Though foederati in name, the Visigoths only acted as allies when it suited them. And at this point in their history, the Visigoths were seeking a suitable place to live, ready to seize land regardless of who might be displaced. So, one of Stilicho's greatest tasks was to keep the Visigoths out of the Western Empire, while at the same time the Eastern Emperor was seeking to force the Visigoths out of the East. The West lost the contest. Leaving the Balkans, the Visigoths, under their chieftain Alaric, entered Greece and then battled their way through to Italy itself. Stilicho fought them at every turn, bargained with Alaric when possible, and sought to prevent their settlement in Italy. He recalled Roman legions from Britain and Gaul to assist him in fighting both the Visigoths and a group of Ostrogoths who invaded Italy in 406. This left both western provinces open to invasion, and the barbarian tribes were quick to seize the moment.

The Visigoths were seeking a suitable place to live, ready to seize land regardless of who might be displaced.

One result of having a poorly-guarded frontier was the massive Vandal invasion of 406 into Gaul, which Stilicho partially obstructed. However, with the increasing chaos, devastation, destruction of lives and property, there was less and less hope for the restoration of Roman law and order. When Stilicho was assassinated by order of Emperor Honorius in 408 (he believed the immensely powerful Stilicho was about to make his own son emperor), things went from bad to worse. Without the restraining influence of Stilicho the Vandal, the city of Rome itself was sacked in 410 by Alaric and the Visigoths.

This was a prelude of what was to come. Just as a breached dam quickly goes from a trickle to a flood, so did the barbarians invade the empire in increasingly huge, unstoppable waves—except for brief occasions when the Romans used other barbarian tribes to stop them. Stilicho had hired Germanic barbarians, as well as Huns, to help him fight the Vandals and the Visigoths, though he was ultimately unsuccessful in pushing back the flood.

Vandals

When the Vandals crossed the Rhine at the end of 406, they entered the Empire not as foederati, but as enemies of Rome. They swept through Gaul as a ravaging tornado, and, having wrought incredible destruction, moved on to Spain. After some years, the Vandals were drawn by the allure of the wealthy and untouched Roman provinces of North Africa, and in 429 they followed their king Gaiseric across the Strait of Gibraltar onto the African continent. It was reported that the whole tribe, 80,000 people in all, made the crossing. This formidable group raced across Northern Africa, capturing the Roman city of Hippo in 430 after besieging it for months (during which Augustine died). They continued on, the Romans finding them nearly invincible. In 435 the Vandals signed a treaty with the Roman Empire to become foederati in Africa, but Gaiseric broke the treaty in 439 when he captured Carthage, the major imperial city in northern Africa.

No longer foederati, the barbarians were establishing their own governments where once Rome had ruled.

On this historic North African stage, the Vandals set up the very first independent German state on Roman soil. Barbarian tribes had been marauding in the empire for decades, but this was something new. No longer foederati, the barbarians were establishing their own governments where once Rome had ruled. From this base, the Vandals now brought devastation to the inner workings of the empire. First, they stopped the grain shipments from Africa to Italy, causing a huge shortage of food in the West, which led to famine conditions. Secondly, they disrupted the flow of trade throughout the empire when Vandal pirate ships took control of the western Mediterranean. They relentlessly captured merchant ships of the empire, laden with goods destined for ports that would never see them.

Recognizing the weakness of his enemy, Gaiseric went on to attack and sack the city of Rome in 455, which made the previous sack of the city seem tame in comparison. An important part of interpreting and understanding this historic puzzle is to keep in mind that the Vandals had embraced the Arian form of Christianity. They not only saw the Roman Empire and its civilization as the enemy but also believed that the Christians of the empire were heretics. Their violent persecution of Catholic Christians led to even more devastation and destruction.

Huns

Meanwhile, on the continent of Europe, the Asiatic Huns—who were perhaps the fiercest and most terrifying of all the barbarians—were wreaking havoc and destruction all over the empire under the direction of their leader, Attila. In a fascinating twist of history, Aetius, the Roman general who would be sent by Rome to repel Attila when he invaded the West, had actually enlisted Huns during previous years to help battle other barbarians.

Aetius had spent some of his youth as a hostage of the Visigoth leader, Alaric, and later as the hostage of the Huns. Attila had also been a hostage in the Roman Empire when he was young. The giving of noble youths to be held as hostages between Rome and barbarian tribes was one means the empire used in forging alliances, as well as in keeping the tribes in check. So Aetius had learned some of the ways of the barbarians in war, while Attila had discovered weaknesses in the empire. Both of them used their knowledge to advantage during these tumultuous events of the mid-400s.

When he grew to manhood, Aetius was made commander over the Roman army in the West, which provided him with the opportunity to effectively rule the region on behalf of the young Roman Emperor Valentinian III. Aetius's major battles against the Germanic barbarians took place in Gaul, and it was there that he used the Huns as his strategic weapon. The Huns were amazing and fearful warriors, who not only commanded their horses masterfully, but could also shoot with deadly accuracy while mounted and moving. Their tactics in charging, retreating, and charging again rendered them terrifying to all those who faced the Huns in battle. No wonder that Aetius, who was a friend of the Huns from his days as a hostage, befriended and made good use of them.

However, the good times between Aetius and the Huns came to an end when Attila turned his attention from ravaging the Eastern Empire to considering the West, which was ripe for picking. When the Emperor's sister, Honoria, sent word to Attila that she wished to wed him to escape an arranged and undesirable marriage, he saw his chance. He seized upon this legal chance to gain power by demanding that his marriage dowry be half of the Western Empire! As is no surprise, Emperor Valentinian III refused the request.

Keep in mind that the Vandals had embraced the Arian form of Christianity.

Thus, in 451, at the Battle of the Catalaunian Plains (also known as the Battle of Chalôns), the two sides met in one of the greatest battles of the early Middle Ages. On the side of the Romans were ranged their occasional allies, the Visigoths (who hated the Huns more than they did the Romans), the Franks, and the Burgundians (another barbarian tribe in Gaul). On the side of the Huns were Ostrogoths and Slavs. When the Visigothic king, Theodoric I, fell in battle, the Visigoths went berserk, overwhelming the Huns. However, the Huns and their allies were able to regain their camp without being routed. And, in fact, Aetius dismissed the Visigoths from service and let the defeated Attila go. It was Attila's first and last defeat.

He returned to Italy in the following year, sacking several cities. Aetius was now powerless to stop him, but famine, the plague, and Pope Leo I kept Attila from overrunning Rome. Attila died in 453, apparently of a nosebleed on the night of his wedding. From this time, the Huns ceased to be a threat to Europe.

When Pope Leo I met with Attila and persuaded him to turn away from the city of Rome, the Church entered a new era. From 425 until 1054 is known as the Early Medieval Church. The main concern of this time is to survive invasions (which will transition from invasions by the barbarians to invasions by Vikings). Our call as Christians, however, is not to merely survive, but to advance. Thus, the Church also took the responsibility and opportunity to spread the Gospel to the Arian and pagan tribes, which required obedience, courage, and grace. During this period of Church history, monasticism also became a prominent feature in the Church. We will examine missions and monasticism in greater detail shortly.

The Church also took the responsibility and opportunity to spread the Gospel to the Arian and pagan tribes.

With the death of Attila and the fading specter of the Huns, when things were actually beginning to look brighter for the Roman people, Aetius was murdered by the fearful Emperor Valentinian in 454. This, along with the tumultuous and disruptive effect of the Vandals upon Africa and the city of Rome, created a huge power vacuum in the region of Gaul. With Aetius gone, there were no other strong Roman leaders. So, the Visigoths, who had helped to defeat Attila, stepped into the gap. Though they remained foederati in name until 475, the Visigoths basically ruled their Roman subjects in Spain and Gaul (to the Loire river) as German overlords.

Franks

The Franks, another of the tribes used to defeat the Huns in 451, were a powerful Germanic tribe who, by the year 480, were firmly entrenched in northeastern France, Belgium, and western Germany. In 481 Clovis became the ruler of a small group of the Franks, but very quickly he gained authority over other Frankish tribes. Having united them, he then used them in battle to bring all of northern Gaul under his dominion by 494. Two years later, Clovis found himself enmeshed in a battle against the Alemanni tribe which did not look hopeful. Appealing to the God of his Catholic Christian wife, Clovis promised that he would convert if he were victorious. And, being true to his word, Clovis converted and was baptized in 496. However, being a tribal king, Clovis was not content to take this step alone. According to the writings of Gregory of Tours, Clovis informed his people that all of them would convert to Christianity when he did, or risk his displeasure.

The conversion of Clovis and his followers to Catholic Christianity (as opposed to Arian Christianity) brought about conflict between this newly converted Catholic barbarian king and the barbarian kings who were Arian. The Romans living in Gaul rejoiced to have a Catholic ruler, and, along with the Roman Church, threw their full support over to Clovis. This gave him the support he needed to go to war against the Arian Visigoths who were living in southern Gaul. They were defeated in battle with Clovis in 507, and fled across the Pyrenees to Spain.

Ostrogoths

In Italy, a series of struggles had led to an Arian Ostrogoth ruling as "King of Italy." This king, Theodoric the Great, had actually been invited by the Eastern Roman Emperor to take his people (perhaps 100,000) to Italy. In Italy, their task was to overthrow Odoacer, the barbarian king who had deposed the last Western Emperor. Their march from the Balkans to Italy is an epic in itself, but the story continued once they arrived in Italy. Theodoric led his warriors to victory in three pitched battles against Odoacer, but when Odoacer took refuge in the impenetrable city of Ravenna, another three years went by before King Theodoric could finally accomplish his mission. Having overthrown and killed Odoacer in 493, he was in no mood to have another strong barbarian king like Clovis on the very doorstep of Italy. So, after the Visigothic defeat of 507, Theodoric made very clear to Clovis that he was not to continue to press south to the Mediterranean. And Clovis complied.

When King Theodoric the Great died in 526, Italy experienced great instability and turmoil between Arian Ostrogoths and Catholic Italians. The new emperor in the East, Justinian I, had just successfully defeated the Vandal kingdom in North Africa in 534, restoring this region to the rule of the Eastern Roman Empire (or, the Byzantine Empire). From this point, the Vandals ceased to exist as a nation, and their name faded from history—except as a synonym for those who willfully destroy or desecrate.

> *A series of struggles had led to an Arian Ostrogoth ruling as "King of Italy."*

Now Justinian I turned his eyes to an Italy ruled by Arian Ostrogoths. For an orthodox Christian ruler to allow heretics to rule the birthplace of the Empire was simply not acceptable. In 535 he sent an army under the command of General Belisarius (the same general who had conquered the Vandals in Africa) to recapture Italy for the Byzantine Empire. The ensuing conflict between the Byzantine armies and the Ostrogoths, which lasted for almost twenty years, brought incredible suffering and untold damage to the land and people of Italy. When it was over, the Ostrogoths ceased to exist as a nation, just as the Vandals and the Huns before them. However, holding onto a distant land is very difficult, so just three years after the death of Justinian I, yet another barbarian tribe, the Arian Lombards, successfully invaded Italy.

Lombards

Shortly before Justinian sent Belisarius to attack the Ostrogoths, a Roman monk by the name of Benedict founded a monastery at Monte Cassino in southern Italy. His experiences with other monastic communities had taught him that moderation and balance in day to day activities would allow ordinary men to flourish as monks. So, for the new monastery at Monte

Cassino, Benedict wrote out a timetable for daily life, which became known as the Benedictine Rule. It combined spiritual disciplines, such as prayer and study, with regular agricultural work, which allowed the monks to be self-sufficient. The Rule also provided time for rest and refreshment. Because of the wisdom and simplicity of this schedule, the monastery flourished during the short time of the Byzantine rule of Italy. When the Arian Lombards invaded that area, however, the monks fled to Rome carrying with them their copy of the Rule. From Rome, the Benedictine Rule disseminated throughout all of Europe, becoming the standard for life and conduct in most Roman monasteries. That is why Benedict is known as the "Father of Western Monasticism."

When it was over, the Ostrogoths ceased to exist as a nation, just as the Vandals and the Huns before them.

By late 569 the Lombards had conquered much of Italy, removing the rule of the Byzantines from all but a few significant areas, such as Ravenna. Sometime in the latter part of the seventh century, the Lombards converted to Catholic Christianity, though no records tell accurately what brought about this doctrinal change.

British Isles

During the time when the Vandals were storming North Africa, the Visigoths were controlling Spain, the Franks were dominating Gaul, and the Ostrogoths were ruling Italy, there were groups of barbarians ravaging the former Roman Province of Britain. Upon the recall of Roman soldiers from Britain during the command of Stilicho, Saxons, Angles, and Jutes had taken advantage of the decreased military power on the coasts to help themselves to whatever spoils they could find. That was not the Britons' only woe, however. Their northern neighbors, the Picts, who had been held at bay by the soldiers manning Hadrian's Wall, made their ferocious presence known once again in England. Joining the Picts in increasing numbers were the marauding Scots from the island of Ireland. (These Scots would eventually give their name to Scotland, the land of the Picts.)

Amazingly, this was the moment that God moved upon the former slave of the Irish, a Christian by the name of Patrick, to return to the land of his captivity in order to share the gospel with them. In approximately 432 Patrick began his mission in northern Ireland. Through his ministry, many of the people of Ireland were converted from druidic paganism to Christianity. This made a huge difference to the land of Britain, as these Christian Scots eventually quit warring against the Britons. But, in the meantime, before their conversion and new peaceful intentions, the British leader of the time, Vortigern (meaning "over king") sought the aid of barbarian tribes to help fight against the Picts and Scots. As we have already seen, this was a solution others in the Empire had tried, with varying results.

Vortigern hired Jutes, Hengist, and Horsa with some hundreds of their followers, to stop the northern invaders. They were completely successful in shutting down the Picts, which removed a tremendous threat from Britain. With the success of Patrick's mission in Ireland and the marriage of Vortigern's daughter to the son of the Irish king (according to British chroniclers), the threat from the Scots ended, as well. Now with the ending of northern hostilities, these hired barbarians, along with their invited Anglo-Saxon friends and relations, were out of work on the coast of wealthy and fertile England. No one left to fight—except, of course, their employers.

When Vortigern was unable to pay the barbarians their wages in 442, they revolted. As one commentator, Gildas, wrote:

> The barbarians . . . were not slow to put their threats into action. The fire of righteous vengeance, kindled by the sins of the past, blazed from sea to sea. . . . Once lit, it did not die down. When it had wasted town and country in that area, it burnt up almost the whole surface of the island, until its red and savage tongue licked the western ocean.

After the first wave of revolt, the Britons retaliated and fought against the Anglo-Saxons whenever they could. Hengist's brother, Horsa, was killed during one of these battles in approximately 455, but Hengist went on to be ruler of the kingdom of Kent. The Anglo-Saxon, or *English,* invaders eventually conquered almost the entire land of Britain, apart from Wales and Cornwall. They set up pagan Germanic kingdoms on what had been Christian British-Roman soil. Unlike their counterparts on the European Continent, these barbarians were not content to live side by side with the native people. Instead, it appears that the Anglo-Saxons either killed or drove off most of the Britons (enslaving some, particularly women), and seized their land.

The Picts made their ferocious presence known once again in England.

This paints quite a horrific picture, doesn't it? Yet, by God's mercy and design, this would become the very site of amazing grace, the place where Christianity would take deep root and eventually send out missionaries to bless the nations. But first, the Anglo-Saxons needed missionaries to come to them. They would come from two sources: the Roman Church and the Celtic Church. They would travel from two places: Rome and Ireland (by way of Scotland).

Celtic Missionaries

Ireland had, as we have already seen, been infused with the gospel by the preaching of Patrick in the mid-400s. This island, which had never been Romanized, took Christianity into its culture and was transformed. In the process, Christianity took on a new look and new approach that differed somewhat from Roman Christianity. This Celtic Church had the flavor of the

By God's mercy and design, this would become the very site of amazing grace; the place where Christianity would take deep root.

Celtic people of Ireland. They were tribal people, related through clans and kin, rather than through political organizations like the Roman Empire. Therefore, their Church functioned on a relational basis, rather than through a hierarchical, political structure. In time, this would lead to a head-on confrontation with the Roman Church. But in the beginning, anyone who was willing to evangelize the pagans was welcomed to the task.

From Ireland, Celtic missionaries began to move throughout England and continental Europe. Two of the best known were Columba, who took a team of missionaries to Iona in Scotland, and Columbanus, the monk who brought the light of the gospel to barbarians in Europe. Columbanus started monasteries in Gaul, moving on to Switzerland, and finally Italy. One of the monks who traveled with Columbanus, Gall, stayed in Switzerland and worked among the Alemanni tribes, who were eventually converted.

From the monastery at Iona, the gospel spread to the northern part of England through the ministry of Aidan, founder of the monastery at Lindisfarne in 635. Aidan was not the first to preach in the pagan land of Northumbria, however. A few years earlier, a Roman monk had been evangelizing under the approval of Edwin, the most powerful Anglo-Saxon king of his time and the first Christian king of Northumbria. But when Edwin was killed, the kingdom reverted back to paganism. The next king, who had been raised at Iona, desired to see Christianity in his realm, so he, Oswald, invited the monks of Iona to send a team for the purpose of evangelization. Aidan, with twelve others, accepted the formidable challenge.

Jesus had said,

You know that the rulers of the Gentiles lord it over them, and those who are great exercise authority over them. Yet it shall not be so among you; but whoever desires to become great among you, let him be your servant.
Matthew 20:25–26

That is how Aidan, bishop of Lindisfarne, lived. He served the people around him, to the point that he sometimes got in trouble with the new king of Northumbria.

One story depicting the humility and

Iron and bronze helmet, Sutton Hoo, Suffolk, England

servant nature of Aidan concerns the king's gift of a horse to Aidan. In those days, only the peasants and poor people walked, while people who were wealthy or held positions of importance rode horses. When the king discovered that Aidan was walking everywhere, he insisted on giving him one of his best horses. Aidan graciously thanked the king for his gift, but when a beggar asked him for alms, Aidan gave him the horse. A short time later, King Oswin invited Aidan to dinner, and coldly reprimanded him for giving his gift horse to a beggar. Aidan replied, "My lord king, surely you can't mean to tell me that that foal of a mare is more important to you than a beggar, the child of God?"

From Ireland, Celtic missionaries began to move throughout England and continental Europe.

Catholic Missionaries

In 596 Pope Gregory the Great had sent a missionary team to the Anglo-Saxons in southern England. Augustine of Canterbury headed this team, and was successful in converting the king, Ethelbert I of Kent. The Roman missionaries continued the work of evangelization, but eventually came into conflict with the Celtic missionaries. The divisive issues that separated them seem unimportant to us today: the style of tonsure, the date of Easter, the nature of a bishop's travel. The deciding issue, however, and the one which typified the differences between Celtic and Roman Christianity concerned the structure of authority in the Church. The Celtic believers looked to their local abbot (the head of the monastery) for direction and clarity, while the Romans were under submission to the pope, whom they considered to be the head of the entire Church.

In 664 a *Synod,* or ecclesiastical council, was held at the monastery of Whitby in England. The abbess of this double monastery (both men and women) was Hilda, who had been trained by Aidan. She, along with the current bishop of Lindisfarne and the bishop of Essex, presented the view of the Celtic Church, while Wilfrid, abbot of Ripon, represented the Roman Church. Wilfrid was able to persuasively argue his case, and the Synod chose that Christian England would henceforth follow Rome.

The barbarian invasions of the West brought about a dramatic transformation in Europe. From a highly structured, highly developed empire, the various lands occupied and settled by Germanic tribes now functioned very differently. Many historians give the early Middle Ages the name, "The Dark Ages," because it appeared that the light of civilization had gone out. The center of power had shifted from the light and airy Mediterranean basin to the gloomy wilds of northern Europe, which was to be the birthplace of medieval civilization. But the lights had not gone out. They were burning brightly from the windows of the monasteries, both Celtic and Roman. ◄

Phase 1

Key People (Church)

Patrick
Chief missionary to Ireland

Benedict
Author of Benedictine rule for monasteries

Columba
Missionary to Scotland

Brendan the Navigator
Celtic missionary possibly to North America

Gregory the Great
Father of the medieval papacy

Augustine of Canterbury
Missionary to southern England

Aidan
Evangelized northern England & southern Scotland

Hilda
Celtic abbess of Whitby

Boniface
Missionary to Germany

▶ Listen to This!

What in the World? VOL. 2

DISC ONE

» Barbarians in Rome (track 6)

» Christianity Among the Goths (track 7)

» The Huns & the Franks (track 8)

» Barbarians & Christian England (track 9)

True Tales VOL. 2

DISC ONE

» Attila the Hun (track 3)

» Saint Columba (track 4)

Digging Deeper VOL. 2

DISC TWO: THE CHURCH IN CHARGE

» Introduction through Missionaries & Monasteries (tracks 1–4)

▶ Read For Your Life

The Holy Bible

» **Missions & evangelism:** Mark 16:15–16; Romans 10:8–15; 2 Corinthians 5:17–21; Ephesians 2 & 3

» **Encouragement in ministry:** 2 Corinthians 4

▶ Talk Together

Opinion Column

» What did you find to be the most interesting aspect, or the most fascinating person, you encountered in your introduction to these early missionaries and the barbarian tribes?

» Imagine you were Patrick's mother or father as he tells you that he is returning to the place of his captivity—Ireland! What would you say to him? To God?

» What do you think were some of the unexpected results of inviting the Jutes' leaders, Hengist and Horsa, to England after the Roman legions left?

» Legendary stories are told about how Patrick encountered opposition from druids as he evangelized Ireland. These encounters provided amazing displays of God's power, showing the native peoples that God was more powerful than their local gods. In what ways do you suppose these events might have paved the way for Ireland to peacefully convert to Christianity?

» There is some evidence that Irish monks, who were known for their traveling ways, may have actually visited the North American continent. The most famous of these voyaging monks was Brendan the Navigator. Imagine you were about to embark on a voyage with Brendan. How would you prepare yourself physically, emotionally, mentally, and spiritually?

Critical Puzzling

» In one of history's great dramatic moments, Boniface, the Apostle to Germany, cut down a sacred oak tree in Geismar (western Germany) which was considered to be the sanctuary of the pagan god, Thor. He did this in order to show the Germans the power of the True God and free them from their fears and devotion to paganism. When he wasn't struck down and killed by Thor, the watching crowd was absolutely astounded. What do you think the people thought about Boniface? How might this have changed people's lives and hearts? Compare this to Elijah's challenge to the prophets of Baal as recorded in 1 Kings 18:17–40.

Key People (world)

Alaric (Visigoths)
Sacked Rome in AD 410

Genseric (Vandals)
Conqueror of Roman North Africa

Attila (Huns)
Sought to conquer Rome

Hengist & Horsa (Jutes)
Anglo-Saxon invaders of Britain

King Arthur (Briton)
Legendary king who defended Britain

Clovis (Franks)
First orthodox Christian barbarian king

Theodoric (Ostrogoths)
Barbarian who ruled Italy with Roman law

» Attila the Hun was known to Europeans as the "Scourge of God." It is interesting to consider why Europe was at the point where scourging would take place. What were some of the issues facing both the Roman Empire and the Church at this point? What specific events in recent history can you think of that caused people in your country to seek God? Do you see any good that comes from this kind of terror?

» Many of the barbarian tribes, including the Visigoths, the Ostrogoths, and the Vandals, converted to the Arian form of Christianity as they came into Europe. What are some of the differences between Christianity and Arianism? In what ways do you think the Visigoths, Ostrogoths or Vandals acted like other Christians, and in what ways did they act like pagans? How do you think their Arianism influenced their actions? *(Hint: Consider what happened when the Vandals sacked Rome in AD 456.)*

▶ Resources for Digging Deeper

Choose a few books that look interesting, or find your own.

MIDDLE AGES

Early Times: The Story of the Middle Ages

Suzanne Strauss Art · Covering the time period from the invasion of the barbarians to the fall of Constantinople in 1453, this book weaves together various aspects of the Middle Ages. **UE+**

The Early Middle Ages

Translated from Italian, this book is one of the best introductions to the early Middle Ages for students. It includes the developments from the AD 300s to 1000. **UE+**

Famous Men of the Middle Ages

John H. Haaren & A. B. Poland, edited by Cyndy Shearer and Robert Shearer · Short, interesting biographies of fascinating personalities from the Middle Ages, this book is a wonderful introduction for all ages. It includes such people as Justinian (Byzantine), Mohammed (Islam), Charlemagne, St. Francis, Marco Polo, and Gutenberg. I would suggest using this book beginning with this Unit, as there are several biographies of Barbarian leaders. **E+**

EARLY MISSIONARIES

Augustine Came to Kent

Barbara Willard · A tremendous story of the coming of Roman missionaries to southern England in AD 597. You will gain much understanding of the difficulties and circumstances facing these early missionaries. **UE+**

Christianity and the Celts

Ted Olsen · One of the InterVarsity Press Histories series, this title is filled with information concerning the spread of Christianity to and through the Celts. It includes fascinating details on this part of the Church. **MS+**

Saint Patrick: Pioneer Missionary to Ireland

Michael J. McHugh · A well written, interesting introduction to Patrick's life and adventures. **E+**

Patrick and Irish Christianity

Tom Corfe · An excellent, factual resource about a most courageous and amazing man, Patrick of Ireland. Well written and interesting. **UE+**

From Jerusalem to Irian Jaya

Ruth A. Tucker · This book is especially helpful for this Unit to examine the missionaries who ministered to the barbarians. **UE+**

The Fields of Bannockburn

Donna Fletcher Crow · This is a sweeping saga of the history of Scotland, told in a storyteller's fashion. It is included in this Unit because of its stories of St. Columba (missionary to the Scots), Ninian, and Mungo. **MS+**

ENGLISH HISTORY

Bede's Ecclesiastical History of the English People

The Venerable Bede · The earliest history written about England, this is a fascinating book to read in translation. Look for it in your library. **MS+**

The Lantern Bearers

Rosemary Sutcliff · The legendary stories of King Arthur are deemed to be based on true events that happened shortly after the departure of the Roman Legions from Britain. This book is a fictional account of what may have occurred, and is absolutely fascinating. **UE i**

Beowulf

Translated by Frederick Rebsamen · If you would like to try Beowulf in the poetry version, the library will be able to provide this book for you. Be sure to read it aloud, with drama. **RA**

Beowulf

Retold by Rosemary Sutcliff · Beowulf is a fascinating poem about early Anglo-Saxon history. If reading the translation listed above is too difficult, Sutcliff's version is fairly tame, and very readable. **E+**

After the Flood

Bill Cooper · This astonishing book looks back into the earliest pagan lists of Anglo-Saxon, Britons, Danish, Norwegian, and Celtic kings, and traces them back to the Table of Nations listed in Genesis 10 and 11. There is also a fascinating chapter on Beowulf showing the relationship between the "monsters" of Beowulf and certain kinds of dinosaurs. **MS+**

BARBARIANS

Why Are You Calling Me A Barbarian?

Birgitta Petrén and Elisabetta Putini · Written for young children, this captivating book introduces some of the dynamics and differences between Romans and "barbarians" through the lives of two children, Martilla and Marbord. **E+**

Attila: World Leaders Past and Present

Steven Bela Vardy · A fascinating look at a man who is considered by some to be the essence of barbarianism and who, to others, is a hero. **MS+**

Barbarians, Christians, and Muslims: The Cambridge Introduction to History

Trevor Cairns · Fascinating, well-written account of the barbarian tribes, the growth of Christianity in England, the Byzantine empire, and the growth of Islam. One of the best all around overviews of this time period, and a valuable resource. **E+**

What books did you like best?

_____

_____

_____

_____

The Internet also contains a wealth of information about Missionaries & Barbarians.

What sites were the most helpful?

_____

_____

_____

For more books, use these Dewey Decimal numbers in your library:

Middle Ages: #970.1

Early Missionaries: #266

English History: #914.2

Barbarians: #936

▶ Student Self-Evaluation UNIT 2, PHASE 1

Dates and hours:_____

Key Concepts

Rephrase the five Key Concepts of this Unit and confirm your understanding of each:

• Motivations for invasion:

_____

• Barbarians' impact on the West:

_____

• The Church's response:

_____

• Celtic missionaries:

_____

• Celtic Christianity:

_____

Tools for Self-Evaluation

Evaluate your personal participation in the discussions of this Phase. Bearing in mind that a good participant in a discussion is not always the most vocal participant, ask yourself these questions: Were you an active participant? Did you ask perceptive questions? Were you willing to listen to other participants of the discussion and draw out their opinions? Record your observations and how you would like to improve your participation in the future:

_____

_____

Every time period is too complex to be understood in one Phase of study. Evaluate your current knowledge of Missionaries & Barbarians. What have you focused on so far? What are your weakest areas of knowledge?

_____

_____

Based on the evaluation of this introduction, project ahead what you would like to study more of in the following Phases:

_____

Phase 2

▶ Research & Reporting

Explore one or more of these areas to discover something significant!

Barbarian Tribes

Research and report on the originating and eventual settling places of one or several of the various barbarian tribes, such as the Ostrogoths, the Visigoths, the Vandals, the Franks, the Saxons, the Angles, the Jutes, and the Huns. Be sure to include a map showing their geographic migrations.

St. Patrick

Discover more about the life and ministry of Saint Patrick. What kind of legends are told about him? What impact did Patrick have on Ireland?

Attila the Hun

Investigate the military tactics of Attila the Hun. Describe his victories and his defeats. In addition, consider the various aspects of his character and his way of dealing with friends and foes. Analyze his life in light of the Scriptures.

Brendan the Navigator

Investigate the life and legendary journey of Brendan the Navigator to North America. Be sure to include information about the attempt in the twentieth century to replicate his travels.

Clovis, King of the Franks

Clovis was the first of the barbarian tribal leaders to convert to Catholicism (rather than Arianism). Research and report on his conversion, and the influential people in his life, including his wife, Clothilde. What dynasty in France did Clovis begin? How did his conversion affect his tribal people?

Theodoric, the Ostrogoth

Discover more about Theodoric. What country did he rule, and by whose authority did he come to power? Why did the Roman people accept him, and why did they distrust him? What was the short-term effect of his rule? The long-term effect? How long were the Ostrogoths able to control this country?

King Arthur

Investigate the legendary life of King Arthur, and examine what is believed to be the basis in fact for this legend. Consider the time period—late 400s to 500s—and report the impact of the departure of the Roman legions from Britain at the time when the barbarians were advancing into the Empire. How does this explain or magnify our understanding of King Arthur and his legend?

Anglo-Saxon Invasion

Discover the reasons for the Anglo-Saxon invasion of Britain. Who were the Britons fighting prior to the Anglo-Saxons? What effect did the Anglo-Saxon invasion have on the native Britons? Who brought the Gospel to these invaders? How did they respond?

St. Columba

Research and report on Saint Columba and his missionary endeavors in Scotland. Why did Columba leave Ireland to go to Scotland? What were the people of Scotland like prior to conversion? What were some of the effects of Christianity taking root in Scotland?

Aidan of Lindisfarne

Founder of the monastery at Lindisfarne in 635, Aidan had a passion for gently sharing the Gospel with all the people he met. Discover the life and influence of Aidan, and the impact he had upon the Anglo-Saxon kingdom of Northumbria.

St. Benedict

Learn more about the life of Saint Benedict, who wrote the governing rules for Roman monasteries in the Middle Ages.

Venerable Bede

Discover and describe the life of the Venerable Bede. Who was he, what did he do, and why was he important? What aspect of his influence affects us today? (Hint: Check the calendar.)

Hilda, Abbess of Whitby

Hilda was a remarkable woman, who headed the Celtic monastery of Whitby, which was a center of Christian literature and art. She hosted the Synod of Whitby in 664, when the Celtic Church lost its struggle with the Roman Church. Research and report on Hilda and the historic Synod of Whitby, describing the influence of each.

Sutton Hoo

Discover the fascinating story of Sutton Hoo, the burial place of an early Anglo-Saxon king (c. 600) in England. Report your findings on this treasure, from an archaeological viewpoint. What does it tell us about life in England in this time period?

Gregory the Great

Research and report on the life and ministry of Gregory the Great. What was his background? Whom did he send to England? What was the impact of this mission? What did Pope Gregory I do for the people of Rome? How did it benefit them?

White Huns

Discover more about the Hephthalites (or White Huns). What is known about them? How did their invasions change the aristocracy of northwest India and Pakistan? What impact did they have upon western China and Persia?

▶ Brain Stretchers

Easter

One of the significant differences between the Celtic Church and the Roman Church in England was the way they figured the date for Easter. The Celts had the same formula as the Orthodox church in the East, while the Roman Church used the formula followed in the West. Research and report on the possible reasons that the Celtic Church knew of, and followed, the Orthodox system.

Arianism & the Barbarians

What are some of the possible reasons for the conversion of so many barbarian tribes to Arianism? How did the Arian beliefs of the barbarians affect the Roman people, both in their attitudes and actions? Discover the life of Ulfilas, Arian missionary to the Goths, and the influence of his life among the barbarians.

Celtic Church

With the resources available to you, research the Celtic church. What were its distinctives? How did it differ from the Roman church? How were these differences eventually settled?

Barbarian Invasions

Investigate the possible reasons for the barbarian invasions. For instance, what might have forced the movement of the Hunnic people, which in turn led to the movement of the Goths?

Create Your Own Research Topic

_____

_____

_____

▶ Timeline

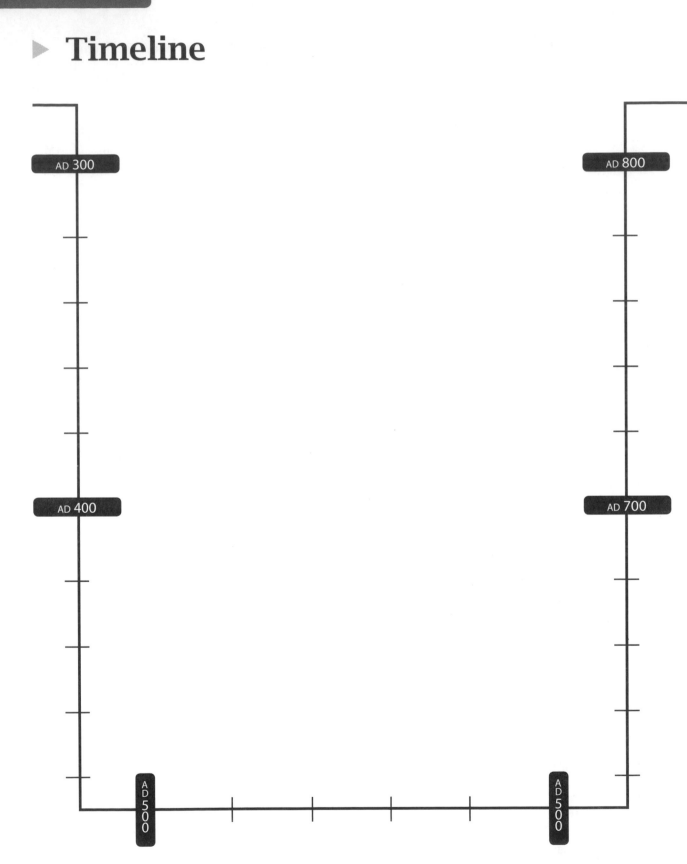

AD 300

AD 800

AD 400

AD 700

AD 500

AD 600

Consider this for your timeline

Consider the number of warrior chiefs from the different barbarian tribes—representing different languages or dialects, different cultures, different points of origin—and how it was the work of the Church to evangelize them all. The nature of missions in the Church changed during the time of the barbarians, since the Gospel was now going not to a civilized but to an uncivilized people. Consider the prominent people of the Church during this time, and notice that a large portion of them were missionaries who had daunting tasks before them.

Key Events

Sack of Rome

Sack of Hippo

Synod of Whitby

Battle of Catalaunian Plains

Battle of Adrianople

CONSIDER:

English derives many of its words from a rich heritage of earlier languages and cultures. If this fascinates you, consider investigating these ancestors of modern English (you may want to ask your librarian for assistance):

Pre-Celtic

Celtic

Latin

Old English

Norse

Norman French

▶ Words to Watch

Remember—The easiest way to learn a subject is to master its terms:

Celtic	Ostrogoths	Visigoths	Vandals
Franks	Angles	Saxons	missionaries
Jutes	Huns	Britons	barbarians
depose	Scots	Picts	monastery
illumine	venerable		

Other words you need to look up:

_____

_____

_____

_____

_____

_____

_____

▶ **Student Self-Evaluation** UNIT 2, PHASE 2

Dates and hours:_____

Research Project

Summarize your research question:

_____

_____

List your most useful sources by author, title, and page number or URL where applicable (continue list in margin if necessary):

_____

_____

Now take a moment to evaluate the sources you just listed. Do they provide a balanced view of your research question? Should you have sought an additional opinion? Are your sources credible (if you found them on your own)? Record your observations:

_____

_____

Evaluate your research project in its final presentation. What are its strengths? If you had time to revisit this project, what would you change? Consider giving yourself a letter grade based on your project's merits and weaknesses.

_____

_____

Letter grade: _____

You have just completed an area of specific research in the time of Missionaries & Barbarians. Now what would you like to explore in the upcoming Phases? Set some objectives for yourself:

_____

Phase 3

▶ Maps & Mapping

Physical Terrain

» Label the Irish Sea, the English Channel, the Black Sea, and the Mediterranean on the outline map.

» Color these areas conquered by barbarian tribes (use different colors for each area): England, conquered by Anglo-Saxons; Spain, Visigoths; France, Franks & Burgundians; Italy, Ostrogoths; northwest Africa, Vandals.

» Label and color the Rhine and Danube rivers.

» Locate and indicate these major mountain ranges: the Carpathians, the Alps, the Pyrenees.

Geopolitical

» Locate and label these places in the British Isles: Iona, the monastery begun by Columba; Northumbria, site of Lindisfarne and the evangelization of northern England by Aidan; Canterbury, center of Augustine's Roman church in England; Kent, site of Horsa's kingdom; Wales, the last stronghold of native Britons. What is the terrain of these different areas?

» Locate and label Hesse and Thuringia (where Boniface evangelized) in Germany. What is the terrain of these areas?

» Draw lines tracing the missionaries of the Celtic church and indicate the major sites where they worked. Draw lines tracing the missionaries of the Roman church, and indicate the major sites where they worked. What kind of geographical difficulties did these missionaries face (i.e., mountains, deserts, etc.)?

Explore

» ***Christian Outreach:*** What is the status of evangelical outreach today to western Europe and the British Isles? What opportunities and what difficulties face those who share the gospel in these areas?

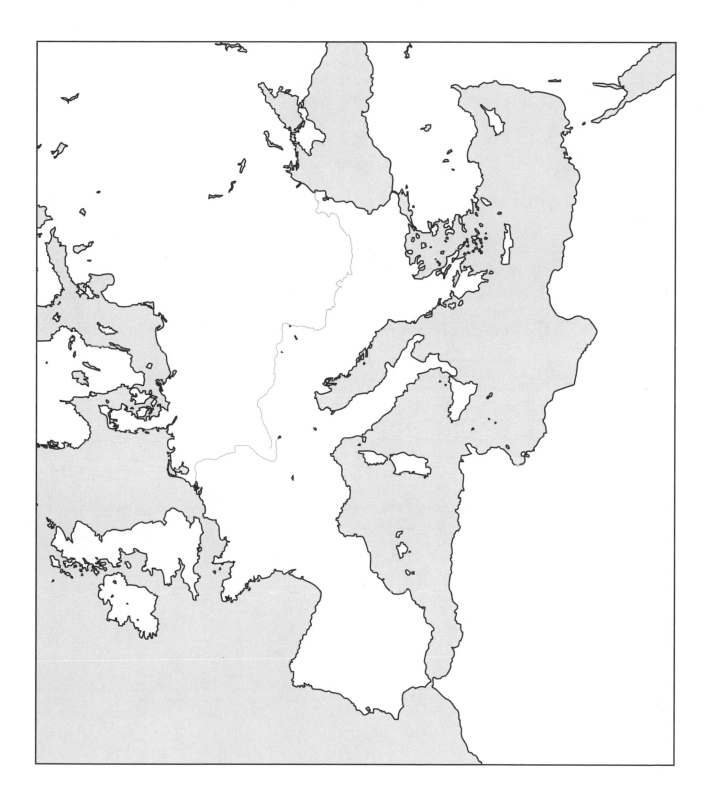

▶ Art Appreciation

Celtic Cross at Iona

The Celtic Cross was a highly decorative, beautiful piece of religious artwork. When made out of stone as a large monument, it seems to have marked the sites of important Christian events, and it may also have symbolized to the local people the protective power of the cross.

> » Examine the details of the stone carvings, the gracefulness of design. What does this say to you about the craftsmen of this time?

> » What words could you use to relate this work of art? How would you describe it to someone who was blind?

Lindisfarne Gospel

The monks of Lindisfarne illuminated their handwritten manuscripts of Scripture with beautiful pictures and colorful designs. The *Lindisfarne Gospel* allows us a glimpse of the remarkable artistry of these men.

> » How would you describe the style of illuminating used by the monks?

> » Why do you think they used illustrations and vibrant designs in these copies of Scripture?

Visigothic Crown of King Recceswinth

The highly mobile barbarians carried both their art and their fortunes with them in easy-to-tote jewelry, weapons, and such. This stunningly beautiful piece shows the level of artistry of the Visigoths.

> » What differences do you see between this and typical Roman art work? Which has more vibrancy, more color?

> » How would you describe this Visigothic crown?

CONSIDER:

The *Lindisfarne Gospel* was created by a remarkable artist, Eadfrith, the Bishop of Lindisfarne between 698 and 721. Since he copied the words as well as created the illustrations—tasks usually done by at least two people, the *scribe* and the *illuminator*—the manuscript has a wonderfully coherent design.

▶ Architecture

Gallarus Oratory

Built between the seventh and eighth century, the Gallarus Oratory is the best preserved early church building in Ireland. With its corbelled stone walls and wise architectural design, this inverted boat-shaped church has remained watertight for centuries.

» Locate a photo of the Gallarus Oratory on the Dingle peninsula, County Kerry, Ireland. How does this architecture differ from that found in Italy during this same time period? How would you describe this building? What do you think it was like to worship in this church?

▶ Arts in Action

Select one or more, and let your artistic juices flow!

Illuminating a manuscript

Select a portion of Bible text to write out as a manuscript. Using a pencil or a fine tip black ink pen, create the outline of an appropriate illumination for your text. Then, with colored pencils (or fine tip colored pens), fill in the outlines. Try to create a look similar to the *Lindisfarne Gospel*, or to the *Book of Kells* (which was created in Ireland).

Barbarian Jewelry

Using the Visigothic crown as your inspiration, create a similar piece of jewelry using beads, wire, metal (or foil) and string. For further information, consult a book on creating simple jewelry from the library.

▶ Science

Herbal Remedies

The medieval monks lived in monasteries which had to produce all kinds of goods for the people living there, including food, clothing, and shelter. They also had to make medicines for the sick. Since they did not have neighborhood drug stores, they created herb gardens to provide herbs for medicinal purposes. Discover more about herbs and herbal remedies that we use today. There are many books and resources you can find on this subject.

> » Purchase an aloe vera plant, and put it in a sunny window. Next time someone in your family gets a sunburn or accidentally burns a finger on something hot, break a piece of the aloe leaf off, and squeeze the juice out onto the burn. Describe the results. You may need to repeat the application. Is this an effective treatment? What other kinds of herbs are used for medicinal purposes?

Ocean Currents

What are the chances of a person finding land starting from the British Isles and going west? What naturally propels a boat or ship on the ocean (if they do not have an engine or oars)? Two things: wind and current. Find books in the library on oceanography, currents, seasonal wind patterns, etc. Also, look for books by Thor Heyerdahl whose voyages across the oceans in primitive vessels are absolutely compelling and hair-raising!

> » To get a simple idea of how a current in the ocean works, try playing "poohsticks." This is a game first mentioned as being played by Winnie-the-Pooh and friends in the book *The House at Pooh Corner*. Standing on a bridge over a stream, have each student or everyone in the family drop a similar size stick (you will want to mark them in some way so they can be identified). Notice how some sticks shoot through the water very quickly, while others lag behind in slower water. See whose stick emerges on the other side of the bridge first. With this in mind, talk about what happens to a boat that sails in the current, like the Gulf Stream in the Atlantic Ocean, as opposed to sailing outside the current.

CONSIDER:

Brendan the Navigator is believed by many to have sailed to the New World in his little boat. That is an amazing thing to consider—a tiny boat sailing on a huge ocean.

▶ Music

Pope Gregory I, called *The Great*, was not only concerned with missionaries and making treaties with barbarians but also with standardizing music. It is from him that we derive "Gregorian Chant" or plainsong. You can understand more about this style from an encyclopedia or dictionary of music.

Discover

Of the Father's Love Begotten

Aurelius Clemens Prudentius (AD 348–413) • Prudentius, native of Spain, was trained as a lawyer and rose to high office in the State, "holding the reins of power over famous cities," serving as a judge. When he was fifty-seven, however, he gave it all up to focus solely on God. His poetry was artistic and powerful, which made later hymn writers call Prudentius the "prince of early Christian poets," and "the Horace and Virgil of the Christians."

Father, We Praise Thee, Now the Night is Over

Pope Gregory I (AD 540–604) • Pope Gregory the Great called himself, "the servant of the servants of God," and was a dedicated leader of the Roman Church. He introduced a simpler form of music to be used in worship, "Gregorian Chant," which is noted for its musical simplicity, its solemnity, its heavenly beauty, and its unity (everyone sings in unison).

O God, Thou Art the Father

St. Columba (c. AD 521–597) • One of the great missionaries to Scotland, he wrote sacred poetry in both Latin and Gaelic. This is translated from his hymn *"Christus redemptor gentium"*.

Try This

» The hymn *Of the Father's Love Begotten* has a plainsong melody line. Sing it slowly, and for the best effect, sing it in an empty hallway or room to get the spine-tingling sense of a Gregorian Chant.

» The tune *Father, We Praise Thee, Now the Night is Over* is also a plainsong. Try singing this as the morning prayer around the breakfast table!

Listen

All Glory, Laud, & Honor MUSIC CD:

Of the Father's Love Begotten
Father, We Praise Thee, Now the Night is Over
O God, Thou Art the Father

▶ Cooking

We can hardly study the Irish without a bit o' good Irish stew and some Irish bread!

Irish Stew

3 pounds potatoes, peeled and thinly sliced
1 pound onions, thinly sliced
1 qt beef stock

Salt & freshly ground pepper to taste
3 pounds stewing lamb, cut in cubes
Chopped fresh parsley for garnish

Line the bottom of a dutch oven or stove-top casserole with a layer of sliced potatoes. Season with salt and pepper. Add a layer of onions with seasonings, then a layer of lamb. Continue layering, seasoning each layer with salt and pepper. End with a layer of potatoes. Pour in the stock and bring rapidly to a boil. Skim the foam off the surface of the stew, then reduce the heat, cover and simmer until the meat is tender, about two and a half hours. Sprinkle stew with fresh chopped parsley. Serves 6.

Irish Soda Bread

4 cups all-purpose flour
1 tsp baking soda
¼ cup sugar
4 tbsp cold butter, cut into small pieces
1 egg

1 tsp salt
1 tbsp baking powder
⅛ tsp ground cardamom
1¾ cup buttermilk

Preheat oven to 375. Lightly grease two 8 inch round baking pans; set aside. Place the flour in a large bowl; add salt, soda, baking powder, sugar, and cardamom. Stir until blended. Cut in butter to make a crumbly mixture. In a separate bowl, beat together the buttermilk and egg; stir into the dry ingredients until just moistened. Turn out onto a floured surface and knead until smooth (2 to 3 minutes). Divide dough in half. Shape each half into a smooth, round loaf; place loaves in prepared pans. Evenly press down each loaf until dough comes to edges of pan. With a floured sharp knife, cut a large cross, about ½ inch deep, in center of each loaf. Bake for 35 to 40 minutes, or until a toothpick inserted in center of bread comes out clean. Makes 2 round loaves.

▶ Student Self-Evaluation UNIT 2, PHASE 3

Dates and hours:_____

Evaluate your projects

List which of the activities listed in this Phase you did:

_____

_____

Rate your enthusiasm: _____

Explain: _____

_____

Rate the precision of your approach:_____

Explain: _____

_____

Rate your effort toward the completion of the project: _____

Explain: _____

_____

Ask yourself what worked and what did not. What would you do differently in the future, and what would you repeat?

_____

_____

How specifically did these hands-on activities enhance your knowledge of Missionaries & Barbarians? What made them worthwhile?

_____

_____

In the first three Phases of this Unit, what aspect of the time period has most captured your imagination? What would you like to creatively pursue to conclude your study?

_____

_____

Phase 4

▶ In Your Own Way . . .

We have seen the dramatically changing scene in Europe as the barbarians invaded the former Roman Empire. We have also examined the powerful witness of the missionaries who brought the good news of Jesus to these fierce barbarians. Now, choose a selection of these activities, or create your own, which will best express what you have learned from this Unit.

LINGUISTICS

Journalism

Imagine you are the investigative, on-the-scene reporter from the *Essence of the Empire* newspaper. You have been assigned the story of a lifetime—interview Attila the Hun (and live to tell about it!). Ask all of the typical questions one would ask of an invading barbarian, and don't forget to ask his opinion about his name on the street: "Scourge of God."

Write a letter to the editor of the *Briton Times* expressing your opinion of the country's invitation to the Jutes to come defend your countrymen. Make a careful assessment of the possible dangers connected with this rash act.

Prose

Columba has asked you to accompany him to Iona, off the coast of Scotland. Keep a journal of the voyage, the initial landing, and Columba's encounter with the druidic king Brude.

Clothilde, wife of the barbarian king Clovis, has asked you to write a carefully worded prayer request to send back home to her folks' church. Knowing that it may be intercepted and misunderstood, compose this heartfelt request for prayer for her husband's salvation.

Poetry

Write a poem from the viewpoint of the besieged Christians of Hippo during the Vandal attack in northwest Africa. Remember that the seventy-five year old Augustine of Hippo dies during this siege by Arian barbarians.

Playing with Words

Complete the following rhyming poem:

A missionary we call Boniface, one day
Cut down an oak that was in folks' way . . .

ART

Painting/Drawing

Create a collage-style painting of the Celtic Church, with its stone crosses, corbelled stone churches, coracles, and the missionaries' victory over druidic powers. Include also the green of the British Isles, the recurring rain and the sea.

Paint or draw your vision of King Arthur, whether it be the legendary king of Camelot or the hardy soldier of legionary descent engaged in fighting the Anglo-Saxons.

Graphic Design

Design an advertisement to enlist "The Few, the Brave, the Godly" to share in Brendan the Navigator's adventures as he sails west into uncharted seas.

Political Cartooning

Draw a political cartoon of the various barbarian hordes piling up on top of each other in their haste to loot the remains of the Roman Empire.

MUSIC

Performance Practice

With your teacher's help, select an appropriate piece of music which expresses some element of invasion by the barbarians, or perhaps, music of the lands where they settled. Prepare and perform the piece for an audience. Communicate with your audience the reason for your selection either in the program notes or in a short speech.

Compose

Write a song of praise and worship in the style of Gregorian Chant. Enlist several people to sing the song with you in unison.

DRAMA

Comedy

Dramatize the story of Aidan's horse, with all its comic elements. Be sure to show the pomposity of the king, the utter surprise of the beggar, and the godly humility and wisdom of Aidan.

Drama

Portray the story of Pope Leo going from Rome to beg Attila the Hun not to invade the city. Remember that Attila is known as the "Scourge of God," and that people throughout Europe trembled at his name.

Reality

Act out "A Day in the Life" of an early monk from either the Celtic or Roman church. Be sure to enroll others, including siblings and pets, as part of the monastery.

Puppetry

Put on a puppet show of one of the power encounters between the God of the Christians and the gods of the pagans during this Unit, such as Boniface versus Thor, the god of the sacred oak tree.

Prop Needs

_____

_____

Costume Ideas

_____

_____

Role/Player

_____

_____

Set Suggestions

_____

_____

MOVEMENT

Pantomime

Pantomime the story of Patrick's life, from his capture by Irish pirates to his slavery and escape, to his heavenly dream and return to Ireland as a missionary.

Dance

Choreograph a dance of Hilda of Whitby, as she encourages the uneducated poet Caedmon to create songs and stories of God's faithfulness.

Miniature Action

Using miniature soldiers, demonstrate the historic battle between the Huns under the leadership of Attila against the combined armies of Romans and Visigoths.

CONCEPTUAL DESIGN

Design-a-Church

Using LEGO® bricks or other building materials, create your own design for a sixth-century Celtic church that would be basically waterproof. For inspiration, consider the Gallarus Oratory.

CREATE YOUR OWN EXPRESSION:

_____

_____

_____

_____

_____

_____

▶ # Student Self-Evaluation UNIT 2, PHASE 4

Dates and hours:_____

Evaluate your projects

- What creative project did you choose:

  _____

- What did you expect from your project, and how does the final project compare to your initial expectations?

  _____

- What do you like about your project? What would you change?

  _____

In Conclusion

Revisit the five Key Concepts from the beginning of this Unit. Explain how your understanding of and appreciation for each has grown over the course of your study.

- _____

  _____

- _____

  _____

- _____

  _____

- _____

  _____

- _____

Record your concluding thoughts on Missionaries & Barbarians:

_____

_____

_____

Byzantines & Muslims

Interior of Islamic mosque

The Cross and the Crescent . . .

While the people of the West were experiencing the disintegration of their empire and way of life under the rule of the barbarians, the people of the Eastern Empire continued on in their orderly Roman fashion for several hundred more years, thinking of themselves as Roman citizens in a Roman Empire. Over the years, however, a step-by-step process of Greek thinking, Greek language, exposure to the cultures of Persia and other eastern countries, and the development of Eastern Orthodoxy brought about such extreme differences that, eventually, this Eastern, or *Byzantine,* Empire became altogether alien to the Latin West.

Byzantine Empire

It was the difference of night and day during the time which many historians term, "The Dark Ages."

The heart of the Byzantine Empire was the city of Constantinople, which bridged West and East geographically and culturally. Because of its prime location, Constantinople served as the chief commercial city of the world in trade and industry for centuries! That meant wealth—a great deal of wealth—for many of its leading citizens. Luxurious articles abounded, such as exotic gems, spices, and silks, which made a tremendous impact on the culture. When you consider the situation for people in the West—where trade had almost ceased and conditions were isolated and primitive—contrasted with the situation in Constantinople, where ships and caravans brought both the latest news and a steady flow of trade goods from Asia, you can begin to understand the impact of all the wealth and trade of Constantinople. It was the difference between night and day during the time, which many historians term, "The Dark Ages."

Into this display of Byzantine wealth and luxury, God sent one of His servants with a much needed message. John Chrysostom, known as *The Golden-Mouthed* for his extraordinary ability to preach clearly and understandably, ministered first in Antioch and later as patriarch of Constantinople. The message to the people of his day was the same as Paul's message in First Timothy 6:17–18:

> Command those who are rich in this present age not to be haughty, nor to trust in uncertain riches but in the living God, who gives us richly all things to enjoy. Let them do good, that they be rich in good works, ready to give, willing to share.

John Chrysostom preached powerfully to his congregations about God's heart in caring for the needy and oppressed. He was such an effective speaker, however, that his message against the abuse of wealth and on sharing with the poor soon gained the notice of powerful (and, perhaps, convicted) enemies who made it their aim to silence him. Though they succeeded with John Chrysostom, they were not able to silence the Word of God—it continued to resound, just as it does today.

Orthodox Christianity

Though the heart of the Byzantine Empire was Constantinople, it could truly be said that the heart of Constantinople was the Byzantine Church. The majesty, the beauty, the art and architecture, the traditions, and the

"Greek-ness" of this branch of Christianity were woven intricately into the very substance of the Empire. *(Author's note: It is important to remember, however, that just as it is not the outward conforming to a set of rules and dogma that makes a person a Christian, so it is with nations. Though the Byzantine Empire and the Orthodox Church were inseparably intertwined, and though the Empire saw itself as thoroughly Christian, it was more often an outward profession than an inward reality.)* One of the defining characteristics of the Byzantine Church was the concern to maintain a right, or orthodox, understanding of doctrine, especially as it concerned the Person and Nature of Christ. As we have seen in previous units, during the time of Emperor Constantine there were disputes concerning whether Jesus was actually the uncreated God or whether He was a lesser degree of divinity (Arianism). This heated debate was not relegated just to Church bishops and theologians, such as in the Council of Nicaea in 325, but was also the intense and opinionated subject of discussion among all classes of society.

Gregory of Nyssa, known as one of the three Cappadocian Fathers of the Orthodox Church, wrote this description of Constantinople during the struggle with Arianism:

> If you ask a person to give you some small change for a large coin, his response is—"What distinguishes the Father from the Son is that He is not begotten." If you go into a shop to buy a loaf, the shopkeeper solemnly informs you that, "The Father is greater than the Son." If you ask your servant whether the water is hot enough for a bath, you have to be satisfied with his assurance that "The Son has been generated out of nothing."

Though the heart of the Byzantine Empire was Constantinople, the heart of Constantinople was the Byzantine Church.

This intense interest concerning theological disputes continued throughout the centuries of the Byzantine Empire, and, in fact, was so important to the peoples of the empire that it occasionally led to church splits. For instance, at the Council of Ephesus in 431, the teachings of Nestorius were condemned. The Orthodox position held that Christ was one Person with two natures, divine and human, whereas the Nestorian position contended that Christ was two persons, divine and human. The nuances of language, especially the Greek language, gave this issue enough fuel to become a raging debate, though it may have been a case of misunderstanding, overblown rhetoric, and hair-splitting arguments. It has been suggested by some historians that Nestorius did not actually believe what he was accused of, and that, in fact, his condemnation at the Council of Ephesus was more of a political maneuver than a matter of heresy. It seems clear that, in the Byzantine Empire, what looked on the surface like divisions within Christianity often were more about political issues, personality clashes, and nationalistic agendas. The political results of the

Council of Ephesus were that a group of Nestorians (those who believed what Nestorius taught) broke away and took refuge in Persia, where they founded the Nestorian Church. It was tolerated in non-Christian Persia for the sole reason that it was NOT Byzantine!

In a similar way, the Council of Chalcedon in 451 condemned the teaching of Monophysitism, which said that the human nature in Christ was swallowed up by the divine, just as a drop of wine dissipates into nothingness in the ocean. Those who continued to hold to Monophysitism, despite the Council of Chalcedon, formed their own churches such as the Coptic Church in Egypt. As we shall soon see, the Byzantine Empire's persecution of these splinter groups might have hastened the success of Islamic conquest in the locations where "heretics" resented the aggressive imperial pressure to conform to the Orthodox Church.

> *The Nestorian Church was tolerated in non-Christian Persia for the sole reason that it was NOT Byzantine!*

Justinian I

Into this maelstrom of theological debate and division stepped one of the greatest of all the Byzantine emperors, Justinian I, who reigned from 527 to 565. He faced significant troubles not only in the Church but in the Empire as well. In the East, war raged against the Empire's perennial enemies the Persians, while in the West, the barbarians had conquered land formerly belonging to the Roman Empire. Justinian believed that his job was to defeat the Persians and the barbarians, reconquering and restoring lands which had been lost. To do that, however, required a large army, a vast treasury, and a willingness to spend both. As it turns out, Justinian was both willing and able.

When he came to the throne, the empire was engaged in an ongoing war with the Persians. After successfully negotiating a very expensive truce with the Persians—paying 11,000 pounds of gold—Justinian turned his sights to the West, where, as noted in the previous unit, he was successful in ousting the Vandals from North Africa and the Ostrogoths from Italy. All of this came at a high cost, however. The citizens back home were disturbed by his reckless military expenditures, and many sought to overthrow him. In the Nika Rebellion of 532, a vast number of rioters gathered in Constantinople to crown a new emperor, setting fire to the center of the city in the process. Though Justinian was ready to abdicate, his wife Theodora courageously addressed Justinian and his court:

> Everyone born into the light of day must die sooner or later; and how could an emperor ever let himself become someone who runs away from danger? If you, my lord, want to save your own skin, you will not find it hard. We are wealthy, there is the sea, and there are our ships, too.

3

> But think first: when you reach safety, will you not regret that you chose flight rather than death? As for me, I stand by the old saying: the best clothes in which to die are the robes of monarchy.

This speech had a steadying effect on the emperor. When all was said and done, Justinian had crushed all opposition and had launched a new building program to restore and revitalize the devastated city. This won him tremendous popularity with the people of Constantinople, even though his spending was extraordinarily lavish and taxes were high. In addition to warring, building, and spending, Justinian established a code of law to which many European nations today are indebted.

One of the most important issues of Justinian's day, and the one where he utterly failed, was in restoring unity to the Christians of his empire. He used the power of the State to try to force those who would not accept the Council of Chalcedon to conform anyway. The Monophysites in the empire—Christians in Eastern Turkey, Syria, Palestine, Egypt, and Spain—all felt the sting of his wrath. It did not bring unity, however. It merely set in motion an increasing discontent with Byzantine rule in these far flung regions of the empire. To many of the persecuted, a change in governments, no matter what kind of change that might mean, would be preferable to staying within Byzantium. When the Arabs came a generation later, many of these disaffected Christians welcomed them with open arms.

One of the most important issues of Justinian's day, and the one where he utterly failed, was in restoring unity to the Christians of his empire.

Rise of Islam

It is amazing how quickly things in history can be turned around. Five brief years after the death of Justinian I in 565, a boy was born in the Arabian city of Mecca. The life and influence of this one, Mohammed, would undo much of what Justinian had labored to accomplish. If we could return to that era of history—the late 500s—we might think that the tribal people living in the Arabian peninsula were a fairly insignificant group, especially compared to the Persians or the Byzantines. However, if we were to keep watching for just a short while, our perspective would radically change as Arab Muslim soldiers captured all of the Persian Empire and half of the Byzantine Empire. We would watch incredulously as this new Islamic Empire grew to include a network of trade routes stretching all the way from Spain to India and China. Within two hundred years, the wealth of the Muslim world would exceed even that of the Byzantines!

This was, indeed, a dramatic event in world history. Though political complexities and intricacies would develop in the Muslim world, the fundamental faith of Islam was easy to understand. Mohammed taught the people that there were five pillars of Islam that one must fulfill:

1. *shahadah*, the Muslim profession of faith;

2. *salat*, or ritual prayer, five times each day;

3. *zakat*, the alms tax levied to benefit the poor;

4. *sawm*, fasting during the month of Ramadan;

5. *hajj*, the major pilgrimage to Mecca.

The Muslim creed required no clergy, no church, and no sacraments. Significantly, in this geographical region, where Byzantine Christianity had divided over difficult-to-understand theological issues, Islam was simple and easy to explain. It was, if you will, a list of items to mark off. "Do these things and you will be a Muslim."

In contrast, true Christianity was, and is, a personal relationship with the One God of the universe through His Son, Jesus. As has already been mentioned, one can outwardly conform to a set of church rules and expectations, but, according to Scripture, that will not make one a Christian. It is the inward change of heart, the believing faith, the new life that makes us children of the Living God. And then, as His children, we behave in ways that please Him. It is the age-old difference between the wisdom of this world and the wisdom of God (1 Corinthians 1:21–25); between those who seek to work their way to God and those who discover that God seeks them (John 4:23); between a religion and a Relationship (1 John 3:1).

It is important that we not relegate this truth to a Sunday-school mind-set (meaning something we only think of in church), but to view history and all of life from this perspective—to think "Christianly." It will help us understand not only the struggles between believers of long ago but also the modern struggles and controversies within different streams of Christianity. It will also help us to understand what the Muslims of the 600s believed and how it contrasted with the reality of Christianity. And not merely a historical understanding—in today's world we need to know how the vibrant message of Christianity can be communicated so that it builds bridges and not just walls.

Jerusalem recaptured

Before the Islamic armies surged out of Arabia, as Mohammed was beginning to preach in Mecca, the new Byzantine Emperor Heraclius came to power. Between Justinian's staggering debt and the incompetence of the various emperors, Byzantium was struggling to survive—610 was not an auspicious year for the Byzantines. The Persians were sitting just across the water from Constantinople, ready to pick up the pieces when it fell; the Slavs, a group of barbarians, were swarming through the Balkans; the Avars, another barbarian tribe, were exacting tribute of the Empire; the army was demoralized; and non-Orthodox Christians were hostile. Heraclius, however, was the right person at the right time. Though the Persians actually captured Jerusalem in 614, along with the rest of Palestine and Syria, Heraclius defeated them in 627. In the peace that followed, all of the Roman lands captured by the Persians were restored to the Byzantines and, in 630, Heraclius entered Jerusalem, walking as a humble Christian pilgrim rather than as a conquering emperor.

One of the most far-reaching ideas that Heraclius enacted for the benefit of the empire was that of setting up the system known as *themes.* In each theme, or military district, the governor was a military man who provided land grants to peasants and soldiers based on their willingness to accept hereditary military service. This brought about a revolutionary effect:

- agriculture, the backbone of the economy of most of the empire outside of Constantinople, was revived;

- peasant-farmers, now free to be landowners, were well-trained soldiers with a personal interest in vigilantly guarding their region;

- the empire no longer had the burden of paying for its entire army, since the soldiers on the themes received their plot of land rather than salary;

- each theme's military was constantly self-renewed without oversight of the empire.

It is the inward change of heart, the believing faith, the new life that makes us children of the Living God.

Unfortunately, for all of Heraclius's brilliant accomplishments, he was unable to stop the Arabic armies from capturing Jerusalem in 637—less than ten years after his reclaiming the city from the Persians. Along with the city of Jerusalem (one of the five patriarchal cities of Christianity), the armies of Islam captured much of the most valuable, most densely populated, and longest-civilized areas of the Byzantine Empire. This included Syria, with the patriarchal city of Antioch; Egypt with the patriarchal city of Alexandria; and Palestine. Heraclius found, much to his astonishment and dismay, that the desert—which had formed one of the frontiers of the empire—was a highway to the Arab Bedouins. This was a wasteland they knew how to cross. And cross it they did.

Islamic Empire

The desert—which had formed one of the frontiers of the empire—was a highway to the Arab Bedouins.

All of the tribes in the Arabian Peninsula eventually converted to Islam, and from that religious and cultural cohesion, the Islamic army began the conquest that would ultimately extend from Spain to the borders of China. But the Muslims did not have a smooth, cohesive transition from following Mohammed's leadership to following the caliphs (rulers), since Mohammed had not set up a formula for succession before he died. At first, the caliphs were elected by a council of elders who had personally known Mohammed. This changed, however, when the fifth caliph, Muawiya, who had served as governor of Syria, contrived to start what is known as the Umayyad dynasty.

Muawiya convinced the council of elders to appoint his son to be the next caliph, which began a hereditary succession to the rule of the Islamic empire. Muawiya also sought to capture Constantinople, using the newly-built fleet of Muslim ships (whose design had come from a Byzantine shipyard, which fell to Muawiya's troops). Though he gained prestige as a caliph fighting against infidel Christians, Muawiya was unsuccessful in gaining Constantinople, largely due to the newly devised *Greek Fire* which the Byzantines used to set fire to the Arab ships. Obviously, it was invented just in the nick of time!

A series of rulers passed in quick succession until 684, when the next powerful Umayyad caliph came to power. Abd al-Malik, who inherited a kingdom torn by factions and infighting, determined to dazzle his people with a spectacular new architectural wonder, the Dome of the Rock in Jerusalem. This was a place sacred to the Jews, the Christians, and the Muslims, since it was believed to be the site of Abraham's sacrifice of the ram instead of Isaac, the site of Solomon's Temple, and the site believed to be the earthly spot where Mohammed ascended to heaven. Abd al-Malik's structure was both a religious and political entity: a place of pilgrimage for devout Muslims, and a shrine firmly within his geographic hold.

Caliph Walid I, successor to Abd al-Malik, reigned at the time when the Islamic Empire reached its greatest extent. It was Walid's general, Tarik, who crossed the straits between Africa and Spain, who gave his name to the massive rock standing there—Gibraltar (*Jabal Tarik*)—and went on with his 7,000 men to defeat, in 711, the 25,000-man army of the last of the Visigothic kings. After this, the conquest of Spain was assured, and within three years, Arab armies were at the Pyrenees.

Shortly after Walid's death, a new emperor seized the Byzantine throne. Leo the Isaurian, or Leo III, was a strong military leader, who was able to defeat the Arabs in their second and strongest attempt to capture Constantinople after a thirteen month siege. Islamic historians said that of the 180,000 Arabs sent to lay siege to Constantinople, only 30,000 returned.

Iconoclast controversy

Leo is better known, however, as the emperor who started the Iconoclast Controversy, which meant that he forbade the use of icons in the Orthodox Church. As a Byzantine ruler, he had authority over both Church and State, and this he powerfully used to bring about the destruction of what he considered to be idols. The Second Commandment given to Moses in Exodus 20:4 specifically forbids the making of images that would be used as objects of worship. Though most Byzantine Christians (and Roman Christians for that matter) approved the use of icons as an aid to worship, there were those within the empire who thought icons, were, in fact, the forbidden images prohibited by God. As a Syrian, it is possible that Leo was influenced by the Monophysites of Syria who tended to disapprove of icons, or he may even have been sensitive to the beliefs of Muslims who were prohibited from any form of representational art and who thought Christians were idolators when it came to their icons. For whatever reason, Leo's position, and that of several future emperors, rocked the empire. It was not merely a matter of theological speculation, either. In 730 Leo III ordered all the mosaics, reliefs, and paintings contained in churches and in public places to be destroyed.

Leo is better known as the emperor who started the Iconoclast Controversy.

Constantinople erupted, but Leo continued his policy, ordering harsh measures against those who would not yield to his position. Many opposed him, including the influential monk John of Damascus, who wrote in defense of icons, "What the written word is to those who can read, the icon is to the illiterate. What speech is to the ear, the icon is to the eye." Pope Gregory II in Rome actually excommunicated Leo, which led the popes of Rome to turn to the Catholic Franks rather than the Byzantines for protection. We will discover, in the next unit, how significant this change was.

Islam divided

The Umayyad caliph who next came to power in the Islamic Empire was named Hisham. He faced uprisings against Umayyad rule in Africa and Iraq, corruption among those governing in the provinces, and Byzantine successes against his armies in Asia Minor. It may be, with all of these enormous issues to deal with, that he was either unaware or unconcerned about a small battle that took place beyond the Pyrenees between his troops and the Franks, but to the people of Europe, this battle was one of the most obviously providential in their history.

In October of 732, an army under Charles Martel, the mayor of the Frankish court, met the army of Abd ar-Rahman, the Muslim governor of Spain. At the battle site between Poitiers and Tours (in France), Abd ar-Rahman was killed, and the Muslim army vanished. Though neither the Arabs nor the Franks realized it on the field of battle, the Muslim tide flowing into Europe was turned at that point. One hundred years after the death of Mohammed, the armies of Islam were finally halted.

As Umayyad rule became increasingly unpopular, the Abbasids—descendants of an uncle of Mohammed—gained military and religious support from a number of dissenting groups. These groups joined under the black flag of the Abbasids, and this army met the Umayyads in battle in 750 at the Great Zab River. The last Umayyad caliph, Marwan II, was defeated and a tremendous change then took place within the Islamic Empire. Rather than looking westward across North Africa and the Mediterranean, the caliphate turned their focus towards Persia and the East. Moving their capital city from Damascus in Syria to Baghdad in Iraq, the Abbasid caliphs made the empire less of an Arab or even a Syrian empire. Instead, they created more and more an opulent Persian rule, culminating in the reign of Harun ar-Rashid.

> "What the written word is to those who know letters, the icon is to the unlettered; what speech is to the ear, the icon is to the eye."

Mosaic of Jesus Christ, Hagia Sophia, AD 1229, Istanbul, Turkey

Islamic civilization

Just as Constantinople was the jeweled city of the Byzantine Empire, so Baghdad sparkled magnificently for the Islamic Empire. Built in just four short years by 100,000 laborers during the rule of Caliph Al-Mansur, this extraordinary city outshone every other for more than seventy years. It was known for its colleges, hospitals, and hotels—and this was in the late 700s! All manner of artists, poets, scientists, philosophers, mathematicians, and linguists flocked to Baghdad, and during the reign of Harun ar-Rashid, beginning in 786, the city reached its height of glory. From all over the empire, luxurious products such as silks, perfumes, precious gems, gold, spices, dyes, glass, furs, porcelain, and ebony flowed to Baghdad, along with slaves from Africa. They came by sea, by river, by caravan, until Baghdad became the greatest trading port in history and, for a short time, the center of the world. Even the great Charlemagne, whom we will meet in the next unit, sent an embassy from Europe to Harun ar-Rashid in Baghdad, and received, in return, the astonishing gifts of a number of elephants and a water clock! Not since Augustus Caesar had one man held such wealth and power as Harun ar-Rashid, and his fame reached not only to Europe but all the way to China.

Though neither the Arabs nor the Franks realized it on the field of battle, the Muslim tide flowing into Europe was turned.

The year after Harun came to power, the Byzantine Empress, Irene (widow of Leo IV), called for another ecumenical church council—the Second Council of Nicaea—to reverse the prohibition against icons while she ruled as regent for her young son, Constantine. Though she was revered for this action by the people of Constantinople, she became an object of horror when she later deposed her own son, had him blinded, and sent him into permanent exile. It is said, "Power corrupts, and absolute power corrupts absolutely." In the life of Empress Irene we see this emerge in living color. Though she governed the Christian Byzantine Empire and functioned as the head of the Church, she was the antithesis of a mother and betrayed the very essence of Christianity, which is sacrificial love.

The emperor who deposed Irene, Nicephorus I, successfully engaged against the armies of Harun ar-Rashid in Asia Minor, but was then killed in battle against the King of Bulgaria. Harun ar-Rashid's successor reigned at the time when a breakaway faction began its own Muslim Empire in Morocco, while at the same time a third Muslim Empire was growing in Spain. This is, in short, the picture of what would continue for hundreds of years—the Byzantines fighting continuously to hold on to a dwindling empire, and the Muslims continuing to divide into various caliphates fighting against each other. We'll see them both as we come to the era of the Crusades. For now, let us remember the amazing splendors we have seen in Constantinople and in Baghdad, while the West continued to languish under its barbarian mastery. A new ruler is on the western horizon, however—the grandson of the Victor of Poitiers. ◀

Phase 1

John Chrysostom
The golden-mouthed preacher

Nestorius
Patriarch and founder of Nestorianism

Leo the Isaurian
Emperor who abolished use of icons

John of Damascus
Defended use of icons

Photius the Great
"The wisest man of the Middle Ages"

▶ # Listen to This!

What in the World? VOL. 2

DISC TWO

» The Byzantine World (track 1)

» Life as an Eastern Emperor (track 2)

» Justinian the First (track 3)

» Mohammed the Reformer (track 4)

» The Hegira & Jihad (track 5)

True Tales VOL. 2

DISC ONE

» The Islamic Empire (track 5)

DISC TWO

» The Byzantines (track 1)

Digging Deeper VOL. 2

DISC TWO: THE CHURCH IN CHARGE

» The Byzantines & Muslims (track 5)

▶ Read For Your Life

The Holy Bible

CONTRASTING CHRISTIANITY'S GOD WITH ISLAM'S CONCEPT OF ALLAH:

» **God's love for us:** John 3:16; John 16:27; Ephesians 3:17–19

» **The father heart of God:** 1 John 3:1; 2 Corinthians 6:18; Ephesians 1:5

» **God's character:** Exodus 34:6–7; Psalm 86:15, 103:8–13

» **God's sacrifice for us:** Isaiah 53:4–6, 63:9

» **Jesus as Savior:** John 14:6; Mark 1:10–11

▶ Talk Together

Opinion Column

» What did you find to be the most interesting aspect, or the most fascinating person, you encountered in your introduction to the history of the Byzantines and Muslims?

» If you were a citizen of Constantinople during the reign of Justinian, in what ways would you have appreciated his use of tax dollars? For what reasons would you be looking forward to his successor? How would you feel about his wars in North Africa and Italy?

» If you had been living in Mecca when Mohammed first started preaching his new religion, how do you think you would have reacted? Do you think you would have had the stalwart courage to tell Mohammed your opinion of his new religion?

» Imagine that it is October, 732, and you are living in the city of Tours in France. Share your thoughts about the anticipated and terrifying invasion by Arabic warriors. What kinds of stories do you suppose people told about what the Arabs had done in other lands they had conquered?

Key People (World)

Justinian & Theodora
Rulers of Byzantine Empire

Mohammed
Prophet of Islam

Abu Bakr
First Caliph

Charles Martel
Frankish leader who stopped the Muslims

Al-Mansur
Founder of Abbasid Caliphate

Irene
Empress who restored icons

Harun ar-Rashid
Ruled at the height of Islamic Empire

Critical Puzzling

» It is very difficult for most Western Christians to comprehend the use of icons in Eastern Orthodoxy. John of Damascus provided this statement to clarify the use of icons: "What the written word is to those who can read, the icon is to the illiterate. What speech is to the ear, the icon is to the eye." In what ways does this explanation help you understand why icons are used in worship? Do you think his statement is valid? What are some ways in which your own culture has used visual images in place of language?

» What seem to you to have been the most important differences between Eastern (Orthodox) Christianity and Western (Catholic) Christianity at this historic time? What are the most important points of agreement?

» In what key aspect are Islam and Christianity similar? How do they differ? How significant are the differences?

» Why do you think Islam was able to conquer so much of the Byzantine Empire so quickly? How did the concept of jihad and the rewards of death in battle impact the soldiers of Islam?

» When the Muslim army was stopped at the Battle of Poitiers, the Islamic surge into Europe was over. Why do you think they ended their quest at that point?

▶ Resources for Digging Deeper

Choose a few books that look interesting, or find your own.

EASTERN ORTHODOXY

Faith in the Byzantine World

Mary Cunningham • One of the InterVarsity Press Histories series, this title is filled with information concerning the historic Orthodox Byzantine Church: its traditions and worldview; its relationship to the Byzantine Emperor; its doctrines. Excellent overview! **MS+**

I Am a Greek Orthodox

Maria Roussou • Written for elementary level, this is an excellent introduction to Orthodoxy for children. It is helpful to know more about Orthodoxy when one is trying to understand the Byzantine Empire, since Orthodoxy was the most significant, defining aspect of the Byzantines. Fascinating! **E+**

Dates with Destiny: The 100 Most Important Dates In Church History

A. Kenneth Curtis, Randy Petersen, & J. Stephen Lang • Two stories are presented, which illuminate the Orthodox Church—John Chrysostom and the Council of Chalcedon. It also has contains a fascinating look at the Battle of Tours (Poitiers). **UE+**

Christian History Magazine ISSUE 54: "EASTERN ORTHODOXY"

Devoted entirely to describing Eastern Orthodoxy, this particular issue of *Christian History* is very enlightening in explaining the differences between Eastern Christianity and Western Christianity. **MS+**

BYZANTINE EMPIRE

Famous Men of the Middle Ages

Haaren & Poland, edited by Cyndy & Robert Shearer • Referred to again in this section because it contains biographies on Justinian and Mohammed. Highly recommended. **E+**

The Fall of Constantinople: World Landmark Books

Bernadine Kielty • This book looks at Constantinople from its beginnings as a city all the way up to its destruction in 1453. Worth the read. **UE+**

Byzantium

Tamara Talbot Rice • A very informative, specific look at the Byzantine Empire. Includes Constantine, Justinian, the Iconoclast controversy, and the Fourth Crusade. Excellent. **MS+**

Byzantium—Greatness and Decline

Charles Diehl • Written in the early 1900's by a distinguished Byzantine scholar, this book gives a fascinating perspective on the Byzantines. **HS+**

Barbarians, Christians, and Muslims: The Cambridge Introduction to History

Trevor Cairns • Fascinating, well-written account of the barbarian tribes, the Byzantine empire and the growth of Islam. One of the best all around overviews. Look for it in your library. **E+**

National Geographic VOLUME 164, DECEMBER 1983: "BYZANTINE EMPIRE"

Filled with gorgeous photographs, maps, and fascinating narrative, this issue of National Geographic would be very helpful in your study of the Byzantines. **UE+**

The Splendors of Byzantium

Dorothy Hales Gary & Robert Payne • A book of photographs from Byzantine artwork and architecture, this is an amazing feast for the eyes as one contemplates the artistry inspired by Eastern Christianity. **UE+**

ISLAM

Unveiling Islam

Ergun Mehmet Caner & Emir Fethi Caner • The authors were raised as Sunni Muslims, and became Christians as young adults. This book is a careful presentation, both sympathetic and uncompromising, of the history and tenets of Islam. It includes a description of the differences between Islam and Christianity, providing believers with insight on ministering to Muslims. **MS+**

Asia: A Christian Perspective

Mary Ann Lind • This book gives a very clear presentation of how Christians can present the gospel to Muslims, showing that the love of Jesus and a changed life will have a tremendous impact upon the followers of Mohammed. **UE+**

Answering Islam: The Crescent in Light of the Cross

Norman L. Geisler & Abdul Saleeb • This comprehensive book examines and critiques Islam from a Biblical basis. It is thorough and exhaustive, and would be especially helpful for students wishing to dig deeply. **HS+**

Reaching Muslims for Christ

Will J. Saal • This book describes the Koran, identifies basic Muslim beliefs, provides doctrinal details to communicate with Muslims, and equips the Christian to be able to effectively respond to Muslims. **MS+**

ISLAMIC EMPIRE

The Islamic World: From Its Origins to the 16th Century

Translated from Italian, this is an incredible book! You will find in it an explanation not only of the difference between Sunni Muslims and Shi'ite Muslims, but also a delineation and explanation of several other "splinter" groups in Islam. **UE+**

The Sword of the Prophet: The Story of the Moslem Empire

Richard Suskind · A great read aloud book, it is written in a very easy-to-read style, much like a novel. **UE+**

Science in Early Islamic Culture

George Behore · A fascinating look at the way science and mathematics developed under the Muslims of AD 800–1100. We receive our Arabic numeral system from these scholars of early Islam—not its invention but its adaptation from an Indian concept. Algebra was modified and given its name by a Muslim mathematician. Medicine, optics, and more are covered in this treasure. **UE+**

For more books, use these Dewey Decimal numbers in your library:

Eastern Orthodoxy: #281.5

Islam: #297

Byzantine Empire: #949

Islamic Empire: #909

What books did you like best?

_____

_____

_____

_____

_____

The Internet also contains a wealth of information about the Byzantines & Muslims.

What sites were the most helpful?

_____

_____

_____

▶ Student Self-Evaluation UNIT 3, PHASE 1

Dates and hours:_____

Key Concepts

Rephrase the five Key Concepts of this Unit and confirm your understanding of each:

- Orthodox Christianity

  _____

- Rise of Islam

  _____

- Seven ecumenical councils

  _____

- Byzantine civilization

  _____

- Islamic civilization

  _____

Tools for Self-Evaluation

Evaluate your personal participation in the discussions of this Phase. Bearing in mind that a good participant in a discussion is not always the most vocal participant, ask yourself these questions: Were you an active participant? Did you ask perceptive questions? Were you willing to listen to other participants of the discussion and draw out their opinions? Record your observations and how you would like to improve your participation in the future:

_____

_____

Every time period is too complex to be understood in one Phase of study. Evaluate your current knowledge of the Byzantines & Muslims. What have you focused on so far? What are your weakest areas of knowledge?

_____

_____

Based on the evaluation of this introduction, project ahead what you would like to study more of in the following Phases:

_____

Phase 2

▶ Research & Reporting

Explore one or more of these areas to discover something significant!

Byzantine Empire

Research and report on the Byzantine Empire, including its fullest expanse of territory and its influence upon the West, North Africa, the Middle East, the Balkans, and Russia. Though we will study the Crusades in a later Unit, you may wish to report an overview of the entire thousand year rule of this empire.

Islamic Empire

Investigate the birth, growth, and flowering of the Islamic Empire during the Middle Ages. Which countries were conquered by the soldiers of Islam? How did they add their distinctive characteristics to Arabic domination? Was there a defining attitude towards Jews, especially in the formative years? What role did Christians play, if any, in the Islamic Empire? Report your findings.

Islamic Dynasties

Discover more about the various ruling dynasties of Islam, especially the Umayyad and the Abbasid dynasties. What were the significant advances or changes that each dynasty brought to the empire? Report your findings.

Justinian and Theodora

Research and report on this early Byzantine Emperor and his Empress. Why was Justinian considered to be the most important emperor after Constantine? How did Justinian and Theodora leave their mark on the Byzantine Empire and the Eastern Church? What is most praiseworthy in their rule? What is most troublesome?

Mohammed

Study the life of the founder of Islam. Describe his early years, his career, his encounter with a supernatural being, and the ongoing results of this meeting. What do Muslims believe about his illiteracy and the writing of the Koran? How did Mohammed gain ascendancy over the Arabian Peninsula?

Battle of Tours

Research and report on this world-changing battle in 732. What happened during the battle? It is not certain why this was the final attempt by Muslims to move northward into Europe, but after researching, suggest your theories. How was Europe impacted by the victory of Charles Martel? How was the Islamic Empire changed by this event?

Seven Ecumenical Councils

Investigate these councils, looking for the major issues, the rulings, and the results of each council. What groups split off to form their own churches in defiance of the rulings? How did these seven councils affect the Orthodox church? How did these seven councils affect the Roman Catholic church? In what ways are Protestant churches following or disagreeing with these seven councils?

Islam

Using one of the books listed in the previous Phase as a starting point, research the belief system of Islam. Compare the Koran to the Bible, and learn what Muslims believe about the Bible. In what ways does the Islamic worldview affect the way Muslim people live their everyday lives?

Eastern Orthodoxy

Research and report on the beliefs and practices of the Eastern Orthodox church. Compare and contrast this with the beliefs and practices of your church.

Mt. Athos

Discover what life is like for the Eastern Ortho-dox monks who live in the large community of Mt. Athos in Greece. Since Orthodoxy has not changed its practices over the years, the way these monks live today will give some insight into monasticism during the Byzantine years. You might want to also investigate the various attitudes Byzantine emperors had towards monks, and include that in your report.

▶ Brain Stretchers

Council of Chalcedon

Research and report on this council. What were the issues? What were the results? What was the "robber synod"? Define Monophysitism. Compare and contrast Cyril of Alexandria with Nestorius.

Evangelizing Muslims

Research and report on the history of Christian missions to Muslims. In what ways has the Church been effective? In what ways has the Church been ineffective? Discover current efforts to minister to people in Muslim lands. What strategies are in place? What have been the dangers to the missionaries and to their converts?

Shi'ite and Sunni

What created these two streams of Islam which are so hostile to each other? Discover the origins of Shi'ite Muslims, their beliefs and practices. Also, investigate the origins of Sunni Muslims, their beliefs and practices. What are some places and contemporary issues where they are in conflict? What results have come from their interactions? Report your findings.

Christianity in the East

As the Nestorians broke off from the Orthodox Church, they moved into Persia. But when persecution broke out in Persia, they fled to the East, taking the gospel with them. Learn more about this early penetration of Christianity into Central Asia and China. One excellent source for this is the article "The Great Missionary Church of the East" by Les Miller, in the book *World Wide Perspectives*, edited by Meg Crossman.

Create Your Own Research Topic

_____

_____

_____

▶ **Timeline**

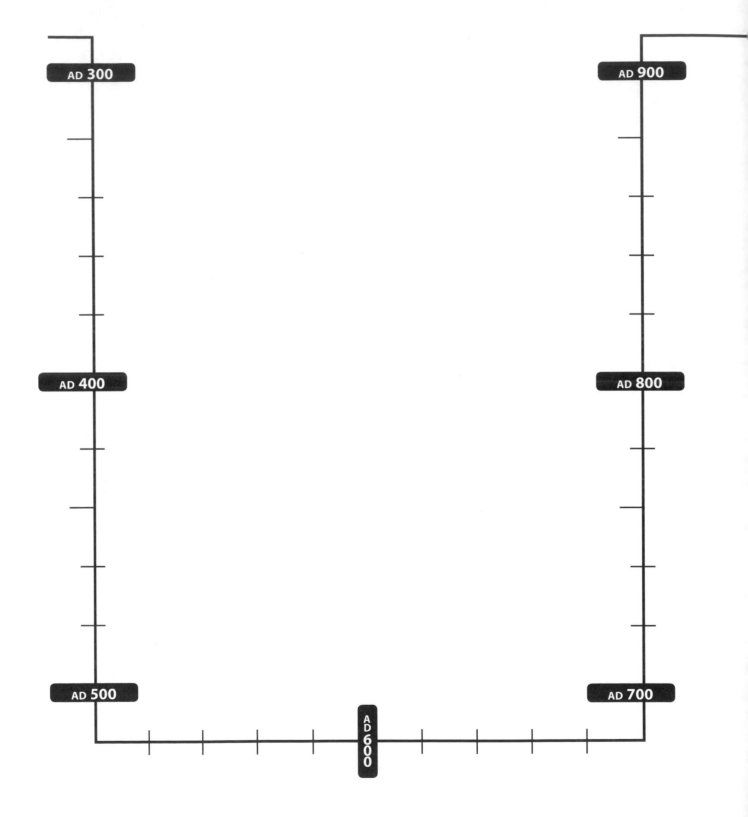

AD 300

AD 400

AD 500

AD 600

AD 700

AD 800

AD 900

Consider this for your timeline

Under Emperor Justinian, many lands conquered by the barbarians were restored to the Byzantine Empire. After his death, however, the Byzantines struggled to hold on to his conquests. In 614 the Persians captured Jerusalem from Byzantine control, leaving the Holy City in the hands of unbelievers. The Byzantine Emperor, Heraclius, went to war against the Persians to reclaim the Holy Land and the "True Cross." After years of struggle, the Persians finally returned all of the Byzantine lands to their former owner. Only eight years later, still during the reign of Heraclius, Islamic armies captured Jerusalem, and this time it would be held by non-Christians (and non-Jews) for more than four hundred years.

Key Events

Building of Hagia Sophia

Hegira

Building of Dome of the Rock

Iconoclast Controversy

Arab invasion of Middle East and North Africa (a span of time)

Ecumenical Church Councils

Battle of Tours

CONSIDER:

You would be astounded to learn just how many words we use in English which come from Arabic and Greek. Here are some examples:

Greek Roots:

tele

scope

hydro

micro

photo

Derived from Arabic:

admiral

apricot

coffee

sherbet

algebra

If you found this fascinating, look for some more examples!

▶ Words to Watch

Remember—The easiest way to learn a subject is to master its terms:

monotheistic	ascetic	orthodox	ecumenical
arabesque	monophysite	icon	iconoclast
veneration	liturgical	tradition	Hegira
jihad	Koran	paganism	Kaaba
prophet	Ramadan	prostrate	caliph
calligraphy	mosque	polytheism	

Other words you need to look up:

_____

_____

_____

_____

_____

_____

_____

▶ Student Self-Evaluation UNIT 3, PHASE 2

Dates and hours:_____

Research Project

Summarize your research question:

_____

_____

List your most useful sources by author, title, and page number or URL where applicable (continue list in margin if necessary):

_____

_____

_____

Now take a moment to evaluate the sources you just listed. Do they provide a balanced view of your research question? Should you have sought an additional opinion? Are your sources credible (if you found them on your own)? Record your observations:

_____

_____

Evaluate your research project in its final presentation. What are its strengths? If you had time to revisit this project, what would you change? Consider giving yourself a letter grade based on your project's merits and weaknesses.

_____

_____

Letter grade: _____

You have just completed an area of specific research in the time of the Byzantines & Muslims. Now what would you like to explore in the upcoming Phases? Set some objectives for yourself:

_____

Phase 3

▶ Maps & Mapping

Physical Terrain

» Using a single color to represent the Byzantines, label and color Asia Minor, the Balkans, Italy, Spain, North Africa, and the Strait of Gibraltar.

» Label and color the Arabian Peninsula (choose a different color to use for Islam). Now, color those areas conquered by the Arabic Muslim armies (even though some of them have already been colored for the Byzantine Empire): Northern Africa, Spain, southern France, Syria, Egypt, Palestine, Persia.

Geopolitical

» Locate and label these cities important to the Byzantine Empire: Constantinople, Ravenna, Alexandria, Antioch, Ephesus, Chalcedon, Nicaea; label these cities important to the Islamic Empire: Mecca, Medina, Baghdad, Damascus, Cordoba.

» Draw a line with a colored pencil or pen indicating the boundaries of the Byzantine Empire at the time of Justinian's conquests. In a different colored pencil or pen, draw the boundaries of the Islamic Empire at the end of the eighth century. How much of the Byzantine Empire remained? How much of Europe was conquered? What kind of geographical terrain did these empires include?

Explore

» *Christian Outreach:* What is the status of evangelical outreach today to the areas conquered by the Muslims? What missions activities are taking place in the lands of the Byzantines? What opportunities and what difficulties face those who share the gospel in these areas?

» *Location, Location, Location:* What made Constantinople such a good place for international trade? What made it so defensible against invaders? Why do you think Constantine chose this prime location for the Byzantine Empire? Is there any other city in Eurasia with the same characteristics?

Art Appreciation

Mosaics of Justinian and Theodora at Ravenna

These mosaics, completed in 548, are a priceless Byzantine treasure located in the Byzantine Church of San Vitale. The Emperor is presented symbolically as both the spiritual and political authority on earth, which had great propaganda value in this Italian city of the Byzantine Empire.

» Examine these mosaics. In what ways are Justinian and Theodora set apart from those people pictured with them? Though it may be difficult to tell, Justinian's robe is purple. What does that signify? What do the halos represent? What else do you notice?

» In what ways could you describe these mosaics? How would you describe the workmanship? What can you learn about the significance of Justinian and Theodora from these mosaics?

Islamic Prayer Rug

In Islam, artists do not depict living creatures, nor do they represent real objects. Instead, they pour their creativity into repeating geometric shapes and arabesques (a pattern based on a design of abstract leaves or flowers radiating out, twisting back in, and out again).

» Look for an example of an Islamic prayer rug in a photo or on the Internet. How would you describe the designs in the rug? How does this differ from Byzantine and Western art?

▶ Architecture

Hagia Sophia

The Byzantine architects attempted to create in their churches a sense of heaven on earth with soaring domes and an immense number of windows to allow light to fill the space. Hagia Sophia, built by Justinian I, is considered to be one of the greatest churches ever built. Though it was converted to use as a mosque after 1453, it is now a museum in Istanbul.

>> Locate a photo of Hagia Sophia. The dome of this church soars 179 feet up into the heavens, and it rests upon a square church. How would you describe this building? What do you think it was like to worship in this church? Why do you think Justinian was reported, after the completion of Hagia Sophia, to have said, "Solomon, I have surpassed you!"?

Dome of the Rock

This mosque is the oldest existing Islamic monument. Built in Jerusalem between 685 and 691, the Dome of the Rock was created as a shrine for Muslim pilgrims, marking the spot where Mohammed was supposed to have risen to heaven. It is located on the site where Solomon's Temple once stood.

>> Locate a photo of the Dome of the Rock. Though the style borrows much from Byzantine architectural techniques, it is distinctively Islamic. How would you describe this structure? If you can locate a photo of the Great Mosque at Samarra in Iraq, compare the two. How do they differ?

▶ Arts in Action

Select one or more, and let your artistic juices flow!

Calligraphy

Calligraphy is perhaps the best known Islamic art form. Though Western calligraphy is quite different than Islamic calligraphy (the alphabet is different, after all), one can gain new respect for this art form by "doing it yourself." Look for an online calligraphy lesson, or choose a book from the library which will help you begin. Try writing out a verse of Scripture in calligraphy, as Islamic calligraphy has historically been used to artistically write words from the Koran.

Mosaic Portrait

Examine photos of Byzantine mosaics, such as the ones from the Church of San Vitale in Ravenna, to see how the artists portrayed eyes, hair, noses, clothes, etc. Then, construct a portrait in mosaics, Byzantine-style, using whatever artistic material you have available (torn construction paper, colored tiles, etc.). If you need help in learning how to make a mosaic, look online or in a book from the library.

▶ Science

The Benefit of Zero

The Muslims, after conquering a people group, set about learning what that group knew. They translated many Greek texts from antiquity about astronomy, math and more, and then used these principles to make new discoveries in science and math. One concept in math, which the Muslims learned from India was absolutely earthshaking: they discovered "zero"! Why was that so incredible? Let's try an experiment to find out:

> » Write out some familiar Roman numerals: I, V, X, L, C, and so on.

> » Now, write several *numbers* in Roman numerals: 33 (XXXIII), 15, 4, 89, 117.

> » Here's the experiment:

> - Add two numbers written out in Roman numerals.

> - Subtract from that answer another Roman numeral.

> - Multiply that answer times III.

> - Divide that answer by VII.

> » Was that easy or difficult? Try doing the same problems using Arabic numbers. Was that easier or more difficult? If easier, do you know why? It is because using the Arabic numerals, we have a ones' column, a tens' column, a hundreds' column, and so on. These columns are made possible because these historic people gave us a "zero" to hold the place in the column until it was needed for a number. These columns make it a snap to add, subtract, multiply, and divide.

CONSIDER:

Just think—before someone discovered zero, arithmetic was a LOT harder!

▶ Music

Music was very significant to the Byzantines. One could learn the doctrines of the church through its music. Some of these hymns, filled with their beautiful imagery, are still accessible to us today.

Discover

Come, Ye Faithful, Raise the Strain

John of Damascus (c. 696–754) • John of Damascus is known as the last of the Fathers of the Greek Church, and the greatest writer of hymns in Orthodoxy.

O, Light That Knew No Dawn

Gregory Nazianzen (329–389) • Gregory Nazianzen was one of the three great theologians in the Eastern Church who helped to overcome the heresy of Arianism. Gregory had a godly mother who read the Bible to him every day. Mothers, take note!

Try This

» Listen to a recording of *Come, Ye Faithful, Raise the Strain* to see if you can hear a change in the meter (or rhythm) of the music. In the Western Church, we often use translated hymns from long ago, with music written in the 1800s, as is this song.

» Become a composer writing a tune (or choose a melody line from a different song) that will allow you to sing the hymn below. Notice that, since the third and fourth lines of each verse are shorter than the first two lines, you might need to change the meter, just as you heard in the hymn by John of Damascus.

O, Light That Knew No Dawn

Gregory Nazianzen

O, Light that knew no dawn, that shines to endless day,
All things in earth and heaven are lustered by Thy ray;
No eye can to Thy throne ascend,
Nor mind Thy brightness comprehend.

Thy grace, O, Father, give, that I may serve with fear;
Above all boons, I pray, grant me Thy voice to hear.
From sin Thy child in mercy free,
And let me dwell in light with Thee.

That, cleansed from stain of sin, I may meet homage give,
And, pure in heart, behold Thy beauty while I live,
Clean hands in holy worship raise,
And Thee, O, Christ, my Savior, praise.

Thy grace, O, Father, give, I humbly Thee implore,
And let Thy mercy bless Thy servant more and more.
All grace and glory be to Thee
From age to age eternally. Amen.

Listen

All Glory, Laud, & Honor MUSIC CD

Come, Ye Faithful, Raise the Strain

► Cooking

Warning: These are absolutely wonderful dishes. You may find them impossible to resist!

Baba Ghannouj

1 large eggplant, unpeeled
¼ cup tahini (sesame-seed paste)
1 large garlic clove, smashed

1 med. size onion, unpeeled
3 tbsp fresh squeezed lemon juice
Salt to taste

Pierce eggplant and onion in several places to let steam escape. Place both in a rimmed baking pan. Bake in a 400 degree oven, uncovered, for about one hour or until eggplant is very soft. Rinse cooked vegetables under cold running water to cool them; then drain, peel, and quarter. Place in a food processor or blender. Add tahini, lemon juice, and garlic. Blend until smooth; season to taste with salt. Let cool to room temperature and serve, or cover and refrigerate until needed (though be sure to serve it at room temperature). Serve in a bowl, or mounded on a plate, with pita wedges that have been heated. Makes about 2 cups.

Pita Bread

1 pkg. dry yeast
1 to 1¼ cups warm water
Pinch sugar
3½ cups sifted flour

1 tsp salt
2 tbsp oil
cornmeal

In a large mixing bowl, dissolve the yeast and sugar in ¼ cup of warm water. Let stand for 10 minutes, then add the remaining water, the salt and the oil. Stir one cup of the flour at a time into the yeast mixture, until it has all been added, to form a sticky dough. (Add a little more flour if dough is too sticky to work with.) Transfer the dough to a lightly floured board, and knead vigorously until smooth, about 10 minutes. Shape the dough into a ball and coat lightly with oil. Cover and let rise until doubled in bulk, about 1 ½ hours. Punch down the dough and form 6 or 7 balls. On a lightly floured board, roll each ball into 6 inch circles that are ¼ inch thick. Dust lightly with flour, cover and let rise again for 15 minutes. Preheat over to 500 degrees. Place the bread on lightly oiled baking sheets dusted with cornmeal. Bake until puffy, about 8 to 10 minutes. Wrap in foil immediately to preserve moistness.

▶ Student Self-Evaluation UNIT 3, PHASE 3

Dates and hours:_____

Evaluate your projects

- List which of the activities listed in this Phase you did:

_____

_____

_____

- Rate your enthusiasm: _____

Explain: _____

_____

- Rate the precision of your approach: _____

Explain: _____

_____

- Rate your effort toward the completion of the project: _____

Explain: _____

_____

Ask yourself what worked and what did not. What would you do differently in the future, and what would you repeat?

_____

How specifically did these hands-on activities enhance your knowledge of the Byzantines & Muslims? What made them worthwhile?

_____

In the first three Phases of this Unit, what aspect of the time period has most captured your imagination? What would you like to creatively pursue to conclude your study?

_____

Phase 4

▶ In Your Own Way…

We have seen the grandeur and controversies of the Byzantine Empire and the Orthodox Church. We have also examined the rise of Islam and its dramatic growth from the Pyrenees of Spain to the western border of China. Now, choose a selection of these activities, or create your own, which will best express what you have learned from this Unit.

LINGUISTICS

Journalism

You have just been nominated vice president in charge of public relations for the Nestorian Church in Persia. Write a press release for the "Muslim Herald" announcing church services in your area. (Remember, you have to walk a very fine line in order that the local imam doesn't think you are a Christian proselytizer.) Be sure to use inventive words that capture the heart of what you want to communicate without using "Christian-ese."

Emperor Justinian has just opened Hagia Sophia to rave reviews. You have been assigned to write a critique of the architectural style, the artistic expression, and the mathematical wonder of a round dome on a square building for the weekly magazine, "The Byzantine Buzz." Only problem is, it cost a fortune… and somebody's got to pay for it!

Prose

Write the Nicene Creed in your own words, expressing the fullness of what each section means to you.

Write the story of the Islamic Empire for Christian children. Be sure to include the major events of the first three hundred years, the capital cities, and some of the scientific and cultural innovations.

Write a letter to a Muslim friend (real or imaginary) describing the concept of a loving Father God. Include the appropriate Scriptures, as well as your own experiences of His love for you. Be sure to write with clarity, using expressions of friendship and paying attention to cultural and religious differences.

Poetry

Write a poem about the first hundred years of Muslim conquest. It could be modeled on *The Charge of the Light Brigade* by Alfred, Lord Tennyson.

Playing with Words

Finish this limerick:
> *There once was fellow named Leo*
> *Who said that icons should not be-Oh!…*

ART

Painting/Drawing

Create an arabesque painting, in the style of Islamic artists. Discover the vibrancy of colors normally used in these paintings, and consider whether you would prefer to use this palette of colors for your own work.

Draw a rendering of a Byzantine church, whether Hagia Sophia in Istanbul, the Church of San Vitale in Ravenna, or another one of your choosing.

Political Cartooning

Create a political cartoon which demonstrates the struggle taking place between Church and State in the Iconoclast Controversy.

Graphic Design

Design a flyer to entice soldiers to settle as soldier/farmers in buffer zone lands adjacent to Muslim territory. The hope is that they will put down roots, so to say, and become a permanent citizen army. So, remember, as you state the reason this relocation would be beneficial, to focus on what would appeal to a soldier.

Sculpting

Sculpt a piece of artwork which evokes a sense of either the Byzantines or the Muslims. You have much to work with, from Greek Fire to scimitars, from minarets to domed churches.

MUSIC

Performance Practice

With your teacher's help, select an appropriate piece of music which expresses some particular aspect studied in this Unit, whether from the rise of Islam or from the Byzantine Empire. Prepare and perform the piece for an audience. Communicate with your audience the reason for your selection either in the program notes or in a short speech.

DRAMA

Comedy

Produce a skit in which Symeon, the "holy fool" of Emesa, teaches a group of aspiring ascetics what 1 Corinthians 4:10 means when it says, "We are fools for Christ's sake." Be sure to include a few of Symeon's personal anecdotes.

Drama

Create a scene from a Coptic church in Egypt, as the church members discuss whether they should fight against the approaching Muslim army or welcome them as the overthrowers of the Byzantines, who have been persecuting your church.

Reader's Theater

Write and read a first person account of the Battle of Tours in 732, from two perspectives: #1) a Muslim soldier mounted on his horse, #2) a Christian peasant watching the battle take place.

Puppetry

Choose one the Seven Ecumenical Councils to reenact with puppets. Be sure to set up the scene by portraying the theological controversy for which the council was convened. You might want to add a bit of audience participation, with "Boo!" for the heretical guys and "Yay!" for the orthodox guys.

Prop Needs

_____

_____

Costume Ideas

_____

_____

Role/Player

_____

_____

Set Suggestions

_____

_____

MOVEMENT

Pantomime

Select one story from *One Thousand and One Nights,* which memorialized the court of Harun ar-Rashid who ruled the Islamic Empire at its most luxurious point. Then prepare a pantomime to tell the story. A few suggestions would be "Aladdin and his lamp," and "Ali Babba and the forty thieves."

Dance

Create a dance depicting the beauty of Hagia Sophia, illuminating the round dome and the square church below. Be sure to choose music that will suggest the soaring dome, and the immensity of the structure.

Action

Portray the extraordinary rapidity of the fall of much of the Byzantine Empire to the Muslims. Invite several participants to portray countries under the Byzantine rule, then have one person, acting as the Muslim army, sweep through the land. When one comes under the domination of the Muslims, they must go down to the ground. Remember, they were only stopped one time— at the Battle of Tours, in France.

CONCEPTUAL DESIGN

Weapon of Fire

One of the major factors for the victory of the Byzantines over the Arabs during the attack of Constantinople in 673 was the use of Greek fire. Launched from the prows of Byzantine ships, this unquenchable fire which burned on contact with seawater, wreaked havoc on the Muslim fleet.

Knowing that Greek fire was both a potent weapon and a potent source of trouble if the method of dispensing it failed, design a modern day launching system capable of shooting this material a substantial distance. Remember that Greek fire erupted into fire spontaneously, and it could only be extinguished with sand.

CREATE YOUR OWN EXPRESSION

_____

_____

_____

_____

► Student Self-Evaluation UNIT 3, PHASE 4

Dates and hours:_____

Evaluate your projects

- What creative project did you choose:

  _____

- What did you expect from your project, and how does the final project compare to your initial expectations?

  _____

- What do you like about your project? What would you change?

  _____

In Conclusion

Revisit the five Key Concepts from the beginning of this Unit. Explain how your understanding of and appreciation for each has grown over the course of your study.

- _____

  _____

- _____

  _____

- _____

  _____

- _____

  _____

- _____

  _____

Record your concluding thoughts on the Byzantines & Muslims:

_____

_____

The Holy Roman Empire & the Vikings

Statue of Charlemagne, Notre Dame, Paris, France

United we stand, divided we fall . . .
Church & State

On Christmas Day, in the Year of Our Lord 800, an epic-making event occurred which would shake the nations of the earth—and would begin Western European civilization. The king of the Franks, Charlemagne, had come not only to observe Christmas but to proudly observe the formality of the crowning of his own son as the king who would eventually follow him. This was a prominent and powerful line of rulers: from Charles Martel to his son Pepin; from Pepin to his son Charlemagne; from Charlemagne to his son, as well. This would be an important service. Conducting it was the friend and beneficiary of Charlemagne, Pope Leo III, who was indebted to Charlemagne for having recently protected him from enemies, restoring him to his papal throne. Unilaterally, Pope Leo took the moment, the crown, and the attention of all of Europe to, without warning and by his own initiative, place the crown on Charlemagne's head. Pope Leo then proclaimed him *Emperor* and bowed before him in the fashion of bowing before emperors. Since the Byzantine emperors had long claimed ownership of Western Europe as part of their Roman Empire, what was it that caused the pope to take such a momentous step and break all political, traditional, and even legal systems?

First of all, when Rome was under threat in the mid-700s, the pope had found no help from the Byzantine emperor. The Byzantines had huge troubles on their own doorstep, diverting all of their attention and energy as they sought to keep the Muslim armies at bay. So the pope looked west to the newly crowned king of the Franks, Pepin, for protection. This incredible connection—between pope and European king—began one of the most significant diplomatic relationships of the Middle Ages.

This action would have an enormous impact upon the papacy for more than a thousand years.

Pepin not only defeated the threatening Lombards in 756, but he also gave several of their cities to the pope, including the Western city of Ravenna, which had belonged to the Byzantines before being captured by the Lombards. This endowment, the "Donation of Pepin," established the territory known as the papal states. From this point, the pope was no longer solely a spiritual leader; he also became a secular ruler of land and people in central and northern Italy. This action would have an enormous impact upon the papacy, as well as on Italy, for more than a thousand years.

Beyond the fact that the Byzantines had been absent when needed, the emperor himself was considered absent. The current Byzantine ruler, much to the horror of the West, was the Empress Irene. It was not merely the notion of a woman as ruler that shocked leaders in the western Church, however. It was the fact that Irene, in 797, had deposed and blinded the legitimate emperor—her own son—in pursuit of imperial power. Because of this, many considered the Eastern throne to be empty. And now the pope found Pepin's son attending Christmas mass.

Secondly, there remained within the worldview of this culture the sense that Constantine's conversion to Christianity in the 300s had ushered in a new era—the time of the Christian Roman Empire. Within this worldview, there was the forceful idea of a Christian empire accomplishing the will of God on earth, which was the Christianization of all people. This meant that the empire should be the secular arm of the Church, aiding her militarily and politically in the business of conversion and in enforcing the policies of the Church. However, with the iconoclast controversy raging in the East, setting at odds the Byzantine Church and the Byzantine emperors, the true business of that empire seemed to be at a standstill. The western Church was looking for an empire, a Holy Roman Empire that could take the kingdom by force, and, providentially, a king had come to church.

Finally, much as the pope was seen increasingly as not merely in charge of the churches in the West but as one overseeing the whole Church, a strong secular ruler was needed—one who could hold together the whole of Christendom, not just reign over a small territory. In Charlemagne, Pope Leo III found someone who fulfilled that final expectation to a *T*.

For the first time since the fall of Rome, someone had stepped into power with the ability to overcome all foes and to weld together many different peoples under one crown. Charlemagne expanded his kingdom year after year, battle after battle, until he reigned over most of Western Europe. He also continued his father's policies of supporting the pope, both through military aid and through enlarging the Catholic Church. For instance, Charlemagne demanded conversion to Christianity when he conquered the Saxon people, giving them a choice of baptism or execution. Fortunately, this policy horrified many of the church leaders of the time, so it was finally dropped in 797. Even with this stain on his character, Charlemagne stood head and shoulders above every other European leader of the previous several hundred years.

In Charlemagne, Pope Leo III found someone who fulfilled that final expectation to a T.

He was the right man for the right job at the right moment, or at least, that was evidently what Pope Leo III believed. At the coronation, Charlemagne was thrust into the exalted ranks of imperial Roman power descending from Augustus Caesar. (They counted him the sixty-eighth emperor from Augustus, from Roman to Byzantine and now to the Franks, having ended the Byzantine line just before Empress Irene.) The main problem, apart from the legal issues and the hostility of the Byzantines, was that the Church had given the imperial crown to the State, rather than the State crowning itself. The question of the hour was, "Does the Church have the right to make an Emperor?" Thus, a struggle was born between Church and State, which would continue to shake the West for centuries.

Vikings

Seven years prior to Charlemagne's crowning, something of an entirely different nature had shaken the British Isles, which lay outside of Charlemagne's empire. To the holy island of Lindisfarne, from which the light of the gospel had radiated throughout northern England in the 600s, came a ferocious assault in June of 793. Unlooked for and wholly unexpected, a terrifying dragon-boat filled with unrestrained and violent Viking raiders landed on the peaceful island. It was not for battle against an enemy army that the Vikings had come to this wealthy monastery, but to plunder and pillage, to kill and destroy. Thus, the Viking Age in all its fury began its nearly three centuries of barbarity at the very spot where God's grace had been poured out.

This was not the only holy place to face the Viking assault. Two years later, the monastery at Iona—another major center from which the message of God's redemption had diffused throughout the British Isles and Europe—was attacked with the same results as Lindisfarne. The coast and monasteries of Ireland suffered, too, under these early attacks by the Viking pirates, with the lure of easy money and unarmed monks drawing them to the very centers of worship and Christian devotion.

The Vikings who went roving throughout the seas were not solely raiding pirates, however.

How sober the words of 1 Peter 4:17 must have sounded in the ears of those who loved the Lord: *"For the time has come for judgment to begin at the house of God; and if it begins with us first, what will be the end of those who do not obey the gospel of God?"* To many Christians, who had been looking for the Second Coming of Jesus, this sudden ferocious attack by terrifying marauders on dragonboats seemed to be the very fulfillment of Scripture—the Apocalypse of Revelation. Revelation 13:1 describes the apostle standing on the sand of the sea and seeing a beast (connected to a dragon) come out of the sea. It fit these medieval monks' experience, and to some, it must have given assurance that the God who had written The Book would eventually triumph despite the devastation.

The Vikings who went roving throughout the seas were not solely raiding pirates, however. There were some who had left their farms in Scandinavia to become traders in the East, as well as the West. The Eastern traders, settling in Russia, traveled south to trade with the Byzantines in Constantinople and the Muslims in Baghdad. Their most popular trading items were furs, amber, and slaves from the North. In the West, Vikings set up cities in Ireland from which they could trade in the British Isles and, when the mood was upon them, raid those same areas. Beyond the raiders and traders, there were settlers looking for new lands to farm in such newly discovered areas as Iceland.

In the early years, though, raiding was the main business of these sea-roving bands of Vikings. It is fascinating to discover that the last fight of Charlemagne's life took place against Danish Vikings. When he was nearly seventy years old, Charlemagne led his troops against Godfred of Denmark, who had landed on the northern coast of the empire. It wasn't much of a fight, since Godfred was killed by one of his own soldiers as Charlemagne approached and the Danes fled before him. Because of the Viking threat, however, Charlemagne went on to fortify vulnerable sites and to establish harbor patrols in his domain in order to deter Viking attacks. These were successful in deterring Viking raids in the empire through the remaining years of his life and the life of his son, Louis the Pious.

Division

Evidently, the Vikings were very aware of what was taking place in Europe. They struck England, which was divided into several petty kingdoms that frequently warred among themselves. Ireland faced the same unwanted attention for the same reasons. But the Holy Roman Empire, as long as it remained united under one ruler, was not touched. This changed when rule passed to Charlemagne's grandsons in 840.

Louis the Pious had bequeathed his territory to each of his three sons, creating a "kingdom" for each, and with the eldest son, Lothair, given authority over the other two as emperor. But with the death of Louis, the two younger sons went to war against Lothair. They forced him to sign the Treaty of Verdun in 843, which essentially ended the empire by dividing it into three wholly separated units: France in the West, Germany in the East, and Lotharingia (or Lorraine), a long, narrow kingdom (including the capital cities of Rome and Aachen) sandwiched in between. This third kingdom became the battle ground as France and Germany each sought more territory. By 888, the wrangling for political territories had resulted in the kingdoms of France, Germany, Italy, Lorraine, and Burgundy.

From the Treaty of Verdun, all unity between these kingdoms—the former Carolingian Empire—was gone. The main focus of the rulers was no longer to rule justly and well nor to defend their borders against Vikings, but instead, to snatch as much territory as possible from their neighboring relatives. Kings sought support by giving land to their nobles, which eventually resulted in strong nobles and weak kings. They also greatly endowed the Church, which gave the popes increasing authority over all of Christendom, including its kings.

More Church & State

Pope Nicholas I, who ruled from 858–867, was the most powerful pope during the time of the Carolingians. He believed that the Church, with the pope at its head, had supremacy over the State and that the pope was the final authority in the Church, in both the East and West. The first point was demonstrated when the personal affairs of Emperor Lothair (son of Louis the Pious) came to his attention. The emperor wanted to divorce his wife on false charges, but she appealed to the pope. After hearing the case, the pope decided in her favor—despite the fact that two Church synods in the northern part of Lothair's kingdom had declared the divorce to be proper. Pope Nicholas in Rome took the stance that the emperor was his ecclesiastical subject, so he nullified the synods and declared, "No divorce!" Concerning

From the Treaty of Verdun, all unity between these kingdoms—the former Carolingian Empire—was gone.

the issue of papal supremacy over the entire Church, when the Byzantine emperor deposed the patriarch of Constantinople and appointed someone else, Pope Nicholas stepped into the fray. Through a series of events, the pope ended up excommunicating the new patriarch who then countered the measure by excommunicating the pope! In taking active measures towards the Byzantine church, Pope Nicholas demonstrated that the papacy believed it had the right to rule in Church affairs worldwide, and to make decisions which all—Byzantine or European, emperor or bishop—must obey.

East vs. West

Part of the church struggle between East and West during this medieval time can be seen in the story of Cyril and Methodius, two brothers sent in 863 by the Byzantine emperor and patriarch (mentioned above) as missionaries to the Slavs. Though they had been invited to come by Prince Rostislav, the ruler of the Slavs, and though they did a phenomenal job of translating the Scriptures and the liturgy into the language of the people (creating the Cyrillic alphabet for the newly written language), these Orthodox Byzantines were seen by the local Catholic archbishop as poachers on European territory. Evidently, he complained about their methods, because it was only a few years before Pope Nicholas I sent for Cyril and Methodius, to have them explain their justification for using a language besides Latin for the holy things of God. He died before he had a chance to question Cyril and Methodius, but the next pope, Adrian II, ended up taking their side in this dispute—provided they would agree to serve as Catholics.

> *Through a series of events, the pope ended up excommunicating the new patriarch who then countered the measure by excommunicating the pope!*

Even this did not relieve the problem. Returning to the field alone (Cyril died in Rome), Methodius was soon tried and thrown into jail by the German clergy in Moravia. He was not freed—even as a Catholic archbishop—until the new pope intervened in the situation. After explaining the use of a Slavic liturgy once more to the pope in Rome (and once more receiving papal approval, though it did not end the troubles in Moravia), Methodius finally returned to Constantinople to seek aid in his mission. At his death, the Slavic liturgy was condemned by Rome and replaced with the Latin liturgy. The Moravian church declined and Methodius's mission seemed a fruitless failure. However, the neighboring ruler of Bulgaria, Prince Boris, welcomed the Slavic liturgy and the Slavic Bible for his people. Within fifteen years, Bulgaria had become the center of Christianity for the Slavic people of Eastern Europe. Though caught in the crossfires of East-West religious hostilities, Cyril and Methodius's groundbreaking work of translation has remained a blessing to the people of Eastern Europe and Russia for centuries.

Back to the Vikings

In the West, the divided empire of Charlemagne had come under increasing attack by the Vikings. It was Matthew 12:25 in living color: "Every kingdom divided against itself is brought to desolation, and every city or house divided against itself will not stand." With shallow-drafted boats, large raiding parties of Vikings began to sail up rivers and wreak havoc in the most unexpected places. France especially, with its wide, flowing rivers, faced brutal devastation inland, where Vikings pillaged at will for more than fifty years. They attacked the city of Rouen in 841 and utterly decimated the city of Nantes in 843. Beginning in that same year, those Vikings attacking France no longer returned to Scandinavia, but wintered on Noirmoutier, a coastal French island, to better position themselves for piratical ventures. By 880 the region of western France had been systematically and thoroughly ravaged. Again, this plundering at will was only possible because of the lack of unity and infighting among the Carolingian rulers and their nobles. In fact, Charles the Fat, who ruled as emperor from 881 to 887, saw his own brothers as a greater threat than the Vikings! Thus, there were no strong rulers on the continent who were prepared to successfully challenge the Vikings.

Alfred & the Vikings

In England, however, an English king faced the Viking threat, and, for the very first time, the Vikings met their match. Alfred, King of Wessex from 871 to 899, defeated the Danish Vikings at the Battle of Edington in 878. In the peace treaty between Alfred and Guthrum, a firm line was drawn between the territory of the English and the Danelaw, land upon which the Danish had settled themselves. (Interestingly, after losing to Alfred, the Danish leader Guthrum converted to Christianity.) Part of the reason for Alfred's continuing success against Viking attack was his strong military presence, shown in a willingness to fortify the land and to patrol the seas. Another aspect of his success, which needs to be considered is found in his God-honoring and just rule. By word and deed, he sought to obey the Lord, and then endeavored to teach his subjects to do the same. Alfred believed, as did others of the time, that the Viking terror in England was God's judgment on the sins of the English people. He thought that by teaching God's Word and His ways, people would gain wisdom, and, thus, live wisely and obediently before the Lord. Since educators were scarce in this decimated region, he invited scholars from Europe and England to come to his court and teach. Alfred himself learned Latin so that he might benefit his people by translating books of theology and history into English. Books such as *Seven Books of Histories Against the Pagans*, written in the 400s, and *The Ecclesiastical History*

The Moravian church declined and Methodius's mission seemed a fruitless failure.

of the English People, written in the 700s, were made available to encourage the understanding that history has God's divine action and purpose behind it.

Cluny

Despite this brief interlude in England, the year 900 seems to have been the low point in European history since the barbarians began invading. To the constant Viking raids was added in this year a new source of destruction: the Turkish Magyars. They ravaged the German kingdoms and the border regions of France, plundering and pillaging everything in their path and draining off what little resources remained. Along with this, one must consider the pathetic spectacle of small, weak kings—the heirs to the mighty empire of Charlemagne—who were constantly at war with each other. It was truly a time of "every man for himself." Into this dark and melancholy moment, though, a bright light began to shine from the new monastery at Cluny. Founded in 909, Cluny led the movement for reestablishing Christian values in Europe after decades of devastation. The second abbot of Cluny, Odo, had the foresight to begin creating a series of daughter monasteries, which would spread eventually across France and Germany. Together they formed a network of interrelated centers holding to the same Christian beliefs and ideals. It was within this network that the Cluniac revival began to touch every level of European society from the highest to the lowest. Monasteries throughout the land were once more focused on heartfelt worship and obedience, and in their schools, Cluniac monks taught the sons of the aristocracy how to rule as Christian leaders. For more than one hundred and fifty years, these monks would be the most influential, behind-the-scene figures in Christian Europe.

The Norman Vikings

To the constant Viking raids was added in this year a new source of destruction: the Turkish Magyars.

Two years after the founding of Cluny, the king of France traded the land of Normandy for peace and quiet. He had finally discovered an effective way of dealing with Viking invasions: hire other Vikings to fight them! Thus it was that in 911, King Charles the Simple made a medieval deal with the Viking leader, Rollo, which worked reasonably well—land for protection. Part of the bargain was that Rollo must convert to Christianity. This was the beginning of a strong relationship between the Normans and the Church in which the Normans eventually played the role of protectors of the pope, as will soon be seen. Apart from ending his troubles with Vikings, however, King Charles the Simple soon found he had far greater troubles. His inability to gather the French nobles to his side resulted in his imprisonment and the loss of his crown, which was the first time this had happened to a Carolingian king. With strong nobles and weak kings, France focused on its own inner turmoil for generations.

Otto

Over in Germany, however, things began to improve, especially during the reign of Otto the Great. Crowned king in 936, he initially faced the huge obstacle of dealing with rebellious nobles, which he dealt with quickly and firmly. He championed the Church in his domain, thereby enlisting the clergy as his allies and supporters. They even became functionaries within his government, since they were among the best educated and most loyal subjects available. In 951 the widowed queen of Italy was taken captive, and she turned to the closest and best ruler available for help—Otto. He marched into Italy, set her free, married her, and then made himself King of the Lombards. His conquests were not over yet, however. When the Magyars attacked in 955, Otto not only defeated them, but quenched their desire to ever intrude on German lands. This is the portrait of a strong ruler, cast in the same mold as Charlemagne. It was evident to the people around him, even in his own day. So, when the pope in Rome was threatened by the same warlord who had formerly captured the queen of Italy, he, too, appealed to Otto for protection. What was the reward for this protection? The imperial crown, given to Otto in 962. It was the reestablishment of the empire in the West, though, with only Germany and Italy included, it was a much shrunken empire compared to that of Charlemagne. The Holy Roman Empire would henceforth be in the hands of German rulers, when not disputed by the pope.

Rus

Further east, the Swedish Vikings had not only set up profitable trading routes to Constantinople and Baghdad in the late 800s, but also established trading centers in the conquered Russian cities of Kiev and Novgorod. (The word "Russia" actually derives from the Scandinavian word "Rus.") In their great strength and ferocity, these Vikings appear to have ruled the indigenous peasants under them. The strongest of the Vikings began the Rurik Dynasty of Russia, which was the royal line of the Russian people until 1598. Though the Russians—both Viking and peasants—were pagans in the beginning, Christianity began to make inroads into the culture by the mid-900s. The defining moment for Christianity in Russia, however, came in 988, when the Prince of Kiev, Vladimir, not only converted to Christianity himself, but forcefully required the people of Kiev and Novgorod to do the same. The stream of Christianity embraced by the people was the Eastern Orthodoxy of the Byzantines, using the Slavic liturgy created by Cyril and Methodius. To cement the relationship, politically

Part of the bargain was that Rollo must convert to Christianity.

and religiously, Prince Vladimir put away his former wives to marry the sister of the Byzantine Emperor. As we will see during the time of the Renaissance, this connection would bear long-term fruit.

Vikings Evangelized

In the momentous year AD 1000, the Viking settlers of Iceland accepted Christianity over paganism.

In the momentous year AD 1000, the Viking settlers of Iceland accepted Christianity over paganism. According to the Icelandic saga, that was the same year Leif Ericson, son of the outlaw who colonized Greenland, was converted to Christianity by the Norwegian king Olaf. His commission to Leif, according to this saga, was to take the gospel back to Greenland. In his journey, however, he was blown off course and landed on the North American continent, which he named "Vinland." After a time of exploration of that lush land, he made his way back to Greenland to share Christianity with the colony. There is a different saga, one from Greenland, which describes Leif's voyage to North America as being the result of hearing another Viking's experience of that land. Many historians credit the Greenland saga as more reliable than the Icelandic, but one way or another, Leif Ericson sailed to North America centuries before Christopher Columbus. And the descriptions of the conversion of the Vikings to Christianity—from Denmark, Norway, Sweden, Iceland, and Greenland—have been well documented. Once the Vikings converted, they ceased raiding, and the terror ended as suddenly as it had begun.

More East vs. West

In the East, the Byzantine emperor had joined the Holy Roman emperor and the pope in an alliance against the Normans, who, in their head-strong and warlike manner, were encroaching upon land in southern Italy belonging to the Byzantines and the Papal States. Unfortunately, the Byzanztine emperor, as part of this alliance, demanded that the patriarch of Constantinople acknowledge the Roman pope as authority over the Byzantine Church. This the patriarch would not do, and in defiance of his emperor and the pope, the patriarch shut down all the Roman churches in Constantinople. He went on to write a letter to the

Viking dragon boats

pope in 1053, telling him all the things the Western believers were doing wrong—things like using unleavened bread in communion. This letter was not well received in Rome, to say the least. Pope Leo IX, sent an ambassador, Cardinal Humbert, to reply to the patriarch's charges and to communicate the Roman position. Neither Cardinal Humbert nor Patriarch Cerularius were patient men, and when Pope Leo IX died, Cerularius ended the negotiation process, utterly dismissing Humbert from his diplomatic role. In response, Cardinal Humbert excommunicated and anathematized (or "banned from the Church") the patriarch and all who criticized the Roman church. Cerularius then anathematized Humbert and his fellow ambassadors. This mutual act is known as The Great Schism of 1054, where the unity between the Church of the East and the Church of the West was finally and completely severed.

Norman Invasion

The Normans were busy, not only in Italy, but in England, as well. In 1066 William, the Duke of Normandy, took a fleet of ships to England, complete with knights and armor, horses and weaponry, and even preassembled wooden forts. Duke William claimed the throne of England upon the passing of his distant relative, King Edward the Confessor, despite the fact that an English earl Harold had just received the crown. In a desperately fought battle, the Normans sought to not only hold onto their toehold of English land, but to completely conquer the English. Just as night was coming, the English King Harold was killed by a chance Norman arrow, and the Battle of Hastings was decided. Duke William followed up this victory by marching his army on London, and when the English nobles finally submitted to him, William the Conqueror was crowned king on Christmas Day 1066.

This letter was not well received in Rome, to say the least.

With this event, England received not only a Norman king but a Norman yoke as well. The tightly-controlled feudalism of Normandy, which William had introduced to successfully subdue the rebellious barons of his Norman lands, was now imported to England. William also granted lands and estates to the Norman barons who had helped him win England, thereby replacing the Anglo-Saxon aristocracy with French-speaking, military-minded, and powerful Normans. England would never be the same.

From the time of Charlemagne to the time of William the Conqueror, much had changed in Europe. After enduring centuries of invasion, Europe finally came to a time of peace. Many small kingdoms had been reformed and reforged in the furnace of conquest to emerge as powerful, united countries. And, as we will see in the next unit, this peace and strength will cause medieval people to look beyond their own borders to see the rest of the world. ◄

Phase 1

Key People (Church)

Alcuin of York
Leading scholar of Carolingian Renaissance

Pope Leo III
Pope who crowned Charlemagne as Emperor

Cyril & Methodius
Missionaries to the Moravians

Pope Nicholas I
One of the most powerful popes of the Middle Ages

Odo of Cluny
Abbot who led Clunaic Reform

▶ Listen to This

What in the World? VOL. 2

DISC TWO:

» Charlemagne (track 6)

» The Vikings (track 7)

» Feudalism (track 8)

» Religion & the Holy Roman Empire (track 9)

» Northern Europe & Britain (track 10)

True Tales VOL. 2

DISC TWO:

» Alfred of England (track 2)

» The Truce of God (track 3)

Digging Deeper VOL. 2

DISC TWO: THE CHURCH IN CHARGE

» Western Politics & Eastern Icons (track 6)

▶ Read For Your Life

The Holy Bible

» **God's deliverance and protection:** Psalm 107, Psalm 127:1

» **God's wisdom for rulers:** Proverbs 8:12–21

» **God's ability to direct kings:** Proverbs 21:1

» **Submission to government:** 1 Peter 2:13–17, Romans 13:1–7

» **God's judgment against a nation and effects of repentance:** Joel 1–2

Talk Together

Opinion Column

» What did you find to be the most interesting aspect, or the most fascinating person, you encountered in your introduction to the history of the Holy Roman Empire and the Vikings?

» Do you think Charlemagne really wanted the pope to crown him emperor? Why or why not? What might be the implications of the head of the Church crowning the head of the empire?

» If you had lived in Charlemagne's domain during his reign, in what ways would you have enjoyed having him as your ruler? In what ways do you think you would have struggled with his rule?

» Imagine you were living on a farm in rural Europe. What would be your reaction when the neighbors started telling you about Viking raids just down the river? What do you think you would do to prepare?

» If you had been a vassal during the time of feudalism, you would have been required to give forty days of military service to the lord of the manor. Why might this have been good for you? Why might it have been bad? For what reasons do you get the impression that knights enjoyed fighting?

» Imagine you were living along the coast of France when your king offers Rollo the Viking some prime real estate just north of you. What is your response?

» If you had been a Saxon living in England at the time of William the Conqueror, how do you think you would have responded to the French Norman knights being given English land?

Key People (World)

Charlemagne
Recreated Western Empire

Alfred the Great
Founder of English nation

Otto the Great
German Holy Roman Emperor

Hugh Capet
First Capetian king of France

Vladimir of Kiev
First Christian ruler of Russia

Leif Ericson
Viking explorer

Canute
Christian king of England & Denmark

William the Conqueror
Norman king of England

Critical Puzzling

» How would you describe feudalism? Why do you think it was successful in the Middle Ages? What do you think are its strengths? What are its weaknesses?

» Why do you think Charlemagne's empire fell apart after his death? What kept it together when he was alive?

» Looking at a map, what reasons can you discover for the Vikings having chosen the British Isles as one of their prime targets?

» There was a constant struggle in the West between emperors and popes concerning their jurisdiction and their rights. What circumstances in the Middle Ages created this struggle? Can you think of any other times in history where this has been the case?

» In what ways, if any, do you think William the Conqueror was good for England? In what ways, if any, do you think he was bad for England?

» What kind of changes came to England because of the Norman invasion?

▶ Resources for Digging Deeper

Choose a few books that look interesting, or find your own.

EARLY MIDDLE AGES

Cultural Atlas for Young People: The Middle Ages

Mike Corbishley • Beginning with the barbarian invasions of Europe, this fascinating book gives an overview of the many elements of the Middle Ages. It is filled with photographs, maps, and informative descriptions of the people, events, and places of the Middle Ages. **UE+**

The Medieval World

Philip Steele • This Kingfisher publication provides a basic illustrated overview of the Middle Ages. Especially recommended for visually-oriented students. **UE+**

Story of the Middle Ages

Michael J. McHugh & John Southworth • Though this book covers the fall of Rome through the Reformation, four of the chapters, beginning with Chapter Three, focus on the time frame of this Unit. Informative and well-written. **UE+**

Early Times—The Story of the Middle Ages

Suzanne Strauss Art • An informative and interesting look at one thousand years of history, this book will provide students with an understanding of how the many and varied aspects of the Middle Ages melded together. **UE+**

The Early Middle Ages

Translated from Italian, this book is a tremendous introduction to the early Middle Ages for students. It includes the developments from the fourth century to AD 1000. UE+

The Middle Ages—The Cambridge Introduction to History

Trevor Cairns • This is a very readable, very interesting overview of the Middle Ages. It covers the Church, the feudal lords, the Crusades, villagers, townspeople, kings, and the end of the Middle Ages. **UE+**

Canterbury Tales

Geoffrey Chaucer, selected, translated, & adapted by Barbara Cohen • This is a delightful, well-illustrated adaptation of Chaucer's tales of medieval people and events. This book makes a wonderful introduction for the whole family. It would be a great read-aloud and discussion book. **E+**

The Rise of the Feudal Monarchies

Sidney Painter • Another from the series The Development of Western Civilization, this book examines the rise and development of feudalism in France, England, and the Holy Roman Empire after the fall of Rome. **HS+**

VIKINGS

The Real Vikings: Craftsmen, Traders, and Fearsome Raiders

Melvin Berger & Gilda Berger • This beautiful children's book is a wonderful, fact-filled, illustrated book about the people we know from history as the Vikings. **E+**

Usborne Internet-Linked Viking World

Philippa Wingate & Dr. Anne Millard • Filled with all sorts of details on Vikings, this well-illustrated book will provide students with a greater understanding of the various elements of life in Viking times. **UE+**

The Vikings, A Horizon Caravel Book

Frank Donovan • This series (*Horizon Caravel*) is wonderful for teaching children about history. The text is interesting and informative, the pictures are wonderful, and the details fascinating. **UE+**

The Story of Rolf and the Viking Bow

Allen French • Set in Iceland in 1010, shortly after the people's conversion to Christianity, this well-written saga is one of those stories you can't put down. **UE+**

The Viking Explorers

Jim Gallagher • The Vikings discovered Iceland, Greenland, and perhaps even North America. Learn more about their travels and experiences in this fascinating book. **UE+**

Viking Quest Series

Lois Walfrid Johnson • In the four books of this series, *Raiders from the Sea, Mystery of the Silver Coins, The Invisible Friend,* and *Heart of Courage,* award-winning children's author Lois Walfrid Johnson weaves a fascinating story of the Viking people. Her careful research provides an in-depth look at this many-faceted culture. Highly recommended! **UE+**

CHURCH HISTORY IN THE MIDDLE AGES

Christian History Made Easy

Dr. Timothy Paul Jones • Though this book covers from the rise of the Church to the present, Dr. Jones has simplified and clarified a subject that is often overwhelming to students. It will enhance your understanding of the medieval Church (both Eastern and Western) and the part it played in history. **MS+**

Faith in the Medieval World

G. R. Evans • This title is filled with information concerning Christianity during the Middle Ages. It will provide students with a better framework for understanding what seems mystifying to Protestant Christians today. **MS+**

CHARLEMAGNE

Son of Charlemagne

Barbara Willard • A wonderfully well-written book about the first Holy Roman Emperor, told from the perspective of his son. This story is historically accurate and sensitive to the complexities of the man Charlemagne. **UE+**

Famous Men of the Middle Ages

by Haaren & Poland, edited by Cyndy Shearer & Robert Shearer • Included in this Unit for its biographies on Charlemagne, Rollo, Alfred the Great, King Canute, William the Conqueror and more. **E+**

Charlemagne—World Leaders Past and Present

Susan Banfield • A very sympathetic portrait of a very significant leader in history, this is one of the best biographies of Charlemagne for young people. Look for it in your library. **MS+**

Two Lives of Charlemagne

Einhard & Notker the Stammerer • The old adage for authors is "write what you know." This book was written by those who knew Charlemagne personally and admired him. Fascinating! **MS+**

ALFRED THE GREAT & ENGLISH HISTORY

A History of the English-Speaking Peoples BOOK ONE

Winston Churchill • This series is a fascinating and delightfully written history by Sir Winston Churchill. As he describes in The Birth of Britain many of the people and events of this Unit—King Alfred, the Danes, William the Conqueror—English history comes to life. Highly recommended! **MS+**

The Dragon and the Raven, or the Days of King Alfred

G. A. Henty • King Alfred is one of the great heroes of English history. This book takes the reader into the time period when the English were trying desperately to throw off the Viking invaders. Written as historical fiction, Henty's books are nonetheless excellent for learning history. **UE+**

The Edge on the Sword

Rebecca Tingle • Another excellent book of historical fiction, this story is about the daughter of King Alfred who was a fascinating and beloved ruler of her people. The book provides a "you were there" look at life in the late 800's in England. **UE+**

The Anglo-Saxon Chronicles THE AUTHENTIC VOICES OF ENGLAND, FROM THE TIME OF JULIUS CAESAR TO THE CORONATION OF HENRY II

translated & collated by Anne Savage • Begun during the reign of King Alfred, the Chronicles are a record of life in England until the mid-1100's. Read for yourself the fear in the hearts of the English as the Vikings strike again. Fascinating. **MS+**

WILLIAM THE CONQUEROR & THE NORMAN CONQUEST

Wulf the Saxon: A Story of the Norman Conquest

G. A. Henty • Historical fiction at its best, this is the story of a young Saxon boy in the service of King Harold before Harold's death in the Battle of Hastings. **UE+**

William the Conquerer

Thomas B. Costain • This out-of-print book is one of the titles in the World Landmark series. It is worth the search to find it, as William the Conqueror comes to life through its pages. Learn about his early life, the battles he had to win in Normandy as a young man, and his claim to the English throne. **E+**

1066—The Year of Conquest

David Howarth • A fascinating and very readable account of the pivotal year when King Edward died, Harold was crowned king, and William of Normandy conquered England. **HS+**

The Little Duke

Charlotte M. Yonge • Learn about life in Normandy after the Viking Rollo settled in France. This story about his grandson (the great grandfather of William the Conqueror) is a fascinating look into the struggles of the late 900's. A great read aloud for every age. **UE+**

What books did you like best?

_____

_____

_____

_____

The Internet also contains a wealth of information about the Holy Roman Empire & the Vikings.

What sites were the most helpful?

_____

_____

_____

_____

For more books, use these Dewey Decimal numbers in your library:

Early Middle Ages: #940.1

Vikings: #948

Charlemagne & Holy Roman Empire: #944

Alfred the Great & English History: #942

Church History in the Middle Ages: #270

William the Conqueror & the Norman Conquest: #942

4

▶ Student Self-Evaluation UNIT 4, PHASE 1

Dates and hours:_____

Key Concepts

Rephrase the four Key Concepts of this Unit and confirm your understanding of each:

• Holy Roman Empire

_____

• Vikinginvasions & explorations

_____

• Norman conquest

_____

• Struggle between Church & State

_____

Tools for Self-Evaluation

Evaluate your personal participation in the discussions of this Phase. Bearing in mind that a good participant in a discussion is not always the most vocal participant, ask yourself these questions: Were you an active participant? Did you ask perceptive questions? Were you willing to listen to other participants of the discussion and draw out their opinions? Record your observations and how you would like to improve your participation in the future:

_____

_____

Every time period is too complex to be understood in one Phase of study. Evaluate your current knowledge of the Holy Roman Empire & the Vikings. What have you focused on so far? What are your weakest areas of knowledge?

_____

_____   _____

Based on the evaluation of this introduction, project ahead what you would like to study more of in the following Phases:

_____

_____

Phase 2

▶ # Research & Reporting

Explore one or more of these areas to discover something significant!

Holy Roman Empire

The Holy Roman Empire—which lasted more than a thousand years—was finally ended by Napoleon in 1806. This unit will consider the first 300 years, so research and report on the early years. Beginning with the exploits of Charles Martel and his son Pepin, trace the beginnings of the Holy Roman empire, its formalization and expansion under Charlemagne, and what happened to this empire in the Middle Ages under the descendants of Charlemagne.

The Vikings

Investigate the culture and exploits of these Scandinavian warriors. You may choose to focus on their raiding of the British Isles and the European continent, the trading with Constantinople, and/or the exploration of Iceland, Greenland, and Vinland (the northern coast of North America).

Treaty of Verdun

In 843 the Treaty of Verdun was signed between the feuding grandsons of Charlemagne. Why was it drawn up? Who did it concern? What was the impact? How does it continue to affect the countries of Europe today?

Otto the First

Research and report on this man who was the first German Holy Roman Emperor. Describe his life, his actions, and what he did to ensure his successor. How did this affect the Holy Roman Empire?

Charlemagne

Research and report on the life of Charlemagne and his conquests. What people groups did he subdue? What were the changes brought into their lives as a result of his conquest? How did he deal with defeat? For what issues is he best remembered?

Alfred the Great

Research and report on King Alfred, known as The Great. What were his accomplishments? In what long-term ways did he influence England? How did he merit the designation *The Great*?

Magyars

Who were the Magyars of Eastern Europe? Research and report on this culture and its place in history. Where did the Magyars live? What did they do? Who conquered them? What modern national people are their descendants?

Peace of God & Truce of God

Learn more about these attempts by the Church to control the violence of feudal knights and rulers. Why were they imposed? How effective were they? Describe how Church leaders would use these tools.

Motte-and-Bailey Castles

Research and report on this type of early fortified European castles, which were the forerunners of stone castles. Of what were motte-and-bailey castles constructed? In what type of terrain were they first located? What was the purpose of these castles?

Donation of Constantine

There is a centuries-old mystery surrounding the Donation of Constantine. Discover more about this document. What was its impact upon Italy and the world? Similarly, describe the Donation of Pepin. What was it? Who gave it? What effect did it have? Who instituted it?

Feudalism

Study feudalism in the Middle Ages. Why was it instituted? Who was involved with feudalism? Where was it most widely used, and why? What were the positive effects of feudalism? What were the negative effects? What caused it to end?

The Danelaw

Study the Danish invasions of England. What were the results of these invasions? What happened to the Danes in England? What was the Danelaw? Where was the land division between the Danish and the English in England?

William the Conqueror

Discover more about William the Conqueror and the Norman conquest of England. In your report, include William's justification for the invasion of England, the results of his rule, and the myriad ways England was forever changed.

Cluny & the Clunaic Reform

Discover more about the monastery of Cluny, and in what ways it was different than other monasteries. What were some of the results of these differences? Where were the daughter monasteries of Cluny located? How did the Clunaic Reform movement influence the West?

Vladimir of Kiev

Research and report on this ruler of Kiev in the Middle Ages. What did he do for Russia? What was his connection to Byzantine Emperor Basil II? What continuing impact did Vladimir have on Russia that continues to this day?

Great Schism

Investigate this permanent break, or schism, between the Roman Catholic Church in the West and the Orthodox Church in the East. What factors were responsible for this schism? Why were the issues never resolved?

▶ Brain Stretchers

Cyril and Methodius

Discover the works of these Byzantine Orthodox missionaries to the Slavs in the 800s. Their influence eventually reached as far as Kiev! Why and from whom did they face opposition? What task did they accomplish which continues to this day?

Church and State

Research and report on the issues of Church and State from the 800s to the 1100s. Describe the various temporal rulers (especially the emperors) and their struggles with the popes. Analyze the problems, then list those facets of the struggles which you recognize to be similar to contemporary conflicts between Church and State. In what ways do you think the lessons of this historic time might be useful to leaders today?

Carolingian Renaissance

Charlemagne instituted what is known today as the Carolingian (pronounced "car-ro-LIN-jee-un") Renaissance. Research and report on this pre-Renaissance renaissance. What were the most important features? How long did it last? Why did it end?

Hugh Capet

Learn more about the Capetian kings of France, beginning with Hugh Capet. How did his kingship affect France? What were the results of his reign? How were the Capetian kings different from the Merovingian kings? –from the Carolingian kings?

Song of Roland

Learn about the "Song of Roland," one of the most significant and important ballads of the Middle Ages. What is it about? How accurate is its portrayal? Read it. Compare it to a poem such as "The Charge of the Light Brigade" or "Paul Revere's Ride."

Alcuin

Study the life of Alcuin, one of the most well-respected educators of the Middle Ages. Describe what he did before, during, and after his work for Charlemagne. Describe his work concerning the Trivium and Quatrium.

Nestorian Christianity in the Far East

By the late 700s the Nestorian Church of the East had evidently penetrated into China, India, Japan, and Korea. Research and report on the spread of Christianity to these people groups in the Far East. One excellent source for this is the article "The Great Missionary Church of the East" by Les Miller, in the book *World Wide Perspectives*, edited by Meg Crossman.

> "The history of the missionary endeavors of the Church of the East undercuts the commonly held idea that God showed his favor only to the European sector of humanity. Courageous Nestorian clergy and lay people long ago extended his blessing to many peoples of the East who are only now being reached and won again for the kingdom. What a joy it will be when those who are coming to faith in Christ today meet their ancestors—Arabs, Persians, Bactrians, Sogdians, Turks, Tibetans, Chinese, Mongols, Indians, and others—in the uncountable throng gathered to praise the Lamb in his glory."
>
> "The Great Missionary Church of the East" by Les Miller, in the book *World Wide Perspectives*, edited by Meg Crossman.

Create Your Own Research Topic

_____

_____

_____

▶ Timeline

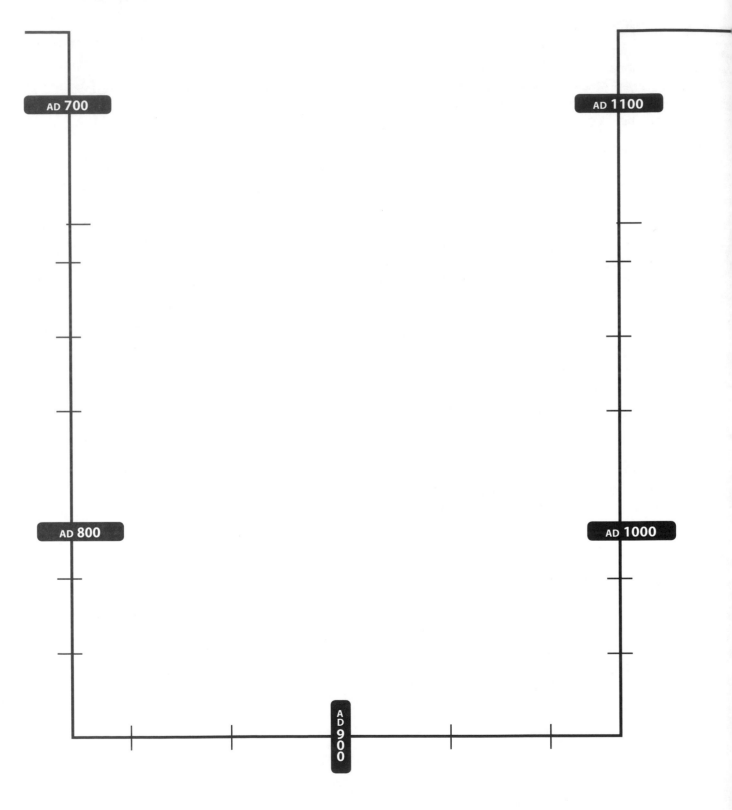

AD 700

AD 1100

AD 800

AD 1000

AD 900

Consider this for your timeline

Notice the connection between the dissolution of Charlemagne's empire and the increase of Viking attacks on Europe. Also, note what is taking place in the Church during this time, both between the Eastern and Western branches of Christianity, and between the Church and the State in the West.

Key Events

Crowning of Charlemagne

Period of Viking invasions

Treaty of Verdun

Normandy established

Battle of Hastings

Orthodox Church in Russia

Beginning of feudalism

Truce of God & Peace of God

Great Schism

CONSIDER:

The English language was impacted significantly by both the Viking and the Norman invasions. Here are some examples:

From the Vikings:

sister

knife

happy

steak

sky

odd

muck

husband

egg

From the Normans:

literature

art

castle

dinner

beauty

biscuit

festival

royal

romance

If you found this fascinating, look for some more!

▶ Words to Watch

Remember—The easiest way to learn a subject is to master its terms:

truce	invasion	serf	knight
motte-and-bailey	feudalism	depose	reform
renaissance	succession	imperialism	medieval
jousting	vassal	simony	dynasty
confer	donation		

Other words you need to look up:

_____

_____

_____

_____

_____

_____

_____

▶ # Student Self-Evaluation UNIT 4, PHASE 2

Dates and hours:_____

Research Project

Summarize your research question:

_____

_____

List your most useful sources by author, title and page number or URL where applicable (continue list in margin if necessary):

_____

_____

_____

Now take a moment to evaluate the sources you just listed. Do they provide a balanced view of your research question? Should you have sought an additional opinion? Are your sources credible (if you found them on your own)? Record your observations:

_____

_____

Evaluate your research project in its final presentation. What are its strengths? If you had time to revisit this project, what would you change? Consider giving yourself a letter grade based on your project's merits and weaknesses.

_____

_____

Letter grade: _____

You have just completed an area of specific research in the time of the Holy Roman Empire & the Vikings. Now what would you like to explore in the upcoming Phases? Set some objectives for yourself:

_____

Phase 3

▶ Maps & Mapping

Physical Terrain

- » Locate and label Iceland, Greenland, and Scandinavia. Choose a color for these areas that represent the Vikings.

- » Locate and label the area of Europe that was included in Charlemagne's Empire (which would not include Spain nor the boot of Italy). Choose a color for this area that represents the Holy Roman Empire.

- » Locate and label the North Sea, the Baltic Sea, the Norwegian Sea, and the Black Sea.

Geopolitical

- » Locate and label these cities and regions which were important to the Vikings: Novgorod, Kiev, Constantinople, Lindisfarne, York, Dublin, Rouen; the Danelaw in England and Normandy in France.

- » Draw a line with a colored pencil or pen indicating the routes of the Vikings when they traded, and another color to indicate their routes when they raided.

- » Locate and label as many of these important cities and regions in the Holy Roman Empire as you can find: Aachen, Reims, Metz, Tours, Rome, Aquitaine, Neustria, Austrasia, Saxony, Bavaria, Burgundy, Lombardy.

- » Draw a line with a colored pencil or pen indicating the boundaries of Charlemagne's Empire in 800. In a different colored pencil or pen, draw the division of the empire after the Treaty of Verdun in 843.

Explore

- » *Viking Archaeology:* Discover these historic sites which were important to the Vikings: Birka in Sweden; Kaupang in Norway; Hedeby in Denmark; Thingvellir in Iceland; L'Anse aux Meadows, Newfoundland, Canada. Locate and label them on a map. What have archaeologists discovered at these sites?

- » *Christian Outreach:* What is the status of evangelical outreach today in the homeland and settlements of the Vikings? What opportunities and what difficulties face those who share the gospel in these areas?

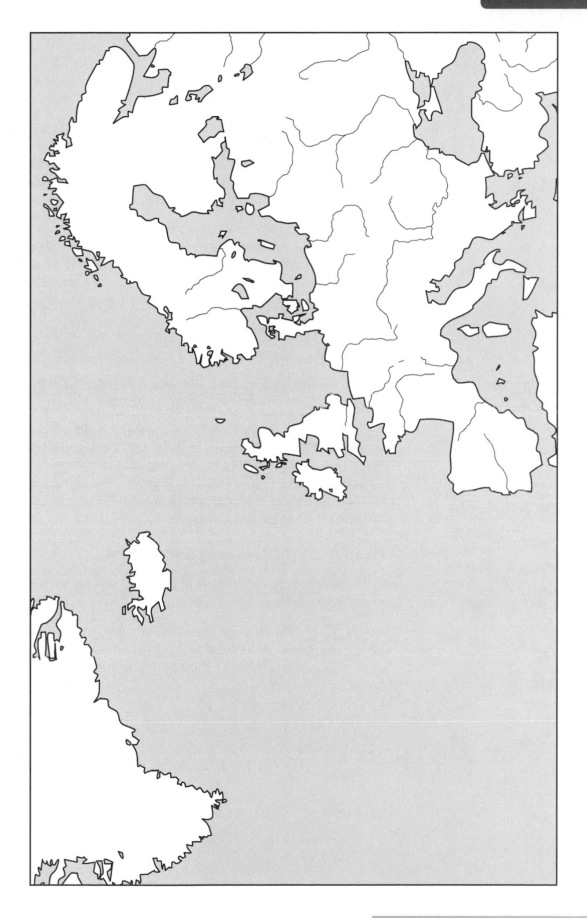

▶ Art Appreciation

Coronation Gospels of Charlemagne—St. Matthew

The *Coronation Gospels* are a Carolingian manuscript of Scripture which was said to have been buried with Charlemagne and was found when his tomb was opened in AD 1000. It is one of the finest examples from the Carolingian Renaissance. The illumination of St. Matthew clearly reflects the Hellenistic-Roman, or Classical, artistic tradition.

> » Examine this illumination. What words would you use to describe this? Look online for an image of St. Matthew from the *Ebbo Gospels,* which was created about fifteen years after the death of Charlemagne. This style is not considered Classical, but is, instead, Carolingian art. How would you compare this illumination with the one listed above?

Bayeux Tapestry

Created to depict William the Conqueror's invasion of England and the Battle of Hastings in 1066, this embroidered tapestry is 230 feet long!

> » This tapestry is wool embroidery on linen, and is almost twenty inches high. How would you describe some of the scenes on the Bayeux Tapestry? Notice the border strips running along the top and bottom of the main scene. They contain various depictions including animals, fables, and scenes from the main work. What artistic effect do these borders create?

Animal Head from the Oseberg Ship Burial

Crafted around the year 825, this example of Viking art was found buried in a Viking ship in southern Norway.

> » Consider the craftsmanship necessary for carving this elaborate head. In what ways is the head realistic? In what ways is it mythical? How would you describe this head to someone who had never seen it?

CONSIDER:

In the city of Bayeux, France, a tradition grew up that Matilda, wife of William the Conqueror, was the woman who created the extraordinary Bayeux Tapestry, though there is no proof of this. Whoever the artist, it is an amazing creation!

▶ Architecture

Palatine Chapel, Aachen, Germany

The style of building during the time of Charlemagne is known as Carolingian architecture. It reinterprets the Roman (Classical), Early Christian and Byzantine styles, making creative changes for northern requirements and a new emperor. To the Christian interpretation of architecture as a symbolic form (such as churches being built in the shape of a cross), the Carolingian architects added high towers, entrances known as "westwork," turrets, elaborate tombs, and chapels.

» Locate a photo of the interior of Charlemagne's Palatine Chapel. This structure was inspired by San Vitale, the Byzantine church in Ravenna which was seen in the previous Unit. Charlemagne's Chapel is unique, however, with its Roman massiveness. How would you describe this structure?

▶ Arts in Action

Select one or more, and let your artistic juices flow!

Portraiture

Examine the illumination of St. Matthew in the *Coronation Gospels* and the *Ebbo Gospels.* Choose the style you would like to imitate (either Classical or Carolingian), and create a portrait in that style. You may wish to draw someone you know seated at a desk, or follow one of these artists in their design of St. Matthew.

Embroidery

Purchase a small piece of plain colored muslin, or other appropriate fabric. Either transfer or draw a scene on the fabric. Next, using several colors of embroidery thread, embroider the scene. Remember, the simpler, the better. Can you imagine embroidering something that was 230 feet long?

▶ Science

The Vikings were among the most amazing shipbuilders in the history of the world. They figured out how to take advantage of the sailing winds using a square sail that could be turned by rope to catch the wind even if it wasn't straight behind them. They also used oars to help steer. This allowed them far greater control and speed. These, along with their shallow drafted boats which allowed the Vikings to sail far upriver and to land on beaches, gave them the elements of speed and surprise. It was good news for boat building, but bad news for the Europeans of the Middle Ages!

Wind-Raising Experiment

» Sprinkle baby powder on a handkerchief. Gently toss a bit of the powder in the air with the handkerchief, next to a light bulb that is off. Now, turn the light bulb on, wait for a few minutes until the bulb gets hot, and try it again. Was there any difference?

Catch the Wind

» On a windy day, take a kite out into an open area (away from power lines and vehicles) and get it airborne. Once you have successfully launched your kite, try to control its course in the sky as it moves up and down in the wind. Then consider how sails on a boat have to catch the wind in order to move that boat through the water.

Make a Boat

» If you have access to the book *Make it Work! Ships* by Andrew Haslam, you could try your hand at making a balsa wood ship with a Viking sail.

▶ Music

The music of this time was the music of the Church. Whether it was King Alfred's fighting song (derived from the Psalms), or Charlemagne's church services in his newly built chapel, songs were designed to glorify God and remind man of who God is. That is a good reminder to us!

Discover

All Glory, Laud, & Honor

Theodulph of Orleans (c. 760–821) • Theodulph of Orleans was an influential poet in the court of Charlemagne. He was another one of the outstanding scholars at court, along with Alcuin and Einhard. He composed this beautiful hymn while in prison, the year before he died. It is a song of praise in the midst of great troubles.

Try This

> » Imagine what it would be like to be in prison in the 800s. If you can create some of the appropriate atmosphere for that scenario (such as cold stone walls), so much the better. Now, imitating both Theodulph as well as Paul and Silas in their prison, sing Theodulph's song. What are the results of praise, even in the midst of trials?

Listen

All Glory, Laud, & Honor MUSIC CD

All Glory, Laud, & Honor

▶ Cooking

Scandinavians—the descendants of the Vikings—have fantastic food! Here is a favorite:

Potato Lefse

2 pounds russet potatoes, peeled and quartered	2 tbsp butter
¼ cup milk	1 tsp salt
3–3½ cups flour	salad oil

Place potatoes in a 3-quart pan and pour in water to cover. Bring to a boil over high heat; then cover, reduce heat, and simmer until tender when pierced (about 20 minutes). Drain. Mash until smooth, then measure; you should have 4 cups. (Do not use more than 4 cups of potatoes in dough!) Place potatoes in a large bowl and stir in butter, milk, and salt. Let cool to room temperature. Gradually stir in about 2 cups of the flour, or enough to make a non-sticky dough. Turn out onto a floured surface and knead gently to shape into a smooth log. Divide into 24 equal pieces, then shape each into a smooth ball; leave uncovered. On the floured surface, roll each ball out to an 8-10 inch round. As you roll, turn dough over frequently to keep both sides very lightly coated with flour. Heat a wide frying pan over medium heat (or heat an electric griddle to 375º); lightly grease with oil. To cook each lefse, first shake off excess flour; then place in pan. Cook, turning frequently, until bubbles form on surface and lefse is dry and lightly speckled with brown, but still soft to the touch (1½–2 minutes). Lefse will puff up briefly, then deflate. Serve warm. Or let cool completely on wire racks, then wrap airtight and refrigerate for up to 4 days. To reheat, wrap in foil and heat in a 325-degree oven for 10 to 15 minutes. Makes 2 dozen.

Be sure to serve the lefse warm with lots of butter and sugar!

▶ Student Self-Evaluation UNIT 4, PHASE 3

Dates and hours:_____

Evaluate your projects

- List which of the activities listed in this Phase you did:

_____

_____

_____

- Rate your enthusiasm: _____

Explain: _____

_____

- Rate the precision of your approach:_____

Explain: _____

_____

- Rate your effort toward the completion of the project: _____

Explain: _____

_____

Ask yourself what worked and what did not. What would you do differently in the future, and what would you repeat?

_____

How specifically did these hands-on activities enhance your knowledge of the Holy Roman Empire & the Vikings? What made them worthwhile?

_____

In the first three Phases of this Unit, what aspect of the time period has most captured your imagination? What would you like to creatively pursue to conclude your study?

_____

Phase 4

▶ In Your Own Way…

We have seen the reunification of Europe under Charlemagne and the Holy Roman Empire. We have also watched the raiding and trading of the Vikings across the British Isles, Europe, Russia, and the Atlantic. Now, choose a selection of these activities, or create your own, which will best express what you have learned from this Unit.

LINGUISTICS

Journalism

The editor of the *Roman Herald* has a hunch in AD 800 that something newsworthy is going to happen in Rome at the church celebration on Christmas Day. You have been assigned to cover the story. Be sure to interview Charlemagne after church!

You are a freelance reporter for the French magazine *Mais Oui!* You have written scathing articles about the seeming inability of your countrymen to defeat the Vikings. Now the news has just broken about Rollo and King Charles III. Go get 'em!

Playing with Words

Finish this limerick:
> The Vikings decided to visit
> A place in a setting exquisite . . .

Prose

Imagine you were one of the monks living at Lindisfarne in 793. Somehow you survived the Viking attack, and have lived to tell the story. Write it in the first person with all of the drama and tragedy the story deserves.

Write a children's book telling the story of Otto the Great and how he became the Holy Roman Emperor.

You have accompanied Leif Ericson on his historic journey across the ocean to Vinland. Despite all odds, you made it all the way back to Greenland. Write your adventures to share with the folks back home.

Poetry

Write an epic poem describing the Battle of Hastings. Is William the Conqueror the villain or the hero in your poem?

ART

Painting/Drawing

Paint a scene from the life of Charlemagne, whether his conquests, the forced conversions of the Saxons, worship at the Palatine Chapel, his coronation, or as the moving force behind the Carolingian Renaissance.

Draw a Viking ship, complete with square sail, ropes, and oars. This could be done either as a schematic or in the setting of the open ocean.

Political Cartooning

Draw a political cartoon depicting the "Truce of God." What kind of expressions are on the faces of the knights?

Graphic Design

Design a T-shirt for the Normans who are about to invade England with Duke William of Normandy. Since the outcome is still undecided, create a motivating, "You can do it!"-type of design.

Help Vladimir, prince of Kiev, convince his subjects that conversion to Orthodoxy is the right step. Prepare an ad campaign for print media, which he can use immediately.

Sculpting

Sculpt in the style of the Carolingian Renaissance—either a small statue or a sculptured book cover such as the front cover of the Lindau Gospels.

MUSIC

Performance Practice

With your teacher's help, select an appropriate piece of music which expresses some particular aspect studied in this Unit, whether from the Holy Roman Empire (courtly, pompous, monarchical) or from the Vikings (sudden appearance, terrifying, oceangoing, exploring the outer limits). Prepare and perform the piece for an audience. Communicate with your audience the reason for your selection either in the program notes or in a short speech.

DRAMA

Comedy

Charlemagne's biographer described him as extremely tall (over 6 feet, which would seem a giant in those days), but, oddly enough, he also had an embarrassingly high-pitched voice. With that in mind, produce a skit where ambassadors of the Saxons come to treat with Charlemagne—a powerful emperor to whom respect is due (and expected!). Unfortunately, no one warned them ahead of time about his voice.

Drama

Portray through drama the story of Cyril and Methodius in their mission to the Moravians beginning in 863. Include the conflict they experienced with the German bishops and their subsequent journeys to Rome along with Methodius's journey to Constantinople.

Puppetry

With the use of puppets, tell the story of Alfred the Great and how he formed the English nation. Include his building of the first English navy, of defeating Guthrum and his Danes, and his encouragement that his defeated foes should be baptized.

Prop Needs

_____

_____

Costume Ideas

_____

_____

Role/Player

_____

_____

Set Suggestions

_____

_____

MOVEMENT

Dance

Choreograph a dance of joy celebrating the Vikings becoming Christians.

Pantomime

Using pantomime, depict what life was like for those living under the system of feudalism. This would include everyone from the king to the serf.

Miniature Action

Create the battle of Hastings with LEGO bricks or other building materials. Describe to assembled visitors the events that took place at this historic moment in 1066.

CONCEPTUAL DESIGN

Viking-Proof Your Home

Knowing that the Vikings can sail hundreds of miles upriver to sack your city, design a foolproof obstacle—moveable and affordable—which will keep these berserkers from getting loose on your soil. You might want to consider franchising this invention for all of Europe!

CREATE YOUR OWN EXPRESSION

_____

_____

_____

_____

_____

4

▶ Student Self-Evaluation UNIT 4, PHASE 4

Dates and hours:_____

Evaluate your projects

- What creative project did you choose:

  _____

- What did you expect from your project, and how does the final project compare to your initial expectations?

  _____

  _____

- What do you like about your project? What would you change?

  _____

  _____

In Conclusion

Revisit the four Key Concepts from the beginning of this Unit. Explain how your understanding of and appreciation for each has grown over the course of your study.

- _____

  _____

- _____

  _____

- _____

  _____

- _____

Record your concluding thoughts on the Holy Roman Empire & the Vikings:

_____

_____

The Crusades & the Mongols

Castle at Carcassonne, Languedoc-Roussillon, France

In the Name of God . . .

We began the last article with a pope *crowning* an emperor. Now, this new era dawns with a pope *deposing* an emperor. The groundbreaking move by Pope Leo III crowning Charlemagne had been made in recognition that he was obviously chosen by God to be ruler of the peoples of Europe. But a new way of thinking had revolutionized the Western Church over the previous 275 years, resulting in Pope Gregory VII formally deposing Emperor Henry IV for disobedience to papal demands. Under the Gregorian reforms (named for Pope Gregory VII), neither the Holy Roman Emperors nor kings had the right to lead the peoples of Europe when it conflicted with or intruded upon the goals of the Church. Pope Gregory VII believed, and passed on, the concept that obedience to God and obedience to the pope were one and the same, and that this obedience to the pope in all matters applied whether one was emperor or peasant, English or Byzantine.

The emperors and kings strongly disagreed (as did the Byzantines). The resulting power struggle between popes and rulers would be one of the defining issues of the High Middle Ages, culminating in the reign of Pope Innocent III (1198–1216), one of the most powerful of all the popes.

A struggle for power had been taking place in the Islamic world, as well. As we saw in unit three, by the beginning of the tenth century three different caliphs were ruling in Islamic lands: the Abbasid caliph in Baghdad, the Umayyad caliph in Cordoba, and the Fatimid caliph in Cairo. The Fatimids were Shi'ites, while the Muslims under the caliphs in Baghdad and Cordoba were Sunnis, which meant there was a tremendous amount of religious, as well as political, tension between these three Islamic regions.

Another aspect of the fragmented empire was that the Abbasid caliphs in Baghdad were, from the mid-900s, mere figureheads. Caliph in name only, the Abbasids had lost their real power to a group of Shi'ite warriors called the Buyids, who effectually ruled the Islamic East until 1055.

Into this mixture a new and volatile ingredient was added—the Seljuk Turks. Newly converted to the Sunnite branch of Islam, these fierce Turkish warriors from Central Asia created a Muslim empire from Iran to Syria and Palestine. They successfully overthrew the Buyids and reestablished Sunni Islamic rule in Baghdad, which was popular with the people. When a Seljuk army defeated the Byzantines at the Battle of Manzikert in 1071, the door was opened for Turkish settlers to pour into the former Byzantine lands of Asia Minor. Though the Seljuks were ruling in Asia Minor, the majority of the population was Christian—Armenians (Oriental Orthodox), Syrians (Monophysites), and Greeks (Eastern Orthodox).

> *Into this brew a new and volatile ingredient was added—the Seljuk Turks.*

The Crusades

To better understand the dynamics of what was taking place in the Muslim world as Europe launched the crusades, we need to understand two sources of instability that were unsettling these lands. First, a medieval group known as the *Assassins* had become one of the great destabilizers in the Eastern lands of Islam. They were a small and violent sect of Shi'ites who believed that to kill a person who opposed the "true faith" was service to Allah. Their goal seems to have been to destroy the Sunni government, so that, eventually, the Shi'ites could take leadership of the eastern Islamic empire. This resulted in the assassinations of numerous Sunni rulers and high government officials (who were Seljuk Turks). One author described the Assassins as "the gravest cancer of the Seljuk empire" because they were terrorists bringing with them all of the accompanying fear and instability of terrorism.

A second source of destabilization and fragmentation was the practice of dividing Seljuk provinces among the sons of a deceased ruler. This quickly resulted in a number of petty principalities ruled by *emirs* (or, princes) rather than a cohesive region ruled and protected by one leader. At the end of the 1000s, these petty principalities in Asia Minor and Syria were engaged in open warfare with one another, as each ruler eagerly sought to take land away from his royal relatives. This meant, for instance, that when the European crusaders approached Nicaea, the other emirs did NOT assist the emir under siege.

Jesus said, "Every kingdom divided against itself is brought to desolation, and every city or house divided against itself will not stand" (Matthew 12:25). That is the picture of what was happening in the Muslim world at the time of the First Crusade.

In Europe, on the other hand, the call for knights to go on a crusade to the Holy Land actually united the people. It gave them a common quest, a common goal, and a common enemy. For those who took the crusader's vow, there were also common hardships: families broken apart for the duration of the crusade, lands unattended by the master, sickness, hunger, fierce heat, and formidable warriors opposing them. Not the least of the hardships was the incredible financial burden imposed on crusading knights. According to recent scholarship, a French knight going on the First Crusade would have needed to spend *four times* his annual income in order to pay the expenses of the trip. How could they afford to go? Often, they mortgaged their lands (or even sold them) to pay for the journey. In fact, Robert, Duke of Normandy, the eldest son of William the Conqueror, seems to have mortgaged his French domain to his younger, covetous brother, King William II of England, in order to pay for his part on the First Crusade. *(William had gone to war twice in an attempt to capture Normandy from his brother. He finally obtained what he sought by exploiting his brother's financial need.)*

Why did these knights vow to make—and to not turn from—what was certain to be a difficult, demanding, expensive, and dangerous journey? Simply put, *Deus Vult!* ("God wills it!"). A Holy War against the enemies of Christ appealed to their medieval sense of right and wrong. They saw the crusades as their Christian duty to retake from the *infidels* the holy lands where Christ had walked. For many, their earnest, medieval faith believed that this service was pleasing to God. For others, it was undoubtedly an opportunity to put their warring skills to profitable use. For all, though, it was an endeavor called by the pope and blessed by the Western Church. Whether or not we see, from our vantage point in history, this enterprise as appropriate and glorifying to God, the people of the time were utterly convinced of its righteousness.

Murdering someone who opposed the "true faith" was service to Allah.

To put the crusades to the Middle East into an understandable framework, take a look at the dates, the major personalities, and the results of each. Understand that from the time Muslim lands were captured in the First Crusade and the Latin kingdom was established in the East, numerous knights and pilgrims continued to come to the Holy Land year after year. Some came for a short time and departed, while others remained for years, eventually dying there. Also, during this time, there were other crusades in Europe: against the Cathars and Waldensians in southern France (known as the *Albigensian Crusade*), against the Muslims in Spain, and the against the Slavic Wends in the Baltic region. Please take a moment to consider the chart below.

A Holy War against the enemies of Christ appealed to their medieval sense of right and wrong.

Crusader States

Let us now pose the question, "What happened in Syria and Palestine as the First Crusade made its way to Jerusalem?" To the powerful caliphs of Cairo and Baghdad, these lands were the frontier of their realms, and, as such,

The Crusade	Pope	Years	Reasons
First Crusade	Urban II	1096–1099	Seljuk Turks, Alexius's Plea
Second Crusade	Eugenius III	1147–1149	Fall of Edessa
Third Crusade	Gregory VIII	1189–1191	Capture of Jerusalem
Fourth Crusade	Innocent III	1202–1204	New Strategy: Attack Egypt
Fifth Crusade	Innocent III, Honorious III	1218–1221	Try Again: Attack Egypt
Sixth Crusade	Gregory IX	1228–1229	Emperor's Vow
Seventh Crusade	Innocent IV	1249	Capture of Jerusalem
Eighth Crusade	(Louis IX's decision)	1270	Loss of territory

were not nearly as important as lands closer to home. The fragmented Seljuk kingdoms in the pathway of the crusaders were, at the moment of their approach, battling for control in a state of virtual anarchy. In other words, the timing of the crusaders was perfect.

After capturing the city of Nicaea in Asia Minor, the crusaders continued their arduous trek toward Jerusalem. At the Battle of Dorylaeum, the Europeans successfully crushed an Islamic army. This gave rise to the rumor that the crusaders were *invincible*. It would eventually be disproved, but for the moment, it provided them with tremendous psychological advantage in this hostile land.

Shortly after this victorious battle, Baldwin, younger brother of Godfrey of Bouillon (one of the leaders of the crusade), left the crusade. He took a small band of knights and soldiers with him to carve out his own realm in the region of Edessa in northern Syria. His tactics and strategies prevailed, and very quickly, Baldwin violently established his own *County of Edessa.* This would become known as the first of the crusader states.

Meanwhile, the crusaders continued on to the city of Antioch, one of the most important cities of the Eastern Church. Though it was virtually impregnable, the crusaders laid siege to it. Laying siege to a city or castle

Major Personalities	Results
Peter the Hermit, Robert of Normandy, Godfrey of Bouillon, Raymond of Toulouse, Bohemend, Baldwin, Stephen of Blois	Capture of Edessa, Antioch, Jerusalem; Establishment of crusader States
Bernard of Clairvaux, Louis VII of France, Conrad III of Germany, Frederick Barbarossa of Germany, Eleanor of Aquitaine	Failure to recapture Edessa
Richard the Lionheart, Phillip Augustus of France, Frederick Barbarossa	3-year truce with Saladin allowing Christian pilgrims to go to Jerusalem
Bonniface of Montferrat, Baldwin of Flanders, Enrico Dandolo	Captured Constantinople, set up Latin Empire
King John of Jerusalem, Legate Pelagius, Francis of Assisi	Failure, rout, lost opportunity to regain Jerusalem
Frederick II, al-Malik al-Kamil	Regained Jerusalem & Bethlehem by diplomacy; 10-year peace treaty
Louis IX of France, Robert of Artois	Rout, failure, capture and ransom of King Louis
Louis IX, Prince Edward of England	Death of King Louis in Tunis, North Africa

was one of the most common means of warfare in the Middle Ages, but when the besieging army was not large enough to seal the city, it became an impossible task. That was the situation at this moment, and would have remained impossible apart from something unexpected.

After eight months of trying to feed the troops and starve the city, the unexpected occurred. The current leader of the crusade, Bohemond, was contacted by a traitor inside the city who wanted to switch sides. Bohemond successfully led his troops into Antioch, and the city then fell to the crusaders. Three days later, a massive Muslim army appeared and laid siege to the city with the crusaders inside. It looked hopeless for the crusaders as they were hungry, sick, and utterly exhausted from the months of constant warfare.

One of the crusaders, Stephen of Blois, escaped from the city, breaking his vows. As he fled north, he met Emperor Alexius Comnenus at the head of a Byzantine army on his way to relieve the crusaders in Antioch, and stopped long enough to convince the emperor that it was a useless gesture. The Byzantines returned to Constantinople, Stephen continued on to Europe, and the crusaders were left to defend their position. The emperor's decision to turn back was seen by the crusaders as betrayal, and drove a wedge of hostility between the Latins and the Byzantines.

> The emperor's decision to turn back was seen by the Crusaders as betrayal.

The crusaders were ultimately rallied to success by the discovery of what they believed to have been an ancient and treasured relic buried inside Antioch, the *True Lance* that pierced the side of Jesus on the cross. Once the Muslim army had been defeated, and the troops given time to recover, the crusaders set their course for Jerusalem. All except for Bohemond, who stayed in Antioch in order to carve out the *Principality of Antioch,* another crusader state.

In June of 1099, the European crusaders at last stood before the city of Jerusalem, which had recently been captured from the Seljuk Turks by the Egyptian Fatimids. After six weeks of siege, including the use of siege engines, the crusaders were able to take the city. After the horrific massacre of the Muslim and Jewish inhabitants, the leaders of the crusade set to the business of holding on to what they had won. Who would rule in the newly Latinized city of Jerusalem? Only one of the leaders had remained neutral amidst the quarreling from Antioch to Jerusalem—Godfrey of Bouillon—and he was elected ruler. Godfrey refused "to wear a crown of gold where Christ had worn a crown of thorns," and took the name, "Defender of the Holy Sepulcher" instead of "king." One month later, Godfrey led his troops in defense of the city against an Egyptian army and won decisively.

With this victory, the First Crusade was over, and the new *Kingdom of Jerusalem* was begun. Most of the crusaders felt their vows had been fulfilled, so they returned to Europe, leaving the new kingdom with few soldiers to defend it. Then, less than a year later, Godfrey died. The remaining leaders of the crusade, now feudal barons of the kingdom, elected Godfrey's brother as the next ruler. Braving fearsome odds to get through enemy territory from Edessa to Jerusalem, Baldwin was crowned King of Jerusalem on Christmas Day in the year 1100—the first King of Jerusalem since the days of Herod. Baldwin's energetic enlargement and defense of the realm over the next twenty years made him the true founder of this feudal, Latin kingdom in Palestine.

After the defense of Jerusalem, one of the other leaders of the First Crusade, Raymond of Toulouse, left to establish his own sovereign realm, the crusader state called the *County of Tripoli.* This county linked the Kingdom of Jerusalem in the south to Edessa and Antioch, the two northern crusader states, which completed the Latin hold on the coastline of Palestine and Syria.

These four Latin states in the East were surrounded at all times by enemies who, naturally, made constant attempts to recapture the land. It made for an uneasy life, since one never knew when the next Muslim raid would take place. This, along with the limited amount of fertile land, made it difficult to attract colonists from Europe. Throughout the duration of the crusader states, one of their most pressing problems was not having adequate personnel to staff and defend their acquisitions. In fact, without the permanent army on hand in Palestine composed of the military orders (the Templars and Hospitalers), the Kingdom of Jerusalem would have maintained only a tenuous hold on its territory.

However, despite this permanent army, in 1144 the Muslim ruler of Mosul and Aleppo defeated the Europeans in the County of Edessa, capturing the first of the crusader states. This loss was the cause of the Second Crusade.

Civil war in England

Back in Europe, less than a decade before the loss of Edessa, the last son of William the Conqueror, Henry I, died in 1135. He left no legitimate sons to inherit his throne, and the barons of England did not want the daughter of King Henry I—the Empress Matilda (also known as Maud)—crowned as their sovereign. Though they had sworn homage to Maud as their future queen before her father died, they quite willingly received her cousin to be their king instead. This new ruler, King Stephen, was the son of Stephen of Blois (the crusader who fled at Antioch) and Adela, daughter of William the Conqueror.

With this victory, the First Crusade was over, and the new Kingdom of Jerusalem was begun.

Unfortunately for the people of England, King Stephen and Empress Maud were each willing to go to war in their respective claims for the crown. The resulting civil war utterly devastated the country until King Stephen died in 1154. Taking his place on the throne was the new and powerful king, Henry II.

Richard the Lionheart's statue outside the British Parliament buildings

Henry was not the son of Stephen. In fact, he was the son of Empress Maud and her second husband, Geoffrey, Count of Anjou. Henry had previously inherited, upon his father's death, many regions in western France. When he married Eleanor of Aquitaine, who brought with her the rule of Aquitaine, Henry then had control of most of western France. Two years later, he became king of England.

The new king Henry II was a powerful, strong, and commanding ruler who instituted judicial policies that are part of the fabric of English-speaking peoples' laws today, such as trial by judge and jury. However, he was also subject to ungovernable rages and fury, which led indirectly to the assassination of the Archbishop of Canterbury, Thomas á Becket, his former friend and now bitter foe. Henry's family problems were also legendary, as his sons and even his wife sought unsuccessfully to overthrow him in battle. He finally died in 1189, a broken and friendless man, betrayed not only by his wife but even by his favorite son, John Lackland.

Saladin

Just prior to the death of Henry II, Pope Gregory VIII called for the Third Crusade to the Holy Land, to retake the Holy City from the Muslims. What had happened in the intervening years to bring about the loss of Jerusalem? The answer can be summarized in one man, Saladin, who unified—both politically and militarily—the Muslims of Egypt and Syria.

Saladin's father had served under the Muslim ruler Zangi, who had captured Edessa in 1144. When he was of age, Saladin entered the service of Zangi's son Nur al-Din, who began the process of unifying the Islamic lands surrounding the crusader states. Saladin (or, *Salah al-Din*) finished it. It was Saladin who formally ended the Fatimid Caliphate in Cairo, becoming its new Sunni ruler. He gathered up the remaining areas of Muslim Syria under his governance and by 1186, the crusader states were now faced with one powerful and united enemy on its borders—an enemy who believed firmly in *jihad* (holy war).

It was at this dangerous moment that Reynauld de Châtillon, lord of the outlying Latin castles of Kerak and Montréal, broke a truce between Saladin and the King of Jerusalem by attacking a Muslim caravan. This foolish action brought jihad to the Kingdom of Jerusalem and resulted in the loss of almost all the knights and foot soldiers of the realm in one battle—the Battle of Hattin—which in turn resulted in the loss of Jerusalem and most of the kingdom.

Saladin's conquest of Jerusalem in 1187 produced shock waves throughout Europe. To know that the City of Jesus was no longer in the hands of Christians provoked the Crusade of Kings, led by the King of Germany and Holy Roman Emperor Frederick Barbarossa, King Phillip II of France (son of Louis VII), and King Henry II of England. When Henry died in 1189, his son and heir Richard the Lionheart *took up the cross* (made his vow), and went on the crusade. It was fortunate for the crusaders that he did, because Frederick Barbarossa drowned in Armenia before even reaching the Holy Land, and Phillip II was not skilled in war. When Richard and Phillip recaptured the besieged city of Acre (which Saladin had previously taken from the crusaders), Phillip believed his vow was completed and returned to France. Richard, a genius in warfare, continued the war against Saladin until 1192, when a three year truce was drawn up between the two opposing leaders allowing unarmed Christian pilgrims access to Jerusalem.

As an interesting side note, Richard also rendered his verdict in the struggle of who was to be the titular King of Jerusalem. Guy (pronounced "Ghee") de Lusignan had reigned as King during the disastrous loss of the city, but when his wife through whom he had claimed the crown died at the siege of Acre, another claimant for the crown stepped up. This man, Conrad of Montferrat, was the uncle of a previous king, giving him blood ties to the throne. Richard reluctantly agreed with the majority, that Conrad should be king and Guy (who was Richard's vassal) should relinquish his claim. To ease the loss of a kingdom, Richard *gave* the island of Cyprus—which he had just captured from the Byzantines—to Guy, who proved to be a much better ruler on Cyprus than he was in Jerusalem. In fact, the Lusignan rulers reigned over Cyprus until the late 15th century. Conrad, the new King of Jerusalem, did not live long enough to enjoy his royal title. The Muslim sect of Assassins murdered him shortly after he was crowned. From this point, a much diminished *Second Kingdom of Jerusalem* was established, with Acre as its capital city.

Taking his place on the throne was the new and powerful king, Henry II.

Magna Carta

After Richard's death in 1199 (he was killed while laying siege to a castle in France), his youngest brother became King John of England, whose poor reputation was well-deserved. Among John's many failings is the fact that he lost the lands in France, which had belonged to his family for generations. He was also such an unpopular and unjust ruler that his own barons forced him to sign the Magna Carta in 1215, limiting for the first time the power of the English king. And in one of his most audacious actions, after defying the pope for years, King John actually *gave* Pope Innocent III the countries of England and Ireland, making himself vassal to the pope when he received them back as papal fiefs!

The Mongols

In the East, a frightening new and invincible power arose in the early 1200s. From the steppes of Mongolia, Genghis Khan and his army rode their Mongol ponies into China, conquering as they went. From there he expanded the territories under his command westward from Beijing to the Caspian Sea, accumulating more land and people than any conqueror before him. When he died in 1227, his sons and grandsons enlarged the realm until it became the greatest land-based empire in history.

One of the grandsons, Hülegü, brother of the famous Kublai Khan, was assigned the task of eliminating the sect of Assassins. In the process of accomplishing this feat, Hülegü captured Baghdad in 1258, which ended the Abbasid Caliphate. This new Mongol threat in the Middle East was seen by some of the crusaders as a gift from God, a means of overthrowing the Muslims entirely. Others saw the Mongols as potentially more threatening than the Muslims. When an Egyptian army under the leadership of the Mamluke general Baybars defeated an army of Mongols in 1260, it signaled both the end of Mongol expansion in the West and the looming destruction of the crusader states in the East.

When Baybars became sultan, he set about emulating Saladin's accomplishments. He once again united Egypt and Syria (which had fragmented after the death of Saladin), and prepared his troops for battle. From 1265 to 1271, he went to war against the crusaders, capturing city after city, stronghold after stronghold. By the time Baybars was finished, the crusaders were nearly beaten. When the final crusader city of Acre, capital city of the Second Kingdom of Jerusalem, was taken by the Mamlukes in 1291, the two hundred year European quest for the Holy Land finally came to an end. ◀

Phase 1

▶ Listen to This

What in the World? VOL. 2

DISC THREE:

» Divisions in the West (track 1)

» The Pope's Call to Action (track 2)

» The Crusades (track 3)

» The Mongols & Marco Polo (track 4)

True Tales VOL. 2

DISC TWO:

» Medieval Europe (track 4)

Digging Deeper VOL. 2

DISC TWO: THE CHURCH IN CHARGE

» The Great Schism & Crusades (track 7)

» Papal Power & Philosophy (track 8)

▶ Read For Your Life

The Holy Bible

» **Urban II's text for crusades:** Mark 8:34

» **God's kingdom not won by sword:** Matthew 26:51–53

» **Preaching the gospel:** Romans 10:8-15, 1 Corinthians 1:17–24

» **Our service to God:** Romans 12

» **Fruit of the Spirit:** Galatians 5:22–26

» **Our approach to life:** Philippians 4:4–9

Key People (Church)

Pope Gregory VII
Investiture Controversy

Pope Urban II
First Crusade

Bernard of Clairvaux
"The Honey-Flowing Teacher"

Thomas Aquinas
Catholic philosopher

Peter Waldo
Leader of Waldensians

Pope Innocent III
Powerful pope

Francis of Assisi
The Franciscan order

Thomas Becket
The martyred Archbishop of Canterbury

▶ Talk Together

Opinion Column

» What did you find to be the most interesting aspect, or the most fascinating person, you encountered in your introduction to the crusades and the Mongols?

» If you had been Henry IV, what would your thoughts have been on the second day at Canossa? Why do you think he continued to wait for Pope Gregory VII?

» Imagine that you were one of the nobles who heard Pope Urban II's call to free the Holy Land from the infidels. In all the excitement, you take the cross and pledge yourself to go on the crusade. Describe your thoughts and expectations.

» If you had been a peasant living in Italy, what do you think your reaction to Francis of Assisi and his friars would have been? How was he different from the other monks?

» Why do you think men would be so attracted to the monastic life when they heard Bernard of Clairvaux? How do you think life would be different for a person who joined a monastery?

» What is your impression of Genghis Khan? Explain why you would have wanted to be a Mongolian under his leadership, or why you would have tried to avoid it.

» If you were Marco Polo's neighbor in Venice in the early 1300s, what would you have thought of his stories about Asia?

Critical Puzzling

» Why do you think the East-West Schism of 1054 has never been healed?

» Why do you think Pope Gregory VII kept Henry IV waiting for days in the snow at Canossa?

» What do you think of Robin Hood? How would you evaluate his actions as either good or bad?

» When Peter Waldo appealed to the pope concerning his group, he was refused permission to operate within the Catholic Church. Yet, when Francis of Assisi made a similar appeal to Pope Innocent III, his group was accepted. What reasons can you think of for these two different papal responses?

» Thomas Aquinas sought to marry together the philosophy of Aristotle, and its dedication to human reason, with divine revelation. What do you see to be the potential benefits or dangers to this approach?

» Richard the Lionheart was absent from England during most of his reign. In what ways do you think this affected his country?

▶ Resources for Digging Deeper

Choose a few books that look interesting, or find your own.

MIDDLE AGES

Medieval Towns, Trade, and Travel

Lynne Elliott · This fascinating book describes for children what life was like in medieval towns, how trade was conducted, and what was involved in traveling. **UE+**

The Medieval World

Philip Steele · Here is a basic, illustrated overview of the Middle Ages. Especially recommended for visually-oriented students. **UE+**

Adam of the Road

Elizabeth Janet Grey · Historical fiction for children and an excellent story introducing many aspects of life in the time of the Middle Ages. **UE+**

The Middle Ages A WATTS GUIDE FOR CHILDREN

Edited by William Chester Jordan · The one hundred articles in this book are a good resource for students. to learn fascinating information about people, places, and aspects of life in the Middle Ages. **UE+**

Life on a Medieval Manor

Marc Cels · Feudalism in the Middle Ages revolved largely around the manor. This well-written book explores what life was like for most people in that time period. **UE+**

A Medieval Feast

Aliki · A medieval feast was not a casual snack thrown on the table! This book shows what kind of incredible preparations were made in the kitchen for the visit of a king. **E+**

Cultural Atlas for Young People: The Middle Ages

Mike Corbishley · Beginning with the barbarian invasions of Europe, this fascinating book gives an overview of the many elements of the Middle Ages. It is filled with photographs, maps, and informative descriptions of the people, events and places of the Middle Ages. **UE+**

Women and Girls in the Middle Ages

Kay Eastwood · There are many books on knights in the Middle Ages, however, finding something which describes the lifestyles for women in this time period is fairly unique. This book does the job very well. **UE+**

The Red Keep

Allen French · A riveting story, this historical fiction depicts life as it was in the 1100s—filled with robber barons, craftsmen, feudalism, and knighthood. Highly Recommended! **UE+**

KNIGHTS, CASTLES, & CATHEDRALS

Castle Diary THE JOURNAL OF TOBIAS BURGESS

Richard Platt · Written from the viewpoint of an eleven-year old sent to his uncle's castle, this award-winning "diary" allows the reader to experience the thirteenth century through the eyes of a child. **UE+**

In the Time of Knights: The Real-Life Story of History's Greatest Knight

Shelley Tanaka · Tanaka's book is beautifully illustrated, not only portraying what it was like to be a medieval knight, but telling the fascinating story of an actual knight in history—William Marshall. **UE+**

A Medieval Castle

Fiona Macdonald · Discover how castles were constructed and how the people in them lived. **UE+**

Knights AN USBORNE INTERNET-LINKED DISCOVERY BOOK

Rachel Firth · Filled with illustrations and explanations, this book provides a great overview of knights. **UE+**

Castles

Philip Steele · This book will provide younger students the opportunity to learn about the construction, the activities, and the inhabitants of castles. **E+**

Medieval Knights SEE THROUGH HISTORY

David Nicolle • Because this book looks at different stages of knighthood—from the early days under Charlemagne to the Teutonic Knights—it is a treasure trove of information. Highly recommended! **UE+**

Cathedral THE STORY OF ITS CONSTRUCTION

David Macaulay • An outstanding resource for learning about the construction of Gothic cathedrals. It is amazing to consider that a cathedral could take one hundred years or more to build! **UE+**

FRANCIS OF ASSISI

Francis of Assisi and His World

Mark Galli • This insightful biography of Francis of Assisi will help students understand the man and his era. **MS+**

Francis of Assisi: The Man Who Gave Up Everything to Follow Jesus

Ben Alex • Written for children, this illustrated biography tells the main episodes of Francis's life. **UE+**

THE CRUSADES

The Crusades

Anthony West • This is a marvelous introduction to the crusades for your entire family. It is based on bits and pieces of surviving journals of crusaders. **UE+**

Knights of the Crusades

Jay Williams • This book contains tremendous information for students about each of the crusades: their purposes, their success (or lack thereof), and the main players. Highly recommended! **UE+**

The Cross and the Crescent

Malcolm Billings • This fascinating book looks at the crusades with understanding of the time, the culture, and the medieval worldview. **HS+**

Winning His Spurs A TALE OF THE CRUSADES

G. A. Henty • Join Richard the Lionheart on his way to the crusades in this exciting story for young people. Written as historical fiction, Henty's books are nonetheless an excellent way to learn your history. **UE+**

NORMAN ENGLAND

The Hidden Treasure of Glaston

Eleanore M. Jewett • Learn about the time period in England of Henry II and Thomas Becket from the perspective of a young boy caught up in the events of this historic quarrel. Well researched and well written, this book is fascinating. **UE+**

Famous Men of the Middle Ages

John H. Haaren & A. B. Poland, edited by Cyndy Shearer & Robert Shearer • Included in this unit for its biographies on Gregory VII and Henry IV, Peter the Hermit, Frederick Barbarossa, Henry the Second and his sons, Louis the IX, St. Francis, and St. Dominic. **E+**

Eleanor of Aquitaine WORLD LEADERS PAST AND PRESENT

Zoe Coralnik Kaplan • This is a fascinating look at one of the most important women of the Middle Ages. Though not a good role model, she had a tremendous impact on England and France, and actually went on one of the crusades. She married two kings and gave birth to two kings, including Richard the Lionheart. **MS+**

A Morbid Taste for Bones

Ellis Peters • The first of several medieval mysteries with Brother Cadfael, the ex-crusader monk. This is a marvelous book for getting a taste of a medieval monastery while solving an armchair whodunit! **MS+**

Ivanhoe

Sir Walter Scott • One of the great classics of all time, this story takes place during the reign of Richard the Lionheart. This historical fiction of the twelfth century is riveting, suspenseful, and wonderfully rich in the characters of the time period. **MS+**

The Magna Carta WORLD LANDMARK BOOKS

James Daugherty • Discover the story of King John and his feud with the nobility of England in this interesting, informative book. What a story! **UE+**

THE MONGOLS & MARCO POLO

Genghis Khan WORLD LEADERS PAST AND PRESENT

Judy Humphrey • This is a very readable, captivating, and even sympathetic biography of the man who conquered much of the known world in his time. **MS+**

Kublai Khan WORLD LEADERS PAST AND PRESENT

Kim Dramer • Kublai Khan was the grandson of Genghis Khan, and the ruler of China. He was the man who employed Marco Polo on diplomatic adventures. **MS+**

Marco Polo: A Journey through China

Fiona Macdonald • Written and illustrated for children, this book will introduce students to the wonders of the world that Marco Polo saw. **E+**

Genghis Khan and the Mongol Horde

Harold Lamb • A very well-written biography describing the young Temjuin who became more and more powerful as he united the Mongols. Eventually, he ruled a larger empire than the Romans. **E+**

The Travels of Marco Polo

Translated by Ronald Latham • The most famous traveler in the Middle Ages, Marco Polo went to the court of Kublai Khan. Read his own descriptions of what he saw and experienced. **HS+**

Marco Polo's Adventures in China

Milton Rugoff • Read in fascinating detail the adventures of one of the most adventurous men to ever live— Marco Polo. Highly recommended. **UE+**

The Adventures and Discoveries of Marco Polo WORLD LANDMARK BOOKS

Richard J. Walsh • This wonderfully written, engaging book about an amazing adventurer is taken from the actual writings of Marco Polo himself. **UE+**

What books did you like best?

_____

_____

_____

_____

The Internet also contains a wealth of information about the crusades & the Mongols

What sites were the most helpful?

_____

_____

_____

_____

> For more books, use these Dewey Decimal numbers in your library:
>
> Middle Ages: #940.1
>
> Knights, Castles & Cathedrals: #623.19
>
> Francis of Assisi: #271
>
> The Crusades: #909
>
> Norman England: #942
>
> The Mongols & Marco Polo: #951

▶ # Student Self-Evaluation UNIT 5, PHASE 1

Dates and hours:_____

Key Concepts

Rephrase the five Key Concepts of this Unit and confirm your understanding of each:

- The Crusades

  _____

- Catholic reformers

  _____

- Medieval dissenters

  _____

- The West in Constantinople

  _____

- The Mongols

  _____

Tools for Self-Evaulation

Evaluate your personal participation in the discussions of this Phase. Bearing in mind that a good participant in a discussion is not always the most vocal participant, ask yourself these questions: Were you an active participant? Did you ask perceptive questions? Were you willing to listen to other participants of the discussion and draw out their opinions? Record your observations and how you would like to improve your participation in the future:

_____

Every time period is too complex to be understood in one Phase of study. Evaluate your current knowledge of the Crusades & the Mongols? What have you focused on so far? What are your weakest areas of knowledge?

_____

Based on the evaluation of this introduction, project ahead what you would like to study more of in the following Phases:

_____

Phase 2

▶ Research & Reporting

Explore one or more of these areas to discover something significant!

An Overview of The Crusades

Going on a crusade to the Holy Land during the Middle Ages was a dangerous undertaking for any who went, and very expensive for knights who brought their horses, pack animals, armor, and weaponry with them. Investigate the causes for the various crusades. Give a general overview of the effects of the crusades upon the Muslims and their governments, upon the Europeans who returned to their homelands, and upon the Europeans who stayed in the Holy Land.

Islam & The First Crusade

Discover the causes given in the West for the First Crusade and the governmental fractures among Islamic rulers in the East, which rendered them less effective against the crusaders. What were the conditions of the various Holy Places when the crusaders arrived in the Middle East? What were the relations between the Byzantines and the Muslims at this point? What did the Byzantine Emperor expect from the West? What were the results of this crusade?

Bernard of Clairvaux & The Second Crusade

Bernard's motto was "To know Jesus and Jesus crucified," and he spent much of his life calling Christians to a life of devotion to the Lord. In this, he sought to minister God's love to those who had strayed from orthodoxy to heresy. He also called kings and nobles to take the cross and go on the Second Crusade. How did he reconcile these two different approaches to those outside of Christianity? Why was the Second Crusade fought and what were the results?

The Mongols

Research and report on the Mongols and their empire. What talents and skills did they possess that allowed them to carve out the largest empire ever seen? What was the attitude of the Mongol leaders concerning religion? Concerning conquered peoples? How was Christianity received among the Mongols?

Richard the Lionheart & The Third Crusade

Discover more about the Third Crusade and its greatest leader. Why did Richard I, known as the Lionheart, go on crusade? Why did King Philip Augustus of France leave the crusade? What attitude did Saladin, the Muslim leader against the Third Crusade, hold toward Richard? How did the Third Crusade end? Why did Richard leave before finishing his quest? Why did Leopold of Austria kidnap and hold Richard for ransom? What was the effect of Richard's ransom and his rule on England?

Saladin

Research and report on Saladin, the Muslim ruler of Syria, Egypt, northern Mesopotamia, and Palestine. How did he come to power? How did his rule change the dynamics between Muslim and Crusading armies? Describe the battles and strategies he used to defeat the crusaders.

King John & The Magna Carta

Research and report on King John, brother of Richard the Lionheart, who signed the Magna Carta. What was it about King John and his rule that caused the barons to force him to sign such a charter? What did he do after signing the Magna Carta that showed his true intentions toward that document? Why did Pope Innocent III condemn the Magna Carta? What was the impact of the Magna Carta on England? On other countries?

The Fourth Crusade

The Fourth Crusade did not advance the cause of the crusaders in the Holy Land. Instead, against the express wishes of the pope, the European knights captured the city of Constantinople and set up a Latin empire that sought to control the Byzantine Empire. Discover why this crusade went astray, including the part played by the Venetians and by the lack of finances.

The Waldensians

Peter Waldo (or Valdes) and his followers, known as the Waldensians, led a Christian reform movement beginning in the latter 1100s in France. Though they embraced a life of poverty and preached the gospel to the poor, they were opposed by the archbishop of Lyon and eventually excommunicated by the pope. With this exit from Catholicism, they sought to live according to Scripture alone—an early prelude to the Protestant Reformation. Research and report on this movement which was labeled as heresy in the Middle Ages.

St. Francis & The Franciscans

Discover more about St. Francis of Assisi. What were the most significant issues of Christian living for Francis? How was this movement started by Francis received by Pope Innocent III? How did this differ from the reception Peter Waldo had from Pope Alexander III thirty years earlier? Describe Francis's missionary ventures, including his attempt to witness to the Muslim sultan. What happened to the Franciscans after the death of their leader?

Investiture Controversy

Investigate this controversy to discover what issues were at stake. Why did Hildebrand want to end lay investiture? What did King Henry IV do to provoke him? What happened at Canossa? How was this controversy ended? What impact did this have on future relationships between kings and popes?

Genghis Khan

Investigate the life and accomplishments of one of the most powerful men to have ever lived, Genghis Khan. What were the circumstances of his childhood? How did he come to power? Describe his military strategies and tactics. How did Genghis Khan influence trade in the countries he conquered? In what ways did he leave a lasting legacy?

Marco Polo & Kublai Khan

Research and report on the travels of Marco Polo to the court of Kublai Khan. What circumstances allowed this adventure to be written down? What was the impact upon the people of Europe when they learned of Marco Polo's travels? What did Kublai Khan accomplish in China? How was this changed by his death? What long term effects did Kublai Khan have on China?

China

Marco Polo's adventures introduced China to Europeans. What did he learn about this ancient and magnificent country? Research and report on China: its history, language, customs, ethnic peoples, and ruling dynasties from antiquity through the Middle Ages.

The Golden Horde

Part of Russia was dominated by a group of Mongols called the Golden Horde. What was their relationship to Genghis Khan? Research and report on the significance of this invasion of Russia. When did it occur? What did this mean to the Russians living under the occupation? Who overthrew the authority of the Golden Horde?

Cathedrals

Research and report on the construction techniques required for building the Gothic cathedrals. Discover how medieval architects solved the problem of supporting heavy masonry ceilings over wide spans. What did they have to overcome? How long did it take to build a Gothic cathedral?

The Inquisition

Learn more about this instrument for combatting heresy in the Catholic Church. Why was Bernard of Clairvaux's method of battling heresy rejected in favor of the inquisition? What were the parameters of the inquisition at its inception? How were these changed? Who was affected by the Inquisition? When did it end?

Henry II & Thomas Becket

Research and report on the struggle in England between Church and State which was demonstrated in the martyrdom of Thomas Becket. What did Henry II require of Becket? Why did Becket refuse? What impact did Becket's martyrdom have upon Henry II? Upon England?

▶ Brain Stretchers

Missionaries to Kublai Khan

Marco Polo reported in his autobiography that Kublai Khan was very interested in learning more about Christianity. Research and report on the response of the Church to the Khan, and about missions to China throughout history.

The Crusades & Reconciliation

There is a modern-day reconciliation movement comprised of Christians who seek forgiveness for the atrocities of the crusaders against Muslims. Research and report on this movement. Where is it taking place? Who is involved? What results are expected? For what reason do some Christians oppose this movement?

The Cathars

Learn about this heretical sect, also known as the Albigensians. What did they believe? How was this related to the gnosticism that existed in the early Church? Why was the Albigensian Crusade proclaimed by Pope Innocent III?

Thomas Aquinas

Thomas Aquinas was one of the great theologians of the Middle Ages. Research and report on his life and writings. Why do some, such as Francis Schaeffer, believe that Aquinas's writings led to humanism, while others, such as the Catholic Church, hold him in very high esteem?

Medieval Universities

The development of universities during this time period shows the changing attitude toward scholarship, learning, and knowledge. Investigate the beginnings of medieval universities. Examine the early universities in different countries. Describe the courses and methods of study. What was the attitude of the Church toward the universities? Study and report on the influence of Muslim universities on Christian universities.

The Mongols in Europe

In 1241 the Mongols invaded Hungary and crossed the Danube into Austria. Investigate the circumstances in Europe before, during, and after the invasion. Estimate the impact on Europe if the Mongols had succeeded. Modern writers attribute the Mongols leaving Europe to their dissatisfaction with the poverty of Europe. Would you agree with this view, or do you believe the evidence shows the providential hand of God in this event?

Create Your Own Research Topic

_____

_____

_____

▶ Timeline

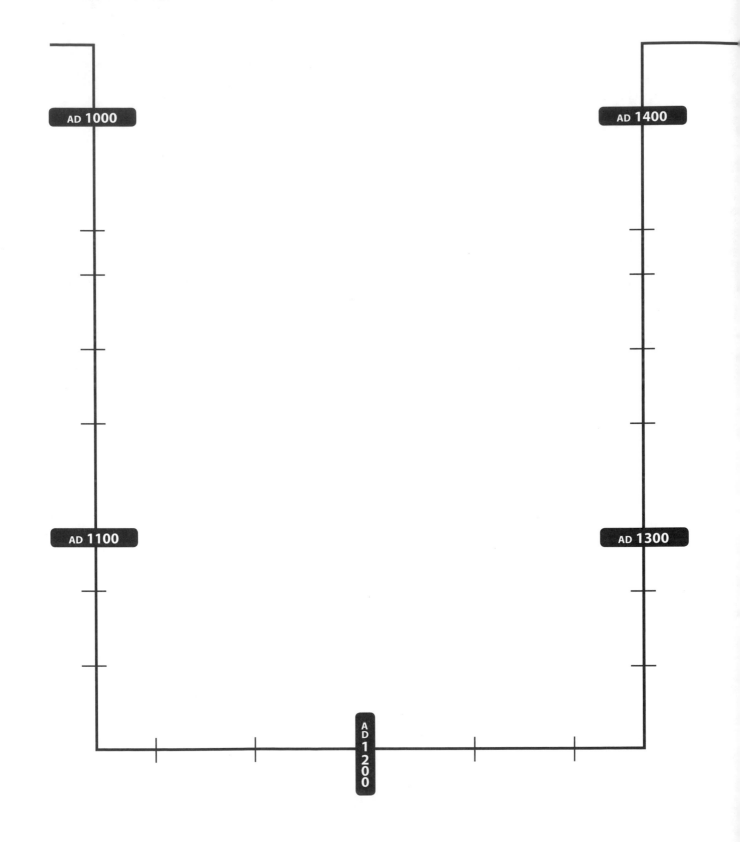

AD **1000**

AD **1400**

AD **1100**

AD **1300**

AD **1200**

Consider this for your timeline

For the first time, the Christians of Europe unite militarily to war in a place beyond the boundaries of their own kingdoms. Think about this moment: when the European knights were spending their time battling one another, the Seljuk Turks had just conquered the Holy Land, the Islamic empire had been splintered into factions, and Pope Urban II was seeking to unite Christendom and restore his papal throne from the antipope. How was this time unique in history?

Key Events

The Crusades

Crusader States

The Latin Empire in Constantinople

Invasion of the Mongols

Beginning of the Inquisition

Signing of the Magna Carta

Martyrdom of Thomas Becket

The Investiture Controversy

CONSIDER:

There are many unusual words associated with the architecture of cathedrals. If you learn what these words mean, you will be able to read historical fiction of this time and learn "where" who did what to whom!

Flying Buttress

Frieze

Nave

Ambulatory

Apse

Arcade

Facade

Transept

Vault

Arch

▶ Words to Watch

Remember—The easiest way to learn a subject is to master its terms:

chivalry	knight's fee	crusade	friars
mendicant	ransom	Inquisition	penance
purgatory	scholasticism	merit	convocation
schism	fealty	pilgrimage	faction
indulgences	Doge	university	excommunication

Other words you need to look up:

_____

_____

_____

_____

► # Student Self-Evaluation UNIT 5, PHASE 2

Dates and hours:_____

Research Project

Summarize your research question:

_____

_____

List your most useful sources by author, title, and page number or URL where applicable (continue list in margin if necessary):

_____

_____

_____

Now take a moment to evaluate the sources you just listed. Do they provide a balanced view of your research question? Should you have sought an additional opinion? Are your sources credible (if you found them on your own)? Record your observations:

_____

_____

Evaluate your research project in its final presentation. What are its strengths? If you had time to revisit this project, what would you change? Consider giving yourself a letter grade based on your project's merits and weaknesses.

_____

_____

Letter grade: _____

You have just completed an area of specific research in the time of the Crusades & the Mongols. Now what would you like to explore in the upcoming Phases? Set some objectives for yourself:

_____

Phase 3

▶ Maps & Mapping

Physical Terrain

» Locate and label the lands of the crusaders: England, France, Germany, Italy, and Sicily. Locate and label the area of Eastern Europe through which the crusaders traveled to get to the Middle East (including Hungary, Romania, and Bulgaria).

» Locate and label the lands where the crusades were fought: Syria, Palestine, Egypt, and Asia Minor.

» Locate and label Mongolia, the land of the Mongols. Locate and label lands that were among those conquered by the Mongols: China, Central Asia (including Kazakhstan, Uzbekistan, Afghanistan, and Pakistan), India, Iran, Russia.

Geopolitical

» Draw lines to show the routes taken by the crusaders, using one color for the journey by land, another for the route by sea. Locate and label these crusader states: Edessa, Antioch, Tripoli, the Kingdom of Jerusalem, Cyprus, the Latin Empire.

» Locate and label these cities important to the crusaders: Tyre, Acre, Antioch, Jaffa, Damascus, Jerusalem, Constantinople, Venice.

» Locate and label these cities important to the Mongols: Beijing, Bukhara, Samarkand, Kiev, Baghdad. Locate and label this city which was important to Marco Polo: Yangchow.

» Locate and label Kublai Khan's kingdom and the area dominated by the Golden Horde.

Explore

» *Christian Outreach:* What is the status of evangelical outreach today in Mongolia and China? What opportunities and what difficulties face those who share the gospel in these areas?

CRUSADER
STATES
INSET

CONSIDER:

Stained glass was, during the time of the Gothic cathedrals, the leading form of painting. Due to medieval glass-making methods, the artist did not paint *on* glass, but *with* glass—using hundreds of small pieces of stained glass assembled like a giant jigsaw puzzle and held together with strips of lead.

▶ Art Appreciation

Melchizedek and Abraham, Reims Cathedral

Sculpted in High Gothic style, this sculpture from the interior west wall shows the fluidity and elegance of Gothic sculpture, as well as depicting Abraham as a medieval knight in the style of mid-thirteenth century knights.

> » Locate a photo of this sculpture (or any sculpture from Reims Cathedral). How would you describe this to someone who was blind? Look at the clothing, hair, facial expressions and posture of the sculpted people. Do they seem realistic or abstract to you?

Stained Glass Windows, Chartres Cathedral

Stained glass in the twelfth and thirteen century cathedrals was both the message and medium of heavenly realities for earthly dwellers. As light penetrated the glass, it brought forth brilliant colors (more brightly colored than most people had ever seen before) and the subject material was from the Bible and from the Church. In a sense, the cathedrals were designed around the stained glass—structures that held the beauty which shone forth with such incandescent hue.

> » Look for photos of any of the stained glass windows from this cathedral. Chartres has a tremendous amount of medieval stained glass which is still in good condition. What colors do you see? Which colors stand out as being most prevalent? How would you describe this art?

▶ Architecture

Notre Dame, Paris

Architects designed and built Gothic cathedrals as lofty and spacious as possible, but with very few stone-filled walls—to allow the jeweled colors from the stained glass windows to bathe worshippers in their heavenly glow. In order to do that, architects had to create an unprecedented technology to support the huge, heavy towers and roofs from the outside. Their solution? Flying buttresses. This made it possible to have incredibly beautiful, delicately formed walls filled with glass, while the ceilings soared more than one hundred feet into the air!

» Locate photos of Notre Dame Cathedral. How would you describe the West Façade (where churchgoers enter)? If you can locate photos which show the view from the southeast, you will see the flying buttresses of Notre Dame. How would you describe flying buttresses? The architects of Gothic cathedrals were more technically daring than any previous architects—creating unprecedented vertical space by lofting heavy masonry ceilings vast distances (112 feet at Notre Dame), then filling the walls (which would have normally supported the ceilings) with glass. Considering this, what questions would you ask a medieval architect?

▶ Arts in Action

Select one or more, and let your artistic juices flow!

"Stained Glass Window"

Try your hand at making a "stained glass window" out of paper. First, draw a design on a piece of white paper, and then go over the outlines with a black crayon. Be sure to press hard! Next, color each of the spaces between the black lines. Finally, pour a little bit of vegetable oil onto a cotton ball. Using the cotton ball, wipe the back of your colored paper. Let it dry, then tape it onto a window and wait for the sunshine!

Sculpting

Examine any of the Gothic sculptures from Reims Cathedral. Using soft sculpting clay, try creating a simple figure wearing a cloak. Consider the folds of the Melchizedek statue at Reims, and then try with your own sculpture to create recognizable folds in the cloak.

▶ Science

Salt was used during the Middle Ages as one of the means of preservation in a time when there was no refrigeration. Think about what you would be able to eat if there were no refrigerators or freezers: foods during winter and spring would mostly be dried, salted, smoked, fermented, or brined (cured in a salt-water solution).

Preserving with salt

» Learn more about salt as a food preserver. Old fashioned kosher dill pickles were made in barrels with salt and vinegar. After a sufficient quantity of time, they were "cured" by the salt, and would remain crunchy and tasty in the brine for months. Try your hand at brining some vegetables, such as cauliflower, cabbage, or cucumbers. (Check a good cook book for recipes.) Note, from cabbage you will get sauerkraut! What other foods are preserved mainly through the use of salt?

▶ Music

Though there are not many hymns remaining from this period, consider the focus, or object, of the composers' hymns. St. Francis of Assisi wrote the joyous song "Canticle of the Sun" (from which was translated the hymn, "All Creatures of our God and King") near the end of his life, when he was blind, sick, and in great pain. What a reminder to us that our God is worthy of all praise, regardless of our own circumstances.

Discover

Jesus, the Very Thought of Thee

Bernard of Clairvaux (1090–1153) • Bernard of Clairvaux was known for his mystical piety, his committed life, his hymns, and his preaching the Second Crusade.

All Creatures of our God and King

St. Francis of Assisi (1181–1226) • There are numerous stories of Francis caring for animals—even preaching to them about God's goodness—and their responsiveness to him. He was even reported to preach to fields of flowers!

Try This

Practice singing "All Creatures of our God and King," and then, after explaining the circumstances in which it was written, sing it to together at a gathering of believers.

Listen

All Glory, Laud, & Honor MUSIC CD

Jesus, the Very Thought of Thee

▶ Cooking

Spices from the East, such as pepper, cinnamon, ginger and cloves, were highly treasured and VERY expensive, hence used only by the very rich. With that in mind, try making this cake, indulging in what would have been a taste reserved for the medieval elite.

Sour Cream Spice Cake

¼ pound butter
3 large eggs
¼ tsp salt
2 tsp cinnamon
¼ tsp nutmeg
1 cup sour cream

2 cups brown sugar
2¼ cup sifted pastry flour
1 tsp baking soda
1 tsp ginger
¼ tsp cloves

Cream butter, gradually add brown sugar. Add the eggs, one at a time, beating well after each addition. Sift the dry ingredients together and stir into the creamed mixture alternately with the sour cream. Turn batter into two greased and floured 8 inch round pans. Tap pans on counter to release excess air in batter. Bake in 350° oven from 25 to 30 minutes, or until cake is done. Cool in pans for 5 minutes before turning out onto cooling racks. Cool completely before frosting.

Nutmeg Frosting

1 cup sugar
1 cup sour cream

1 cup light brown sugar
½ tsp ground nutmeg

Combine the two sugars and the sour cream in a saucepan. Cook over medium heat, stirring constantly, until mixture reaches the soft ball stage (235° on a candy thermometer). Remove from heat and cool to barely lukewarm. Add the nutmeg and beat with an electric mixer until frosting is of spreading consistency. Add a few drops of milk if necessary. (Hint: If you can find whole nutmeg, grate it fresh for this recipe—the taste will astound you!)

▶ Student Self-Evaluation UNIT 5, PHASE 3

Dates and hours:_____

Evaluate your projects

- List which of the activities listed in this Phase you did:

_____

_____

_____

- Rate your enthusiasm: _____

Explain: _____

- Rate the precision of your approach:_____

Explain: _____

- Rate your effort toward the completion of the project: _____

Explain: _____ _____

Ask yourself what worked and what did not. What would you do differently in the future, and what would you repeat?

_____

_____

How specifically did these hands-on activities enhance your knowledge of the crusades & the Mongols? What made them worthwhile?

_____

_____

In the first three Phases of this Unit, what aspect of the time period has most captured your imagination? What would you like to creatively pursue to conclude your study?

_____

_____

Phase 4

▶ In Your Own Way...

We have seen European warriors go on crusades to the Middle East, Constantinople, and even southern France. We have also watched the conquests of Genghis Khan and his descendants, which created the largest land empire to that point. Now, choose a selection of these activities, or create your own, which will best express what you have learned from this Unit.

LINGUISTICS

Journalism

Emperor Alexius I has requested that Europe send mercenaries to help fight the Seljuk Turks. Since you are the ace reporter for the daily *Constantinople Sun*, you have been assigned to cover the story of the advancing crusader army. (Remember, you are Byzantine, not European.)

You are in charge of hiring the medieval architect and the contractor/builder for your city's Gothic cathedral. Write want ads for the employment section of the paper. You have high expectations, so be specific.

As an eyewitness observer, write your opinion for Pope Gregory VII concerning the sincerity of Emperor Henry IV's repentance at Canossa.

The Venice news show, "Strange But True," has asked you to interview Marco Polo. Be sure to have him describe Kublai Khan's palace! (No one will believe it, though.)

Prose

Imagine you were a Waldensian (a follower of Peter Waldo), and had accompanied him to the Third Lateran Council in Rome. Write home to tell your friends and family what happened concerning Pope Alexander III's ruling on your group's poverty and preaching. Include how the news impacted Peter, and what new plans are being considered.

You are Eleanor of Aquitaine, and your son, the newly crowned Richard I of England, has just released you from prison. Write your story, including the reason your husband, Henry II, imprisoned you. Knowing the vagaries of royal politics, be careful of what you say.

Poetry

Finish this poem:

If ever you start a crusade . . .

ART

Graphic Design

Genghis Khan is launching an advertising campaign in preparation for his upcoming invasion. The ad is directed towards his countrymen who have been complaining that his empire is currently large enough and needs no further conquests. You have been hired to change their mind.

Design the graphic for a road-tour jacket for the Polo family to wear when they present travelogues in Venice concerning their eastern travels.

Cartooning

Draw a political cartoon depicting the penitence of Henry II after the murder of Thomas Becket. You need to decide if Henry was sorry because Becket was killed, or whether he was sorry that he got blamed for it.

Painting/Drawing

Create a collage of the major crusades, which contains a key scene, person, or element for each crusade depicted.

Paint or draw a scene from the story of Robin Hood. You might want to include Prince John, or even King Richard the Lionheart.

Stained Glass

Make a project (lampshade, box, etc.) with stained glass. There are stained glass kits which contain all that is required for this type of art. (CAUTION: ADULT SUPERVISION REQUIRED.)

MUSIC

Performance Practice

With your teacher's help, select an appropriate piece of music which expresses some particular aspect studied in this unit, whether from the crusades (martial, religious, Greek, Arabic to name a few possibilities) or from the Mongols (swift moving, Central Asian, galloping horses, are a few other possibilities). Prepare and perform the piece for an audience. Communicate with your audience the reason for your selection either in the program notes or in a short speech.

DRAMA

Drama

Present dramatically the events of the Fourth Crusade and the resultant Latin Empire in Constantinople. Sound effects, backdrops, and props would be helpful for your audience!

Puppetry

With the use of puppets, tell the stories of two brothers: Richard the Lionheart and John Lackland, especially focusing on their on-again/off-again relationship. Don't forget the story of the Magna Carta!

Comedy

Give a comedic performance of a "Day in the Life" of one of the workers building the Gothic cathedral of Notre Dame. Include the kinds of things that you have to deal with on a regular basis, and the unappreciative remarks people have been making about the flying buttresses.

Prop Needs

_____

_____

_____

Costume Ideas

_____

_____

_____

Role/Player

_____

_____

_____

Set Suggestions

_____

_____

_____

MOVEMENT

Pantomime

Using pantomime, depict Urban II's journey across the Alps to Clermont, and then, to the assembled French nobles, his call for the First Crusade. Stir up your audience as he stirred his, only don't use words!

Action

Using dramatic action, depict the life of Francis of Assisi, from his careless youth to his remarkable encounter with the Muslim Sultan in 1219.

Dance

Choreograph a dance showing the Mongol conquests, region by region. You might want to use a number of short sections of music, which would help represent these different areas.

CONCEPTUAL DESIGN

Translator

The Polos don't have time to learn all of the languages they will encounter on their travels. Design a hand-held translator for them which they could use to ask anyone they meet for help with the directions to Cathay and back. It might utilize graphics, maps, words—you decide!

CREATE YOUR OWN EXPRESSION

_____

_____

_____

_____

_____

_____

▶ Student Self-Evaluation UNIT 5, PHASE 4

Dates and hours:_____

Evaluate your projects

- What creative project did you choose:

  _____

- What did you expect from your project, and how does the final project compare to your initial expectations?

  _____

- What do you like about your project? What would you change?

  _____

In Conclusion

Revisit the five Key Concepts from the beginning of this Unit. Explain how your understanding of and appreciation for each has grown over the course of your study.

- _____
  _____

- _____
  _____

- _____
  _____

- _____
  _____

- _____
  _____

Record your concluding thoughts on the crusades & the Mongols:

_____

_____

Seeds of the Reformation
& the Late Middle Ages

Key Concepts

- Hundred Years' War

- Western Church in crisis

- The printing press

- Exploration & trade

- Fall of Constantinople

Trebuchets at the Château de Castelnaud, Perigord, France

More Than Conquerors . . .

The late Middle Ages boiled into a seething cauldron of struggle, battle, terror, and strife. It seemed to many (especially for the Orthodox Byzantines who experienced the fall of Constantinople) like the Apocalypse of the book of Revelation. As we shall discover, this time period endured much of the description Jesus gave of the end of time:

> For nation will rise against nation, and kingdom against kingdom. And there will be famines, pestilences, and earthquakes in various places. Matthew 24:7

Yet, amazingly, in the midst of this devastation, God powerfully raised up courageous servants who spoke truth and life to His people.

The Ottomans

Our story begins with the collapse of Seljuk rule in the mid-1200s. The vacuum of power this created was soon filled in Anatolia (Asia Minor) by a Turkish warrior clan, the Ottomans. There was a fiercely religious aspect to these new rulers, and with their reinvigorated spirit of *jihad* they drew enthusiastic Muslim warriors (*ghazis*) from surrounding Islamic lands. The weakened Byzantines were no match in Anatolia for these warriors, and by the 1330s the Ottomans had captured it all. This was the beginning of a new heroic age of Muslim conquest, with the Byzantine Empire and its city of Constantinople as the goal.

> *The capture of Constantinople in 1204 by Europeans had fragmented the empire.*

The Byzantine Empire was, by this time, debilitated and frail. The capture of Constantinople in 1204 by Europeans had fragmented the empire. Though the Byzantines were able to recapture the city in 1261, it was a mere shadow of its former glory and power. Different emperors tried their own strategies for strengthening the empire. For instance, the emperor who ousted the Europeans, Michael VIII, tried forestalling the West from recapturing Constantinople by joining the Orthodox Church to the Catholic Church (which ended in political disaster) while his son, Andronicus II, tried strengthening the economy by dramatically reducing the size of the army and eliminating the navy (which left the Byzantines nearly defenseless). The one real strength remaining to the Byzantines was a fierce commitment to Orthodoxy.

In the West, kingdoms were rising against kingdoms. England's King Edward I went to war against Wales (and won), went to war against Scotland (which he lost, then won, then posthumously lost again), and tried to go to war against France. France's Philip IV rose up against England over its lands in France, defied Pope Boniface VIII over "who was subject to whom," and challenged the Knights Templar with charges of blasphemy.

In 1309 Europe was subjected to the shock of the pope moving from Rome, from whence the pope had always ruled, to Avignon, just across the river from France and Philip IV. Akin to moving the planet Mars to the center of the universe, this relocation seemed wrong, unnatural, and wholly unsuitable—especially to the English people, who lived on the constant edge of war with the French.

Hundred Years' War

When the new ruler of France, Philip of Valois, came to the throne as Philip VI, tensions between the two countries increased to the breaking point over French lands owned by the English king Edward III, and coveted by Philip. In the upcoming contest of strength, France appeared to be in the best position for winning: rich agricultural lands and the great wealth that accrued from them, a vastly superior population base, and the most powerful army on the continent. England, however, had a secret weapon. The English long-bow (used first by the Welsh) was quick to fire—three to four times faster than the French crossbow—and flew one-hundred fifty yards. At sixty yards it would penetrate armor. The longbow was strictly a defensive weapon, but when the English were on French ground and the French armies attacked, this defensive weapon annihilated the enemy. Through the murderous success of the longbow, Edward III and his vastly outnumbered English army won the battle of Crécy in 1346 because half his army were longbow archers.

An observer of this struggle between France and England (known to later generations as the Hundred Years' War) might question how two countries both subscribing to belief in Jesus Christ could go to war with each other, since the Bible clearly states:

> He who says he abides in Him ought himself also to walk just as He walked. 1 John 2:6

> Therefore if your enemy hungers, feed him; if he thirsts, give him a drink; for in so doing you will heap coals of fire on his head. Romans 12:20

These medieval rulers were able to religiously observe Christian ceremonies without having their hearts or their actions affected.

Though they had managed to justify their earthly crusades against the Muslims as doing God's work and obeying the pope's call, how could they possibly justify this war?

The answer lies in our ability as human beings to *compartmentalize* our faith. Just as people today may go to church on Sunday and leave all Christian thought behind as they walk out the door, so these medieval rulers were able to religiously observe Christian ceremonies without having their hearts or their actions affected.

Perhaps part of the reason for this compartmentalization can be found in the lack of knowledge of God's Word. In those days, the position of the Catholic Church was that only the clergy were allowed to read the Bible. Since they only permitted the Bible to be written in Latin (a dying language understood only by a small, well-educated group of clergy and scholars), few of the clergy really knew what it said. The official Catholic position was that allowing non-clergy direct access to the Bible produced heretical groups such as the Waldensians, so there was no desire or motivation to see the Bible produced in the *vernacular,* or everyday language, of the various people groups in Europe. That position (and many Catholic doctrines) would soon be challenged by an Englishman named John Wycliffe.

Western Church in crisis

Briefly, before looking at the impact of John Wycliffe, let us consider the pestilence that stalked both East and West in the mid-1300s. The Black Death—*the plague*—seems to have originated in China and was first transmitted to the West in 1347 when a besieging Asian army catapulted plague-riddled corpses into a trade city of the Genoese on the Black Sea. The disease was transmitted by fleas on rats; thus, the plague entered the port cities of the Mediterranean aboard rat-infested trading ships. But no one at the time understood how this plague was carried from place to place, and they had no idea how to stop it.

Since they only permitted the Bible to be written in Latin, few of the clergy really knew what it said.

It was a pestilence of tremendous proportions, with a death toll unmatched by any previous epidemic or war—approximately 25 million people died in Europe alone. The terror of this sudden death, striking unexpectedly and without regard for wealth or status, is beyond our comprehension. This, combined with the trauma of the Avignon papacy and the spectacle of the Hundred Years' War, left people of the mid-1300s searching for relief and answers from a wide range of dark sources, including a macabre fascination with death, unbiblical mysticism, and seeking to pacify God by wounding themselves. Without direct access to the Light of the World, these traumatized people walked in great darkness.

Out of this maelstrom a fresh voice was soon heard with the resounding thunder of an Old Testament prophet. John Wycliffe, a famous scholar and theologian at Oxford in the 1360s, had been called by King Edward III as religious advisor to the royal court of England. The main question Edward III wanted answered was whether England actually owed its unpaid taxes to the pope. These were the feudal taxes left over from King John's gift of England to the papacy. That was distasteful enough, but now the pope had left Rome and was living under French control in Avignon. All of Parliament as well as the royal court were delighted with Wycliffe because, in essence,

The printing press heralded the mass publication of literature.

his position was whether the pope be Italian or French, England didn't owe him any money. As Wycliffe continued past that issue onto insightful questioning of other papal decrees and Catholic doctrines, he began to powerfully influence the English nation. Though he lost royal favor and support when he repudiated the central Catholic doctrine of transubstantiation (believing that the bread and wine of Communion becomes the actual body and blood of Jesus Christ), Wycliffe endured the loss of position and prestige by organizing a group of scholars to translate the Bible from Latin into English. He also gathered a group of disciples, known by the derogatory name of *Lollards,* who went out to preach the good news to the poor. They believed that the people needed direct access to the Scriptures as well as edifying preaching, which was an unorthodox concept in that day, and soon became labeled as heresy.

What do people hear when they are exposed for the first time to the Word of God? Messages such as, "God has provided His Son to be your redeemer," and "In God's family, we are all loved and are members one of another." Perhaps one of the most surprising Scriptures to the late Middle Ages was from Galatians 3:28: "There is neither Jew nor Greek, there is neither slave nor free, there is neither male nor female; for you are all one in Christ Jesus." To the listening ears of peasants under the weight of poor wages, high prices, and the spectacle of wealthy aristocracy eating their fill, it must have been a dramatic and liberating thought.

Unfortunately, there were those preaching at the same time as Wycliffe and the Lollards, who brought a twisted version of the truth. One charismatic ruffian by the name of John Ball preached this inflaming message:

> Good people, things will never go well in England so long as goods be not in common. . . . By what right are they whom we call lords greater folk than we? On what grounds have they deserved it? Why do they hold us in serfage? If we all came of the same father and mother, of Adam and Eve, how can they say or prove that they are better than we, if it be not that they make us gain for them by our toil what they spend in their pride? They are clothed in velvet, and warm in their furs and their ermines, while we are covered with rags. They have wine and spices and fair bread; and we oatcake and straw, and water to drink. They have leisure and fine houses; we have pain and labor, the rain and the wind in the fields. And yet it is of us and of our toil that these men hold their state.

His position was whether the pope be Italian or French, England didn't owe him any money.

The peasants, stirred up with a sense of their own value in God's eyes (based on Wycliffe's teaching) and the unfairness of a few lording it over the many (John Ball's teaching), in 1381 rose up in revolt—known as the Peasants' Revolt or *Wat Tyler's Rebellion.* Appealing to the young King Richard II, they sought relief from unfair taxes and exploitation. To the great detriment of their cause, they were destructive and violent, which gave the authorities freedom and license to hunt them down, ending the revolt. It gives one pause to consider how similar this revolt was to the reaction of the peasants exposed to Martin Luther's message, which we will discover in the next Unit. How important it is to have the whole counsel of the Word of God!

> For you, brethren, have been called to liberty; only do not use liberty as an opportunity for the flesh, but through love serve one another. Galatians 5:13

What a difference this truth would have made in the lives of the peasants of 1381.

The message of God's Word leapt across the Channel from England to Eastern Europe through the everyday affairs of state. King Richard II married Anne of Bohemia, whose brother happened to be the king of Bohemia. Diplomatic doors were opened between the two countries, and students from Prague began to come increasingly to study at Oxford. The education they received went beyond the regular scope of study, however, when these Bohemian students were exposed to the teachings of Wycliffe. Eagerly embracing this

Scripture seed, they took it home where Bohemia was struggling under the German yoke of the Holy Roman Empire. There it found fertile ground and grew mighty under the preaching of John Huss in Prague, along with a corresponding nationalism. When the Council of Constance met in 1414, one of its tasks was to deal with the spread of the Wycliffe *heresy*, and the council called for John Huss to come and answer these charges. Since it was a dangerous thing to respond to this call (people were being burned as heretics in England and on the Continent), King Sigismund of Hungary and Germany offered a safe conduct pledge to Huss—that he might come to respond to the charges and return safely home. The king's word was not worth the paper it was printed on, for when the council found Huss guilty of heresy, he was executed. Bohemia ignited into war. The *Hussites* (followers of John Huss) battled for their lives against the Imperial army led by Sigismund. For a time they won against all odds, but eventually through their own dissensions and fragmentation, they went back under the yoke of the empire. In a bizarre turn of events, Sigismund (brother of the former king) was himself made king of Bohemia in 1436.

> The message of God's Word leapt across the Channel from England to Eastern Europe.

Fall of Constantinople

In the East, the Byzantine empire had shrunk steadily under the

Timetable of the Late Middle Ages

	Islam	Byzantines	French	English
1280–1300	Rise of Ottoman Turks: Osman I	Emperor abolishes imperial navy, 1284; sailors defect and build fleet for Ottomans	Philip IV; 10 year war with England beginning 1294; conflict with Pope Boniface VIII.	Edward I subdues Wales; Wars of Scottish Independence; expells Jews, 1290
1300–1320	Ottomans defeat Byzantines at Nicomedia, 1302	Inflation and near famine in Constantinople	Captures Boniface for trial; strong pressure on Clement V—papacy in Avignon; Jews expelled, 1306	Edward II loses Battle of Bannockburn; Robert the Bruce reigns king of Scotland
1320–1340	Muslims capture Byzantine cities in Anatolia: Bursa, Nicaea, Nicomedia, Scutari	Civil war between claimants for throne; Emperor uses Turks to help fight against other enemies in Eastern Europe	Charles IV dies without heirs; Philip of Valois assumes the throne, threatens Edward III's lands; beginning of Hundred Years War, 1337	Edward II abdicates in favor of Edward III; beginning of Hundred Years' War; Parliament grows more powerful
1340–1360	Gallipoli first Ottoman foothold in Europe, 1354; permanent army created—first time since Roman Empire	Second civil war; Emperor's daughter married to Ottoman sultan—Turks gain thorough knowledge of Balkans; Black Death decimates Constantinople	Defeated at Battle of Crécy; Black Death, 1347–1350; King John II captured at Battle of Poitiers	Edward III, after victories and treaty, granted most of south-western France; Black Death arrives 1348: in some areas, 50% of population dies

nibbling efforts of the Ottomans. In 1354, when the city of Gallipoli (on the European side of the Dardanelles) experienced a massive, destructive earthquake, the Ottoman mercenaries who had been employed by the Byzantine emperor quickly moved to occupy, rebuild, and fortify the city. This provided them with their first base in Europe, and from there they began military action against the European countries in the Balkans. In 1362 the Ottomans captured Adrianople, renamed it Edirne, and made it their capital city. This completed a virtual encircling of the isolated city of Constantinople, surrounding it on all sides with Ottoman forces.

The warriors were unified in a common cause—similar to the European crusaders setting off for the Holy Lands in the late 1000s.

Why were the Ottomans able to accomplish this feat that no previous Muslim military had been able to do? The answer lies partly in the Ottoman policy of passing the empire in its entirety to one son, rather than the Seljuk approach of parceling pieces of the empire out to every son. At this point in time, the Ottomans were also well organized with a permanent, well-paid, well-disciplined army. The warriors were unified in a common cause—capturing Constantinople—and this gave them a strength currently lacking among the Europeans and Byzantines. Interestingly enough, this is similar to the European crusaders, united in purpose and vision, setting off for the Holy Lands in the late 1000s. Just as the Europeans were now fragmented and embroiled in civil war (which prevented them from sending a sufficient military force to offset the Ottomans),

Holy Roman Empire	Church	East	Trade, Inventions, & Exploration
Teutonic knights conquer all of Prussia; Rudolf I, first Hapsburg king of Germany	Nestorian archbishop in Beijing, under protection of Kublai Khan	Defeat of Sung Dynasty; Kublai Khan sets up Yüan Dynasty; Marco Polo in China	Florence leading city in commerce & banking; Venice leading city in trade
Emperor Henry VII provokes hostility in Italy: pro-papal forces against pro-imperial forces	Beginning of Avignon Papacy: French popes—Europe shaken by the spectacle	Muslim Tughlak Dynasty begins in Western India with Delhi as capital	Trade fairs in France & The Netherlands; Canary Islands rediscovered; Genoa at its peak of power
Louis IV, German king & Holy Roman Emperor, declared heretic by French pope for political reasons; declares pope heretic in return	William of Ockham & Marsilius of Padua write against pope, flee to Louis IV's empire; Brethren of Common Life started in The Netherlands, 1334	Nestorians & Roman Catholics are permitted in China during Yüan Dynasty	
Charles IV, king of Germany & Bohemia, Emperor 1355–1378: moves capital of Empire to Prague	Black Death causes many to question ability of clergy for inability to stem the plague; monasteries are among the hardest hit during Black Death	Firoz Shah in India (Tughlak Dynasty) systematically persecutes Hindus who refuse conversion to Islam	Hanseatic League officially founded, 1356; Ibn Battuta, geographer, explores Sahara Desert; early cannons effectively used in Hundred Years' War

so had the Seljuks been divided and at war with one another during the time of the First Crusade.

Remarkably akin to the response of the Byzantine emperor to the threat of Seljuk Turks, so now was the Byzantine emperor's appeal to the pope for help. Knowing that only a fully-accepted union between Orthodox and Catholic would motivate the West to come to their aid, Emperor John VIII came in person to the Council of Florence in 1439 to submit to the authority of the pope. The attitudes of the people in the Orthodox East had never changed, however. Their sentiment was expressed thus, *"Better the turban of the Prophet than the tiara of the pope."*

Though the official union of churches was celebrated in Hagia Sophia in 1452, the majority of people refused to attend and resolutely chose to take their chances against the Ottomans. With their background of more than one thousand years of successfully withstanding besieging land armies (the assault of the Venetians and crusaders in 1204 took place on the sea and would not have succeeded on land), the people of Constantinople readied themselves for the inevitable attack by Mehmet II, ruler of the Ottomans.

There was a significant difference in the Ottoman preparations for this siege, however. Mehmet II, a young and fiercely determined sultan, was a student of history (including daily readings about Caesar and Alexander the Great) and a proponent of the newest and best technologies. His administrative skill proved formidable when his army, his huge array of cannons (including the largest cannon ever made), and his new fleet of ships arrived on the doorstep

	Islam	Byzantines	French	English
1360–1380	Edirne first Ottoman capital in Europe, 1362; Byzantine Emperor made vassal, 1363	Surrounded by Ottomans in Europe and Anatolia; Emperor begs West for help	2nd wave of Black Death; Charles V wins back much of what was lost to England	Wycliffe preaches reform; Richard II comes to throne as 10 year old
1380–1400	Ottomans win Battle of Kossovo, 1389—Balkans under Ottoman rule; Catholics defeated in Battle of Nicopolis, 1396	Ottoman siege of Constantinople, Emperor tours the West seeking aid	Charles VI (the Mad); his brother made Duke of Orléans; Charles favors Clement VII as pope; negotiates with Richard II	Lollards sent out to preach to the poor; Wat Tyler's Rebellion, 1381; Henry IV usurps throne, Richard II murdered
1400–1420	Ottoman sultan loses to Tamerlane, 1402; civil war between sultan's sons	Byzantine ambassador to West hired to teach Greek Literature in Florence	Duke of Burgundy has Duke of Orléans assassinated, civil war begins; loss at Agincourt	Barons rebel against Henry IV; Henry V wins at Agincourt; opposes Lollards
1420–1440	Ottoman expansion in Europe: Muslims win Battle of Varna, 1444; 2nd Battle of Kossovo, 1448	New Muslim siege of Constantinople, 1422; Union of Churches (Catholic & Orthodox), 1439	Treaty of Troyes makes Henry V heir; Joan of Arc helps Charles VII to be crowned at Rheims	Henry V dies young; 9-month-old Henry VI king of England & (disputed) king of France
1440–1460	Mehmet II captures Constantinople, 1453, makes it Ottoman capital—Istanbul	Union of Churches in Hagia Sophia, 1452—bitterly resented by most; End of Byzantine Empire, 1453	Charles VII reunifies France; ends Hundred Years War 1453	Anarchy in England; end of Hundred Years War—all territory in France lost except Calais

of Constantinople in April of 1453. As soon as the cannons were set up, he began a merciless pounding on the impenetrable walls of Constantinople. He also found a way to drag his ships across land, bringing them into the enclosed safety of the Golden Horn—much to the horror of the Byzantine fleet. It took seven weeks of heart-wrenching artillery pounding, breathtaking sea battles, and all-out assaults before the Ottomans were finally able to break through the defenses of the city. To the people of Constantinople, it was the end of their empire and the end of life as they had known it. To the faithful in Christ Jesus, it was difficult but not the end of their world. They knew the truth of Romans:

> For I am persuaded that neither death nor life, nor angels
> nor principalities nor powers, nor things present nor things
> to come, nor height nor depth, nor any other created thing,
> shall be able to separate us from the love of God which is in
> Christ Jesus our Lord. Romans 8:38–39

The year 1453 was a cataclysmic year. It saw the end of the Byzantine Empire, the end of the Hundred Years' War (which France finally won), and the beginning of a new technology, one that would bring greater changes to the world than even the might of cannons. In the city of Mainz, Germany, Johannes Gutenberg was beginning to print Bibles on his newly invented printing press. The reverberations of that event have not yet been silenced. They continue to ring out across the world in nearly every language. And, as we shall see in the next Unit, the printing press would unleash a revolution of thought. We call it the Reformation. ◄

Holy Roman Empire	Church	East	Trade, Inventions, & Exploration
Wenceslas king of Germany & Bohemia, king of Romans	Avignon Papacy ends; Great Schism begins—Europe divided between two popes; Wycliffe's teachings impact England	Tamerlane, Turkish Mongol; Ming Dynasty in China	Hanseatic League forces Denmark to share its profits
Germany in anarchy for a decade; Sigismund of Hungary defeated by Ottomans, 1396	Wycliffe oversees English Bible translation; his Lollards repudiate indulgences, clerical celibacy, transubtatiation	Tamerlane begins 35 successful campaigns across Asia; Delhi sacked	Venice wins long war against Genoa; Medici in power in Florence; Byzantines use cannons against Ottomans at siege of Constantinople
Sigismund now also king of Germany, extends phony safe conduct to John Huss for Council of Constance	Wycliffe's writings influence Bohemia's John Huss; Great Schism healed, Huss condemned & executed	Tamerlane ravages Georgia, conquers Damascus & Baghdad, captures sultan	Prince Henry sends out voyages of discovery; Portugese sailors rediscover Madeira; sail past Bojador
Hussite wars: 1st crusade against Hussites, Sigismund defeated; Sigismund becomes king of Bohemia, 1436	Council of Florence, 1439: union of Orthodox & Catholic; Joan of Arc condemned as heretic		Portugese sailors discover Azores; capture first African slaves; gold dust found in West Africa
Hapsburg Frederick III, last of emperors crowned by pope in Rome, 1452	Unitas Fratrum: organization of Hussites formed in Bohemia; Hagia Sophia made a mosque	Lodi Dynasty: last dynasty of Delhi sultanate of India	First large-scale artillery attack used by Ottomans at Constantinople (68 cannons); printing press invented

Phase 1

Key People (Church)

Dante
Wrote Divine Comedy

Pope Boniface VIII
Absolute power for pope

John Wycliffe
English reformer

Catherine of Siena
Influential Italian mystic

John Huss
Bohemian reformer

Pope Martin V
First Pope after Great Schism

Thomas a Kempis
Wrote The Imitation of Christ

▶ Listen to This

What in the World? VOL. 2

DISC THREE:

» Disintegration of Monarchy (track 5)

» The Hundred Years' War (track 6)

» European Conflict: West & East (track 7)

» Heresy & Heroism (track 8)

True Tales VOL. 2

DISC TWO:

» Prince Henry the Navigator (track 5)

Digging Deeper VOL. 2

DISC TWO: THE CHURCH IN CHARGE

» Francis of Assisi & Fall of Constantinople (track 9)

▶ Read For Your Life

The Holy Bible

» **Heart of early Reformation in England & Bohemia:** Zechariah 4:6,10; Isaiah 58; Psalm 51

» **Indictment of false shepherds & hypocritical Pharisees (Wycliffe's description of monks):** Ezekiel 34; Matt 23:1–12

Pertinent to the vision and teaching of the early Reformers, compare Ezekiel 34 and Matthew 23 with the following:

» **Jesus is the Good Shepherd:** John 10:1–18

» **Following Jesus:** Luke 9:57–58; Philippians 3:8–14

» **Christianity in action (God's love):** 1 Corinthians 13

Talk Together

Opinion Column

» What did you find to be the most interesting aspect or the most fascinating person you encountered in your introduction to the Seeds of Reformation and the Late Middle Ages?

» If you had been living during the beginnings of the Hundred Years' War, what do you think your attitude would have been toward the war if you were French? If you were English?

» Imagine you were a loyal churchman living in England during the Hundred Years' War. What would be your concerns when you learned that the pope was French and was living in Avignon?

» If you had been a French soldier anytime during the Hundred Years' War, you would probably have been very disheartened and ready to quit. What do you think your impression of Joan of Arc, when she appeared on the scene, might have been? How do you think her presence—and the amazing victories that followed—would have impacted you?

» The Black Plague was an incomprehensible terror to the people during the 1300s. Can you imagine one person out of every four dying suddenly from this horrible disease? In what ways do you think it might have changed the way people thought about God? After the plague had passed, how were their lives and societies changed?

» What do you think about Edward I's decision to invade Scotland? If you think he was justified, explain your reasons. If you think he was wrong, explain your reasons.

» If you had been living in England at the time when Wycliffe's translation of the Bible became available, do you think you would have been afraid of displeasing the Church authorities by hearing it read? In what ways do you think having the Bible in their own language impacted the English people?

Key People (World)

Edward I
Sought to conquer Scotland

William Wallace
Led Scottish resistance

Philip the Fair
Absolute power for French monarch

Tamerlane
Nomadic Asian conqueror

Henry the Navigator
Sent ships down African coast

Joan of Arc
Led French troops to victory over English

Gutenberg
Moveable type printing press

Mehmed II
Ottoman sultan who captured Constantinople

Critical Puzzling

» Why might this statement, "The Emperor derives his power from God, not from the Pope," be important during this time period? What do you think would be some of the possible repercussions of this new idea?

» In what ways do you think Wycliffe's Poor Preachers might have affected England? To whom did they minister? How were they different from the *mendicant* (or "begging") friars of the time, like the Franciscans and Dominicans?

» What do you think are some of the more significant results of Gutenberg's technological breakthrough?

» Why do you think the fall of Constantinople in the East was such an important event for Western Europe? How do you think it may have affected trade and exploration?

» Tamerlane was a powerful, violent Mongol conquerer, and was known as "the Scourge of God and the Terror of the World." Why do you think the Byzantines were thankful for him? Why do you think almost everyone else was terrified of him?

» William Wallace is considered by many to be the Father of Scotland. Why do you think this was the case? How do you suppose his courage in life and death became a challenge and encouragement to other Scots?

» What changes in perspective might have developed as reports came back that Prince Henry's ships were exploring further south in Africa?

▶ Resources for Digging Deeper

Choose a few books that look interesting, or find your own.

CHURCH HISTORY

Christian History Made Easy

Timothy Paul Jones • This book has a tremendous, insightful chapter on the late Middle Ages, and the need people had for God's reality in their own lives. **UE+**

The 100 Most Important Dates in Church History

Curtis, Lang, & Petersen • Several articles concerning this time period can be found here. **UE+**

Church History in Plain Language

Bruce L. Shelley • Mentioned again in this Unit because of the clear presentation of the historical context of the Babylonian Captivity of the Church, the Great Schism, and the lives of John Wycliffe and John Huss. **MS+**

LATE MIDDLE AGES

The Late Middle Ages

Translated from Italian, this book is one of the best introductions to the late Middle Ages. It includes the developments from AD 1000 to the mid-1400s. **UE+**

Fourteenth-Century Towns

Edited by John D. Clare • This book looks at the culture and everyday lives of the people living in the 1300s.

(Note: Though there are great pictures and helpful descriptions, the tenor of the book is fairly bleak.) **UE+**

Life in a Fifteenth Century Monastery A CAMBRIDGE TOPIC BOOK

Anne Boyd • This is an in-depth look at monks and monasteries at the end of the Middle Ages. Though it describes a monastery in England, information is also given about the dissolution of English monasteries after the Reformation. **UE+**

HUNDRED YEARS WAR

St. George for England: A Tale of Cressy and Poitiers

G. A. Henty • Henty provides students with an understandable and fascinating look at the early years of this war between France and England. **UE+**

The Hundred Years' War

Desmond Seward • Published in England, this wonderful book is a "play-by-play" description of the battles in the Hundred Years' War between England and France. **MS+**

At Agincourt: A Tale of the White Hoods of Paris

G. A. Henty • Discover another dynamic of the struggle in France—the enmity between the rulers of Burgundy and Orleans. The English victory at Agincourt, which took place in the latter part of the Hundred Years' War, is a significant part of this story. **UE+**

JOAN OF ARC

Joan of Arc WORLD LANDMARK BOOKS

Nancy Wilson Ross • This is an excellent look at one of the most significant figures in the 1400s—Joan of Arc. **E+**

Joan of Arc

Diane Stanley • Carefully researched, thoughtfully written, and beautifully illustrated, this book provides a gripping imagery of Joan of Arc's life. **UE+**

The Story of Joan of Arc

E. M. Wilmot-Buxton • Originally published in 1914, this well-researched book provides a thorough look at the Maid of France and the final years of the Hundred Years' War. **MS+**

SCOTTISH HISTORY

In Freedom's Cause

G. A. Henty • A story of William Wallace and Robert the Bruce, this book is a thrilling recounting of these Scottish heroes of the early fourteenth century. Written as historical fiction, Henty's books are, nonetheless, excellent for learning history! **UE+**

Scottish Chiefs

Jane Porter • This 1921 classic is a stirring rendition of the lives of the Scots who would not bow to England's Edward I. Worth the read! **MS+**

ENGLISH HISTORY

A March On London: Being a Story of Wat Tyler's Insurrection

G. A. Henty • The Peasants' Revolt of 1381 is explained in this fascinating historical novel by Henty, one of the world's great storytellers. **UE+**

Both Sides The Border: A Tale of Hotspur and Glendower

G. A. Henty • This book tells the story of the revolts against Henry IV in his early reign. **UE+**

The Door in the Wall

Marguerite de Angeli • A story of a young boy in old England who perseveres, through what seems to be insurmountable obstacles, to serve his king. Set during the time of the Scottish wars, this book is a wonderful tale. **E+**

The Hawk and the Dove

Penelope Wilcock • A favorite, this story is set in the early 1300s in a monastery in England. This is not only historical fiction, but it is a depiction of Christian love and sacrifice toward the people with whom we live. It is precious—a rich, rare treasure of a book. **MS+**

A History of the English-Speaking Peoples

Winston Churchill • Volume One, *The Birth of Britain,* takes the reader from the time of the Romans through the War of the Roses in English history. Churchill's insightful descriptions will help students make their way through the Hundred Years' War as well as the time of Richard II and Henry IV. Highly recommended. **MS+**

GUTENBERG

Fine Print A STORY ABOUT JOHANN GUTENBERG

Joann Johansen Burch • Discover the amazing story of the man who invented movable type, and the difficulties he overcame to create the technology of printed books for the world. **E+**

Ink on His Fingers

Louise A. Vernon • The story of Gutenberg and the printing of the first Bible, this book for younger students is well worth the search. **E+**

JOHN WYCLIFFE

The Beggars' Bible

Louise A. Vernon • Written for younger students, Vernon's book will transport you to the time of John Wycliffe and Oxford University. Wonderful! **E+**

Morning Star of the Reformation

Andy Thomson • This is the biography of John Wycliffe, the English scholar of the 1300s who gave England the Bible in her own language, sent out men to preach the

Good News to the poor, and inspired John Huss and the later Reformers in their pursuit of truth. **UE+**

John Wycliffe, Man of Courage PUBLISHED BY AMBASSADOR INTERNATIONAL

This fascinating account tells of Wycliffe's impact on England. It sets the stage—long before Wycliffe was born—with King John's submission to Innocent III in 1213 and England's continuing response to the demands of the papacy. **MS+**

TAMERLANE

Tamerlane WORLD LEADERS PAST AND PRESENT

Dennis Wepman • This book contains fascinating insights to this ruthless conqueror, including the fact that his capital city, Samarkand, was covered by a vaulted, glass-windowed roof!! **MS+**

HISTORICAL FICTION

Canterbury Tales

Geoffrey Chaucer; selected, translated, and adapted by Barbara Cohen • A delightful, well-illustrated adaptation of the medieval tales by Chaucer, this book is a wonderful introduction for the whole family. **E+**

Otto of the Silver Hand

Howard Pyle • Historical fiction about the time of the Robber Barons of Germany, this book is an excellent, though troubling, look at the end of the Middle Ages. **MS+**

Men of Iron

Howard Pyle • A classic tale of treason and justice, set in fifteenth-century England. You won't be able to put it down! **MS+**

The Lion of St. Mark

G. A. Henty • The story of Venice, even when it is not fictionalized, is among the most interesting in all of history. Add Henty's touch, describing the struggle Venice had against Genoa in the late 1300s, and you'll find yourself unable to put the book down! **UE+**

EARLY SEA FARING EXPLORERS

Henry the Navigator THE WORLD'S GREAT EXPLORERS

Charnan Simon • This is a wonderful biography of Prince Henry of Portugal, the man who encouraged the discoveries of ocean navigation. He was a fascinating man, and this is a fascinating description of him. **UE+**

First Ships Around the World A CAMBRIDGE TOPIC BOOK

Walter D. Brownlee • Written by a Master Mariner, this is an in-depth look at fourteenth- through sixteenth-century ships, and at Magellan's voyage around the world. It contains a tremendous description of sails, masts, and rigging for "landlubbers." **UE+**

What books did you like best?

_____

_____

_____

_____

The Internet also contains a wealth of information about the Seeds of Reformation & the Late Middle Ages.

What sites were the most helpful?

_____

_____

_____

_____

For more books, use these Dewey Decimal numbers in your library:

Church History: #270

Late Middle Ages: #940.1

Hundred Years' War: #944

Joan of Arc: #944

Scottish History: #941

English History: #942

Tamerlane: #950.2

Gutenberg: #686

John Wycliffe: #200

Historical Fiction: #823

Early Sea Faring Explorers: #946

▶ # Student Self-Evaluation UNIT 6, PHASE 1

Dates and hours:_____

Key Concepts

Rephrase the five Key Concepts of this Unit and confirm your understanding of each:

- Hundred Years' War:

  _____

- Western Church in crisis:

  _____

- The printing press:

  _____

- Exploration & trade:

  _____

- Fall of Constantinople:

  _____

Tools for Self-Evaulation

Evaluate your personal participation in the discussions of this Phase. Bearing in mind that a good participant in a discussion is not always the most vocal participant, ask yourself these questions: Were you an active participant? Did you ask perceptive questions? Were you willing to listen to other participants of the discussion and draw out their opinions? Record your observations and how you would like to improve your participation in the future:

_____

_____

Every time period is too complex to be understood in one Phase of study. Evaluate your current knowledge of the Seeds of the Reformation & the Late Middle Ages. What have you focused on so far? What are your weakest areas of knowledge?

_____

_____

Based on the evaluation of this introduction, project ahead what you would like to study more of in the following Phases:

_____

Phase 2

▶ Research & Reporting

Explore one or more of these areas to discover something significant!

An Overview of The Late Middle Ages

From the early 1300s to the mid-1400s, a tremendous amount of activity took place: earthshaking events, fascinating people, significant developments in the Church, important universities founded, exploration and discovery, and technological breakthroughs. Research the overall impact of the late Middle Ages, and report what you discover.

Prince Henry the Navigator

Prince Henry was an amazing person in history. Research and report on his life and work. What did he accomplish? What kinds of work did he pay to have done? Show how this laid the foundation for the tremendous Age of Exploration.

The Rise of African Slavery by Europeans

Prince Henry of Portugal influenced more than exploration and navigation: Europe's African slave trade began when Prince Henry's ships brought back the first black Africans as slaves. Research and report on this aspect of exploration and discovery.

Hundred Years' War

Research and report on the Hundred Years' War. Who were the key people? What were the issues—both in the early years of the war and in the latter years of the war—for England and for France? How was each country affected by this war in terms of politics, finances, and trade? How was the Peasants' Revolt of 1381 in England tied to the Hundred Years' War? Consider the development of military strategy and weaponry during this war.

Describe the battles of Crécy, Poitiers, and Agincourt, and the siege of Orléans.

Joan of Arc

Learn more about this young French woman who led French troops to victory. To what did she attribute her success? How did the French people receive her? What was the response of the English toward Joan? In what ways did the French king benefit from Joan's actions? Report your findings.

The Wars of Scottish Independence

The story of Scotland's struggle against English rule is as great an adventure as any fictional book could provide. Study and report on William Wallace, Robert the Bruce, and Edward I of England.

Avignon Papacy

Also known as the "Babylonian Captivity of the Papacy," this situation created enormous tension between the Roman Catholic Church and various European countries. Investigate the issues involved and how this impacted England, France, Germany and Italy. How was Philip IV of France involved? What was Catherine of Siena's role in the resolution? Was it fully resolved? What was the overall effect of the Avignon Papacy?

The Great Schism of the Western Church

The Great Schism was an outgrowth of the Avignon Papacy. Research and report on this struggle for power between the popes of the Western Church. How did this schism influence people's view of the papacy? What were some of the results in Western European countries? How did it conclude?

The Black Plague & the Decline of Feudalism

Learn about the Black Plague, also known as The Black Death. How did it cause feudalism to decline? What were the results of this decline? What impact did towns with markets and commercial trade have on feudalism? What took the place of feudalism and how did it develop?

John Wycliffe & Reforming England

John Wycliffe played a major role in England's history, both politically and religiously. Investigate his part in the struggle between England and the papacy. Why did John of Gaunt, brother to the king, defend Wycliffe? In what ways was Wycliffe an early reformer in the style of the Protestant Reformation? How did his followers influence the nation? In what way was Wat Tyler's insurrection considered to have been tied to Wycliffe?

John Huss & Reforming Bohemia

John Huss learned of Wycliffe's teachings, and, taking them to heart, preached powerfully in Bohemia. Though his people were deeply affected by his message (for both religious and nationalistic reasons), the end of his life was quite different than that of Wycliffe. Learn more of this influential man's life and work and of the impact he had on Bohemia.

History of Printing

Research and report on the history of printing. Where did paper come from? How were books created before movable type was invented? How did the technology of printing develop after Gutenberg? Compare it with the process used today.

The Fall of Constantinople

The last city of the Byzantine Empire was captured by the Ottoman Turks. After more than nine hundred years of successfully defending itself against the Muslims, why did the city fall in 1453? How had the circumstances changed? How was Mehmed II the right man for the job of taking Constantinople? What was the effect in the Islamic world of the fall of Constantinople? What was the effect in Christendom?

The Rise of the Ottoman Empire

Research and report on this powerful six-hundred-year-old empire. Where did the Ottomans come from? How did they come to power? In what ways were they affected by the rule of the Mongols and the defeat of the Seljuk Turks? How were early Ottomans viewed by the rest of the Islamic people of the Middle East? How did the decline of the Byzantine Empire accelerate the growth of power of the Ottomans?

Tamerlane

Investigate the life and times of Tamerlane, or Timur the Great. How were his conquests similar to that of Genghis Khan? How were they different? Learn more about Tamerlane's military strategies, which he based on Genghis Khan's tactics. How much land did Tamerlane personally conquer? How does that compare to other conquerors in history?

The Hanseatic League

Discover more about trade and commerce in the late Middle Ages by studying the Hanseatic League of Germany, which was created by German merchants and northern German towns in the late 1200s to protect their commercial enterprises.

▶ Brain Stretchers

Boniface VIII

Boniface VIII claimed that the pope had authority over every living person. Research and describe his time as pope, and the significance of his statement. Compare and contrast Boniface VIII with Gregory VII.

Conciliar Movement

Investigate the conciliar movement at the time of the Great Schism. What was its impact? How did Martin V view the conciliar movement?

Brethren of the Common Life

Research and report on the Brethren of the Common Life. Where did this group begin? How was this a reform movement of the Church? What were the hallmarks of this movement? Read Thomas a Kempis's devotional *The Imitation of Christ,* which is considered to be the most influential book, apart from the Bible, in Christian history. Compare and contrast this with a modern devotional.

The Janissaries

Learn about the Janissaries, who were the elite troops of the Ottoman Empire. Discover why the Ottomans chose to use Christian youths taken from their parents for this service. Report your findings.

The Orthodox Church after the Fall of Constantinople

Discover what happened to the Orthodox Church in Constantinople (renamed Istanbul) under the Muslims. Which country took up the position as leader of the Orthodox Church after 1453? What was their rationale for this advance to the forefront of Orthodoxy?

Create Your Own Research Topic

_____

_____

_____

▶ Timeline

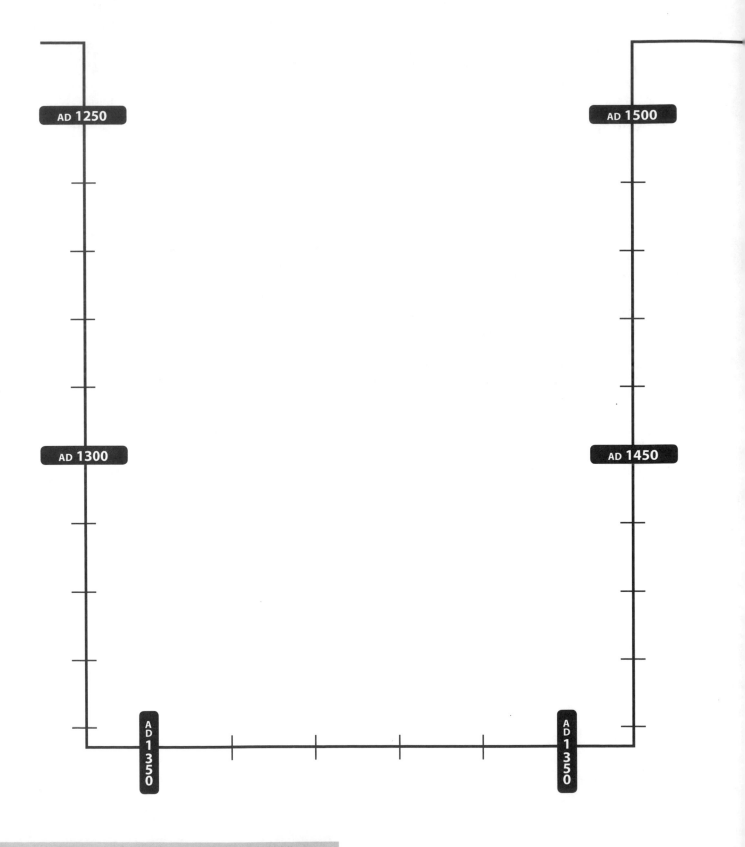

AD 1250

AD 1500

AD 1300

AD 1450

AD 1350

AD 1350

Consider this for your timeline

This time period begins a process of shaking and changing Christian nations dramatically, with events such as the "Babylonian Captivity of the Papacy," the fall of Constantinople, and the voyages of discovery down the coast of Africa. It also brings a tremendous liberty to people to think and to question as printed books and pamphlets become widely available. In the East, the rise of the mighty Ottoman Empire brings a consolidation of Islamic power and causes Eastern Europe to feel threatened. In Africa, the people learn to fear the European ships as slaves are captured and taken away, never to be seen again. All in all, this is a tumultuous and turbulent time.

Key Events

Portuguese explorations of African coast

Scottish Wars of Independence

The Hundred Years' War, including the major battles

Avignon Papacy

Great Schism

Black Plague

Fall of Constantinople

Invention of the printing press

CONSIDER:

This is an excellent time to become more familiar with the terms of weaponry and war. There are many books in the library, as well as online, showing the many different kinds of weaponry used during the Scottish Wars of Independence, the Hundred Years' War, and the assault on Constantinople. Look for these words as you read about the battles, sieges, and wars!

catapult

ballista

trebuchet

claymore

chainmail

halberd

quarterstaff

flanged mace

long bow

crossbow

lance

dirk

longsword

pike

▶ # Words to Watch

Remember—The easiest way to learn a subject is to master its terms:

trade	commerce	captivity	revenue
Unam sanctam	confiscate	conciliarism	reformation
mariner	papal see	treaty	truce
monopoly	caravel	slavery	plague
antipopes	janissaries	navigator	breach

Other words you need to look up:

_____

_____

_____

_____

_____

_____

_____

▶ # Student Self-Evaluation: UNIT SIX, PHASE TWO

Dates and hours:_____

Research Project:

Summarize your research question:

_____

List your most useful sources by author, title and page number or URL where applicable (continue list in margin if necessary):

_____

Now take a moment to evaluate the sources you just listed. Do they provide a balanced view of your research question? Should you have sought an additional opinion? Are your sources credible (if you found them on your own)? Record your observations:

_____

Evaluate your research project in its final presentation. What are its strengths? If you had time to revisit this project, what would you change? Consider giving yourself a letter grade based on your project's merits and weaknesses.

_____

Letter grade: _____

You have just completed an area of specific research in the time of the Seeds of the Reformation & the Late Middle Ages. Now what would you like to explore in the upcoming Phases? Set some objectives for yourself:

_____

Phase 3

► Maps & Mapping

Physical Terrain

» Locate and label Portugal—the land of Prince Henry the Navigator—and the north-western edge of Africa.

» Locate and label the major area where the Hanseatic League was located, as well the Baltic Sea, where much of its ocean-going trade was centered.

» Locate and label the land of the Hundred Years' War, France. As part of this exercise, locate the area of the Avignon Papacy (which is now a part of southern France).

» Locate and label Bohemia, the land of John Huss (now located in the Czech Republic).

Geopolitical

» Locate and label these important battle sites of the Hundred Years' War: Agincourt, Crécy, Poitiers. Also locate and label the cities of Orléans and Rheims (where the kings of France were crowned).

» Locate and label these cities important to the early Reformation: Oxford, London, Prague.

» Draw lines showing the flow of scholars to Italy from Constantinople, and the conquests of Mehmed II from Anatolia into Constantinople and the Balkans.

» On a world map or globe, discover how far Prince Henry's sailors traveled down the coast of Africa. You will need to first locate Cape Bojador (in modern Western Sahara), which was the southernmost point sailors were willing to go prior to Prince Henry.

Explore

» *Christian Outreach:* What is the status of evangelical outreach today in western Africa? What opportunities and what difficulties face those who share the gospel in these areas?

» *Slavery:* After passing Cape Bojador, Portuguese sailors began to take slaves from Africa as part of their commercial enterprises. Investigate the geographical locations of the African slave trade to Europe, beginning in the mid-1400s.

▶ Art Appreciation

Well of Moses by Claus Sluter, 1395–1406
Chartreuse de Champmol, Dijon

One of the artistic styles of the late 1300s and early 1400s found in France, especially under the patronage of the Duke of Burgundy, is called the Franco-Flemish or "International" Style. The most famous of these artists was Claus Sluter from the Netherlands.

» Locate a photo of this sculpture. Notice the vibrancy and intensity of these sculptures. Do they seem realistic or abstract to you? In fact, do these sculptures look like real people? Look at the clothing, hair and facial features. Consider the postures of the sculpted people, especially Isaiah and Daniel. How would you describe their attitude?

The Adoration of the Lamb by Jan van Eyck, completed 1432, Ghent Altarpiece, Belgium

Jan van Eyck was one of the greatest artists to have ever lived. Not only did he masterfully use the newly developed oil paint to create a depth and luminosity of color, but his use of biblical imagery and symbolism is unparalleled in history.

» Look for the central painting of this altarpiece, which shows a Lamb standing on an altar. Give as many of the details as you observe in this painting. How does it tell the story of salvation? Notice the way van Eyck paints even the grass beneath. How would you describe this painting to someone who had never seen it? How would you represent it without words?

CONSIDER:

In this painting, van Eyck shows the Lamb of God, giving His blood on the altar as a sacrifice. But the joyous proclamation of this painting is that the Lamb is not dead! He is alive! Consider that van Eyck finished this awe-filled painting in 1432—almost eighty years before the Reformation began.

▶ Architecture

St. Maclou, Rouen, begun 1434

Increasing wealth in the late Middle Ages allowed for the growth and importance of towns. Because of this, we see more and more elaborate cathedrals, civic buildings, and town palaces of the rich. Some of the names of the more elaborate gothic styles are: Perpendicular (England), Flamboyant Gothic (France), and Manueline (Portugal).

> » Locate photos of the church of St. Maclou in Rouen, France. The style of architecture used is Flamboyant Gothic. The word *flamboyant,* which is French, means "blazing" or "flaming." Can you see how this architecture got its name? How would you describe the ornamental stonework, or tracery, over the windows?

▶ Arts in Action

Select one or more, and let your artistic juices flow!

Beginning Oil Painting

Why not try oil painting? This medium, which dries much more slowly than other paints, allows for a greater freedom in blending and manipulating the paint when it is applied to the canvas. There are books and videos available in libraries and bookstores, or you might try a "paint by numbers" for your first oil painting experience.

Paint Sampler

Oil paints are a much different medium than watercolor or tempera. Try making a "sampler" of different painting mediums. You might want to create the same scene using as many different types of paints as possible. Which do you prefer?

Carve a Sculpture

Mix a batch of plaster of paris and pour it into a clean cardboard milk container. When it dries to the "damp" stage, unmold your uncarved sculpture, and begin creating a masterpiece! Suggestions for carving utensils would be a knife (a *fettling* knife is commonly used by sculptors) or chisel. (Use caution with younger children.) Then, after the plaster has dried, use sandpaper to remove any marks made by the knife. Once the carving is finished, use wet strips of cotton to buff the plaster to a smooth surface. Finally, coat the sculpture with a few coats of milk to seal it.

▶ Science

In 1337 a man at Oxford, William Merlee, attempted the first scientific weather forecasts. Nowadays, with all of the technology used for weather forecasting, it may be hard for us to appreciate what it was like before this science was developed.

Forecasting with hair

» Did you know that human hair will tell you how humid it is? Human hair will be very stretchy when the humidity is high and no stretch when the humidity is low. Try an experiment with a few long hairs. Using a ruler, measure how far a hair can stretch. Record the results, and repeat the process for several days. At the same time, record how "sticky" the weather feels to you, or check the newspaper for humidity levels. How smart was your hair in predicting the humidity?

» Clouds are an excellent guide for forecasting the weather. Learn about the different kinds of clouds and the kinds of weather they indicate. Then keep a weather journal, daily recording the kinds of clouds you have observed, and the kind of weather which followed. Can you begin to predict the weather? Anticipate the weather conditions based on the correlation between clouds and weather over the past days and weeks.

Music

According to the Harvard Dictionary of Music, Germany was the earliest nation to begin singing hymns in its own language. The enthusiasm for singing hymns to God in one's own language was one of the many foretastes of the Reformation.

Discover

To Avert from Men God's Wrath

Jan Hus (1369–1415) • This is the oldest hymn of the Moravian church. It was translated into German by Martin Luther.

Good Christian Men Rejoice

A Latin carol of the 14th century • A favorite Christmas hymn, this was translated into English by John M. Neale. The melody is a German tune, also from the 14th century.

Listen

All Glory, Laud, & Honor MUSIC CD

To Avert from Men God's Wrath by Jan Hus, the Bohemian Reformer

To avert from men God's wrath, Jesus suffered in our stead;
By an ignominious death He a full atonement made;
And by His most precious blood brought us, sinners, nigh to God.
Hither each afflicted soul may repair, though filled with grief;
To the sick, not to the whole, the Physician brings relief;
Fear not, therefore, but draw nigh, Christ will all your want supply.

But examine first your case, whether you be in the faith;
Do you long for pardoning grace? Is your only hope His death?
Then, how e'er your soul's oppressed, come, you are a worthy guest.
He who Jesus' mercy knows is from wrath and envy freed;
Love unto our neighbor shows that we are His flock indeed;
Thus we may in all our ways show forth our Redeemer's praise.

Try This

Sing a rousing, robust version of *Good Christian Men Rejoice*. What effect do the words have on you? Explain whether you think the melody is an appropriate one, given the words of the hymn. What other style of music or melodies might work well with these words? Experiment!

▶ Cooking

During the time of the Avignon Papacy, the popes lived in Avignon, which is today part of southern France. This area is known as Provence, and from this region come some of the most marvelous dishes in French cooking.

Tomatoes Provençal

6 firm ripe tomatoes, 3 to 4 inches in diameter
1 cup coarse, dry white bread crumbs
1 tsp finely cut fresh basil
1 tsp salt
⅓ to ½ c olive oil

Salt (for sprinkling on tomatoes)
½ cup finely chopped fresh parsley
1 clove garlic, minced
Freshly ground pepper

Preheat oven to 375º. Cut the tomatoes in half crosswise, or make wedge shape cuts all the way around the tomato to cut it in half. Scoop out the seeds. Sprinkle the inside of the tomatoes with salt and turn them upside down to drain. In a large mixing bowl, stir together the bread crumbs, parsley, basil, garlic, the 1 tsp salt, and a little bit of pepper. Add enough olive oil to moisten the stuffing, but still leave it crumbly. Fill each tomato half with about 2 tbsp of the crumb mixture, patting it in and letting it mound up a little in the middle. Arrange the tomato halves in one or two lightly oiled shallow baking dishes; do not crowd them! Sprinkle a few drops of oil over each half. Bake in the upper third of the oven for 20–30 minutes, or until the tomatoes are tender but not limp. With a wide metal spatula, transfer the tomatoes to a heated platter and serve them hot.

Bon Appetit!

▶ # Student Self-Evaluation UNIT 6, PHASE 3

Dates and hours:_____

Evaluate your projects

- List which of the activities listed in this Phase you did:

  _____

  _____

- Rate your enthusiasm: _____

  Explain: _____

  _____

- Rate the precision of your approach:_____

  Explain: _____

  _____

- Rate your effort toward the completion of the project: _____

  Explain: _____

  _____

- Ask yourself what worked and what did not. What would you do differently in the future, and what would you repeat?

  _____

  _____

- How specifically did these hands-on activities enhance your knowledge of the Seeds of the Reformation & the Late Middle Ages? What made them worthwhile?

  _____

  _____

- In the first three Phases of this Unit, what aspect of the time period has most captured your imagination? What would you like to creatively pursue to conclude your study?

  _____

  _____

Phase 4

▶ In Your Own Way...

We have seen sailors probe the coasts of Africa under the guidance of Prince Henry of Portugal; England and France at war for more than one hundred years; French popes in Avignon while the mainstream pope resides in Rome; Wycliffe and Huss challenge the institutional church; and Joan of Arc lead France toward victory. In the East, the Ottoman Turks have successfully captured Constantinople, the last bastion of the Byzantine Empire. Now, choose a selection of these activities, or create your own, which will best express what you have learned from this Unit.

LINGUISTICS

Journalism

The year is 1453. The Hundred Years' War has finally come to an end. Your editor for the English paper *News From Abroad* has asked you to write a recap for the readers. Remember that your audience doesn't want an in-depth description, and is not happy with the loss of its French territory. Your job is to remind them of their former victories and the accrued glory.

You are a Portugese sailor on one of Prince Henry's sailing vessels. Your captain has informed the crew that you are going to sail past Cape Bojador. Write your parents and tell them what others are saying about what might happen, and then share your own opinion of the likely outcome. Don't worry your parents!!!

Interview Martin V, the pope elected at the end of the Great Schism, for the Church magazine,

The Insider. Ask his opinion about the Avignon papacy and the Great Schism. Discover for your readers whether Pope Martin has any idea how to keep this from happening again in the future!

Playing with Words

Finish this limerick:

Now, Johann invented, one day,
A way to print books that would stay . . .

Prose

Write and illustrate a story for children about the life of John Wycliffe or John Huss. Be sure to show how their lives impacted the Church and their respective countries.

Write a first person account of the Battle of Stirling Bridge from the perspective of a Scottish participant. Remember, the Scots were the underdogs!

ART

Painting/Drawing

Paint in the style of Jan van Eyck. It may be a biblical scene, a portrait, or a scene from everyday life. What aspect of his painting style do you wish to imitate?

Draw a depiction of the fall of Constantinople, with the Ottomans overwhelming the Byzantine walls. Be sure to show that the Ottomans outnumbered the Byzantines by about fifteen to one and had the largest cannon yet built.

Graphic Design

Create a T-shirt for the French soldiers who were led by Joan of Arc. As you create the design, keep in mind that these soldiers might be quite disgruntled at the lack of honor given their champion by the newly crowned king. Articulate their enthusiasm and honor.

Design a full-color sales brochure for the Hanseatic League. Their business is moving product (buying from one place and selling to another). Your job is to accelerate the pace.

Cartooning

Create a political cartoon showing merchants devising unexpected ways to outwit the robber barons of Germany.

MUSIC

Compose

Compose a song which laments the fall of Constantinople in 1453. If it is from the perspective of a Greek Orthodox believer, the lament might reflect the death of the empire and the loss of Hagia Sophia. If from the perspective of the West, consider the previous losses of the Crusades, and that this might seem to be the final loss of Christian lands in the East to the Muslims.

Performance Practice

With your teacher's help, select an appropriate piece of music which expresses some particular aspect studied in this unit, whether from the Hundred Years' War or the Early Reformation. Prepare and perform the piece for an audience. Communicate with your audience the reason for your selection either in the program notes or in a short speech.

DRAMA

Comedy

Depict Johann Gutenberg in his efforts to create the first moveable type printing press. Remember, if it had been easy, he wouldn't have been the first.

Drama

Create a scene showing a strategy meeting of military leaders who have been given the impossible task of stopping Tamerlane. They might want to interview a survivor of one of Tamerlane's assaults.

To the English, Edward I was a good king, to the Scottish he was a usurping tyrant. In dramatic form, tell the story of this (in)famous king.

Puppetry

With puppets, portray the story of Robert the Bruce and the lesson in perseverance he learned from the spider in the cave. Be sure to give the spider a starring role!

With the use of puppets, produce a children's version of the Hundred Years' War. Your goal is to help younger children understand the reasons for the war, and how people in each country felt about the war in its various phases.

Prop Needs

_____

_____

Costume Ideas

_____

_____

Role/Player

_____

_____

Set Suggestions

_____

_____

MOVEMENT

Pantomime

Pantomime the sailors aboard Prince Henry's ship, endeavoring to get beyond Cape Bojador. If there is a small group working on this presentation, one could portray the captain who is under Prince Henry's orders, while the others act the part of very reluctant, fearful sailors.

Miniature Action

Choose one of the battles of the Scottish Wars of Independence or of the fall of Constantinople, then create a miniature of that battle to display what happened.

Dance

Catherine of Siena, a Catholic mystic of the late Middle Ages, reconciled the French pope at Avignon to the idea of returning the papacy to Rome. Choreograph a dance which reflects her peacemaking labors. Remember that the whole Western Church had been scandalized by this situation.

CONCEPTUAL DESIGN

Desktop Publishing

Gutenberg's invention is all the rage. Unfortunately, it is large and bulky, unsuitable for carting from town to town. Your job is to design a portable printing press using the new technology of moveable type—one that will fit on top of a table. This miniaturized version of Gutenberg's press will aid and support itinerant preachers as they create individualized tracts for each village and city they visit.

CREATE YOUR OWN EXPRESSION

_____

_____

_____

_____

6

► # Student Self-Evaluation: UNIT 6, PHASE 4

Dates and hours:_____

Evaluate your projects

- What creative project did you choose:

  _____

- What did you expect from your project, and how does the final project compare to your initial expectations?

  _____

- What do you like about your project? What would you change?

  _____

In Conclusion

- Revisit the five Key Concepts from the beginning of this Unit. Explain how your understanding of and appreciation for each has grown over the course of your study.

  - _____

    _____

  - _____

    _____

  - _____

    _____

  - _____

    _____

  - _____

    _____

- Record your concluding thoughts on the Seeds of the Reformation & the Late Middle Ages:

  _____

  _____

The Renaissance & the Reformation

Key Concepts

- The Renaissance
- The Reformation
- The Age of Exploration
- The New World
- The Scientific Revolution

Michelangelo's Pieta in St. Peter's Basilica in Rome

The Just Shall Live By Faith . . .

The year AD 1500 is considered to be the start of the High Renaissance, the celebrated *rebirth* of art, architecture, literature, and philosophy in Italy as people looked back to the cultures of the ancient Greeks and Romans. It is amazing, however, to see that historians name AD 1527 as the end of the Renaissance. Twenty-seven years makes just a small splash in the history of the world, yet artists, teachers, writers, philosophers, photographers, students, filmmakers, and even tourists spend much time and money to see the highly visible remains of the High Renaissance. One might wonder why it ended so abruptly. The answer is simply that 1527 was the year the troops of the Holy Roman Emperor sacked Rome.

Within those three brief and tumultuous decades, another event took place, which has had an even greater, continuing impact on our world. On

7

October 31, 1517, a German monk posted on a cathedral door his criticism of the lucrative industry of selling *indulgences,* which monetarily profited the Western Church but crippled spiritually ignorant people. With the help of the printing press, the tiny spark of his one action blazed into a consuming fire, birthing the Reformation and Counter-Reformation. This seismic impact shook the Roman Catholic Church to its core, violently split Europe into division between Protestant and Catholic countries, contributed to the rise of nationalism, promoted Bible translations into the languages of the people, and provided a fresh impetus to carry the message of the gospel to the world.

Strife in Europe

The tiny spark of his one action blazed into a consuming fire.

How did all of this come about? What were the circumstances, which led to the chasm-like break—both culturally and spiritually—from the Middle Ages? To begin to answer these questions, let us consider the state of wars, civil wars, exploration, and greed developing in Europe since 1453.

Almost immediately after the end of the Hundred Years War, a civil war, known as the War of the Roses, broke out in England. As the descendants of Edward III struggled for power, they generated a *war between relatives* as one branch of the royal family, known as the House of Lancaster, fought another branch, known as the House of York. This devastating war, which brought turmoil to England for thirty years, finally resolved with the ascension of Henry VII, father of the infamous Henry VIII.

Other regions of Europe were also facing issues of strife and division. Peasants in the German area of Salzburg, facing impossible taxes levied by their archbishop, began a revolt in 1458, which spread to other areas of Germany. Thirty years later, Flemish towns in the Netherlands rose in rebellion against the Hapsburg ruler, Maximilian I (who would soon be Holy Roman Emperor). The French king, Charles VIII, embarked on a war with Italy to capture Naples for himself, which embroiled the French in an ongoing series of wars in Italy for the next fifty years. Italy itself continued to be a battlefield between various European rulers intent on adding a piece of Italy's glory to their crown. Spain, which was united in 1479 due to the marriage of Ferdinand of Aragon and Isabella of Castile ten years earlier, labored to finish the *Reconquista*—the recapture of all of Spain from the Muslim Moors.

Ferdinand and Isabella's triumph over the Moors in 1492 allowed them enough breathing space to finance an Italian's westward voyage to Asia. As we are well aware, Christopher Columbus's epoch-making journey did not bring him to the East but rather to an entirely new world for the Europeans. The shifting of the balance of power from the Mediterranean to the Atlantic slowly commenced as Spain's conquests brought it to the forefront of Europe—as the new colonies in Central and South America increasingly poured silver and gold into its treasuries. The native people of this new world, who were by far the greater treasure in the eyes of the One who created them, were not prepared to defend themselves against these Spanish conquistadors and the diseases they brought with them. Tragically, what profited Europeans decimated the indigenous people of the Americas. Vast numbers of them died as a result of this contact.

In the same year that Columbus sailed west across the Atlantic, a Spaniard by the name of Rodrigo Borgia came to power as Pope Alexander VI. This was not to be a model papacy—while still a cardinal, Borgia had been rebuked by the reigning pope for living as a *Renaissance prince,* a synonym for greed and corruption. Unfortunately, his unscrupulous, pleasure-loving lifestyle was not changed by his new station in life. Ultimately, with a blatant disregard for morality and an unquenched desire to promote his family to positions of power and wealth (which is called *nepotism*), Alexander VI unwittingly contributed to the Reformation.

One of the most outspoken of Alexander VI's critics was the Italian preacher Girolamo Savonarola. Brought to the Renaissance city of Florence by Lorenzo de' Medici in 1490, Savonarola proved to be less of an ornament to the Medici rule of Florence and more of a fierce watchdog, vocalizing against the Medicis as well as against tyranny, corruption, and the paganism lurking inside Renaissance culture and the Roman Church. After Lorenzo's death in 1492, Savonarola prophesied the coming of a foreign army to Florence—which happened in 1494 when Charles VIII of France invaded Italy. Negotiating with the French king, Savonarola was able to spare the city. Thus began his own rule over Florence, and his attempt to create a Christian republic in the heart of Italy that might reform the State and the Church. It lasted but a short time. With Savonarola's loyalty to the king who had invaded Italy but spared Florence, and with his outspoken preaching against the excesses and abuses of the Roman clergy (including the pope), Savonarola's enemies in Italy worked hard to remove him from power. In 1498 they successfully seized him, orchestrated a mockery of a trial, and executed him. Though he was a loyal Catholic in word and deed, his eight years of powerful preaching against the evils of his time give evidence, yet again, of the circumstances within the Church and the Renaissance, which brought forth the Reformation.

> Tragically, what profited Europeans decimated the indigenous people of the Americas.

Beyond the borders of Europe, the Ottoman sultans who had already established their capital at Constantinople continued the process of consolidating power in the Balkans of Europe, the lands of the eastern Mediterranean, and Anatolia in Asia Minor. This steady growth of the Ottoman empire would soon come to the attention of the rulers of Europe as they were threatened on their very door step, at the siege of Vienna in 1529, by Suleiman I.

Warring Popes in the Renaissance

> *With Italy in shambles and under foreign attack, Pope Julius II went to war.*

The sixteenth century had dawned on an Italy that was being torn apart, not only by foreign armies, but by its own papal army fighting for control of the Papal States. Commanding this army was the notorious Cesare Borgia, illegitimate son of the Spanish Pope Alexander VI, and the inspiration for Machiavelli's book *The Prince*. Unbelievably, the purpose of Borgia's military attacks on various Italian cities—using the papal army—was to fashion for himself his own private state within Italy. It all came to naught, however, when his father died, leaving him without papal support or finances. In fact, not only was the new pope Julius II, who came to power in 1503, not a supporter of the Borgias, he was their bitter enemy. This seems understandable when we learn that the Borgia pope had sought to assassinate him!

With Italy in shambles and under foreign attack, Pope Julius II went to war. He is known to history as "the warring pope" and the "savior of Italy" since he led the fight to restore the Papal states and to oust the French

	Germany	Italy	Britain	Holy Roman Empire	Switzerland
1516-1520	1517: Luther protests indulgences 1518: Luther refuses to recant at Diet of Augsburg 1519: Luther questions infallibility of pope 1520: Luther burns papal bull; beginning of Anabaptists; Lucas Cranach: "Luther" portrait	1516: Michelangelo: "Moses;" Raphael: "The Sistine Madonna" 1517: Leo X publishes bull for 5-year peace in Christendom 1518: Raphael: portrait of Leo X with his cardinals 1520: Papal bull giving Luther 60 days to recant	1516: Princess Mary born, daughter of Henry VIII 1520: England signs commercial treaty with France	1519: Charles I becomes Charles V, Holy Roman Emperor	1516: Erasmus publishes Greek NT 1518: Zwingli goes to Zurich to be "People's Preacher" 1519: Swiss Reformation begins 1520: Zwingli denounces monasticism, purgatory and relics
1521-1525	1521: Charles V condemns Luther at Diet of Worms; translation of NT into German begun 1524: Protestant princes meet at Ulm against Charles V; Peasants' Revolt—50,000 killed 1525: Luther marries	1521: Leo X excommunicates Luther: "heretic"; Pope Leo X dies 1523: Clement VII becomes pope 1524: French driven out of Italy 1525: Spanish & Germans defeat French and Swiss—Fr. king imprisoned, Charles V master of Italy	1521: Henry VIII proclaimed "Defender of Faith" by Leo X 1525: Tyndale's English translation of NT printed & smuggled into England	1521: Charles V grants Ferdinand of Austria the Hapsburg possessions in Germany 1523: First martyrs of Reformation	1523: Zurich abolishes religious ornaments 1525: Anabaptists expelled from Zurich; Zurich abolishes Catholic Mass

from Italy. He was also the pope noted as being the foremost "Patron of the Arts." It was Julius II who convinced Michelangelo to paint the ceiling of the Sistine Chapel, utilized Bramante as his architect, and hired Raphael to paint frescoes in the Vatican. Though this has provided the world with some of the most beautiful art and architecture from the High Renaissance, it did not profit the spiritual condition of the Roman Church, which was, at this point, equally in shambles.

There is no substitute in the Church for the work of God's Spirit.

Interestingly enough, Erasmus (who would become a pivotal scholar and satirist of the Renaissance/Reformation) had the opportunity to see in person the triumphant Julius II leading his army into an Italian city in 1506. It was an unforgettable and unsettling sight, one which he memorialized in a famous satire, *Julius exclusus e coelis.* Martin Luther, the German monk who launched the Reformation, also encountered Pope Julius II in Rome while on a diplomatic mission for his monastery. That experience, along with the general state of the Church in Rome, left Luther utterly disillusioned.

During the early 1500s, though there were occasional glimmers of life and vitality within a small selection of the Western Church, there was much

Spain/Portugal	France	Ottomans	Asia/Africa
1516: Archduke Charles becomes Charles I	1516: Pope Leo X & Francis I sign agreement: French kings choose clergy; da Vinci invited to France	1516: Selim I defeats Egyptians, takes Syria	1516: Ming dynasty continues in China; African slave trade continues to supply slaves to Caribbean & America—used in mining and agriculture
1517: Charles I arrives in Spain from Netherlands; Portuguese reach China		1517: Ottomans rule Egypt, Syria, Palestine, Arabia	
1518: License to import 4,000 African slaves to Spain's American colonies; Spanish discover Mexico		1520: Suleiman I—the Magnificent—is new Ottoman Sultan	1517: Portuguese set up a factory on island of Ceylon (Sri Lanka)
1519: Cortez in Mexico—brings Arabian horses to North America; Magellan begins earth's circumnavigation; Spanish explore Gulf of Mexico—Florida to Vera Cruz			1518: Barbary States of Tunis and Algiers; East Asian porcelain arrives in Europe
1520: Magellan passes Straits of Magellan into Pacific; chocolate brought to Spain from Mexico; Portuguese traders in China			
1521: Cortez conquers Aztecs; Magellan killed in Philippines; Spanish explore N. American coast to S. Carolina (Atlantic)	1525: Francis I imprisoned by Charles V until 1526 when Treaty of Madrid signed	1521: Ottomans invade Hungary	1525: Babur, descendant of Genghis Khan & Tamerlane, invades Punjab (Pakistan)
1522: Ignatius Loyola begins "Spiritual Exercises"; Magellan's expedition completed by the remaining sailors; Spanish discover Peru		1522: Suleiman I captures Rhodes from Knights of St. John	
1523: Portuguese are ousted from China; Spanish found town of Jamaica		1525: 7-year peace treaty signed with King of Hungary	
1524: Spanish discover Hudson River			

that was dead and decaying. And the visible heart of the Western Church, Rome, seemed to many to have rotted to the core. We must remember that there is no substitute in the Church for the work of God's Spirit, His life and His resurrection power. No amount of artistic beauty or formalized ritual will suffice if the supernatural vitality of Christ is not present in the congregation. This was the crisis for many Christians in this time.

> *The same desire for profit shown by the Portuguese also fueled the Spanish conquistadors.*

Age of Exploration

Before we look at the Reformation, which was in part the God-breathed response to this crisis, let us consider what was taking place during this same time of the Portuguese race against the Spanish for the spices and wealth of the East. Remember that the Portuguese, under the initial sponsorship of Prince Henry the Navigator, had been slowly and steadily exploring further and further south along the west coast of Africa.

	Germany	Italy	Britain	Holy Roman Empire	Switzerland
1526-1530	1529: Zwingli and Luther disagree about Lord's supper 1530: Charles V declares Protestants theologically defeated; Protestant princes form Schmalkaldic League against Charles V	1527: Armies of Charles V sack Rome, imprison Pope Clementine VII; end of High Renaissance	1528: Reformation begins in Scotland; Henry VIII seeks divorce from Catherine of Aragon	1526: Anabaptists settle as "Moravian Brothers" in Moravia (part of Bohemia) 1528: Anabaptist burned at the stake in Vienna 1529: Turks lay siege to Vienna unsuccessfully	1529: Civil war erupts between Protestants & Catholics
1531-1535	1534: Luther's translation of Bible into German printed	1534: Paul III becomes pope	1531: Henry VIII Supreme Head of Church in England 1533: Cranmer annuls marriage to Catherine; Henry marries Anne Boleyn; Henry VIII excommunicated; Princess Elizabeth born 1534: Church of England separates from Rome; "Oath of Succession" recognizes Elizabeth as heir 1535: Several Catholics executed for refusing to sign Oath; Holbein: portrait of Henry VIII	1535: Charles V conquers Tunis; frees 20,000 slaves	1531: Zwingli killed in battle

In 1488 Bartholomew Diaz rounded the Cape of Good Hope, the southernmost tip of Africa, becoming the first European to do so. This opened the door for the Portuguese sea route eastward to India and the Spice Islands. However, it would be nearly ten years before the Portuguese voyaged through that open door. In the meantime, as we have seen, Christopher Columbus laid his startling proposition before Ferdinand and Isabella of Spain, a journey *west* to the spices. This was not to be a step-by-step, Portuguese-style approach to a new sea route to Asia. It was a one-throw-of-the-dice gamble based on Columbus's beliefs that, first, only 2,500 miles separated Asia from Europe if one traveled westward and, second, it would be clear sailing on the ocean—no landmass lay between them.

Think about it. This was, for the Europeans of that time, a mad race to the Asian finish line, with the victors taking the spoils. The Portuguese were slow but Columbus, as it turned out, was wrong. Not only is Asia approximately 10,000 miles west of Europe but

A German Augustinian monk and professor took the momentous step of arguing against the practice of selling indulgences.

Spain/Portugal	France	Ottomans	Asia/Africa
1526: Portuguese in New Guinea 1528: Venezuela colonized 1529: Franciscan mission in Mexico 1530: Portuguese colonize Brazil	1529: Treaty of Cambrai between Francis I & Charles V—France relinquishes Italian possessions	1526: Ottomans kill king of Hungary in battle 1529: Ottomans attack Austria	1526: Babur, crowned in Delhi, founds Mogul dynasty 1530: Emperor Babur dies
1532: Pizarro leads expedition to Peru; Sugar cane cultivated in Brazil 1533: Pizarro executes Inca ruler 1534: Loyola founds Jesuits	1533: Reformation in France; John Calvin converted 1534: 24 Protestants martyred in Paris; Calvin flees to Switzerland; Cartier first voyage to N. America 1535: Cartier's second voyage—reaches Quebec & island of Montreal	1532: Ottomans attack Hungary	

there were, in fact, *two* connected landmasses between Europe and Asia. Thus, Portugal emerged as the victor in this contest when Vasco da Gama arrived in Calicut, India on May 20, 1498.

Getting to the finish line first did not provide the Portuguese with the spoils they had anticipated. Da Gama found that the people of India were far more sophisticated than he expected, and his cheap trade goods—which had been acceptable along the coast of Africa—were not enticing to the Hindu ruler or hostile Muslim traders. No treaty between the spice countries of Asia and Portugal was made on this voyage. It was on da Gama's second voyage that he finally was able to cement alliances, often through the use of savage military force. All the violence, treachery, and cruelty done by *Christian* diplomats against Hindus and Muslims defied God's clearly stated commands in the Old and New Testament. And all these things were

	Germany	Italy	Britain	Holy Roman Empire	Switzerland
1536-1540	1539: Religious Truce of Frankfurt grants limited toleration of Reformation in Germany	1536: Michelangelo: "Last Judgment" on altar wall of Sistine Chapel 1537: Pope Paul III gives oral approval of Loyola and Jesuits 1539: Michelangelo makes new plans for the Capitol, Rome 1540: Jesuits receive official confirmation from pope	1536: Queen Anne beheaded; Queen Jane Seymour; Dissolution of monasteries 1537: Queen Jane dies after giving birth to Prince Edward 1538: Cromwell orders a copy of English Bible to be set up in all English churches 1540: Henry VIII marries Anne of Cleves—annulled; marries Catherine Howard	1536: Tyndale martyred near Brussels	1536: Calvin's Christian Religion Institutes; Erasmus dies 1538: Calvin expelled from Geneva
1541-1545		1541: Francis Xavier sails for India (Jesuit missionary) 1542: Xavier sets up mission to Portuguese area of India; Pope sets up Inquisition 1545: Pope Paul III calls for Council of Trent (1564) Counter Reformation; Xavier sets up Jesuit mission in Spice Islands	1541: John Knox leads Calvinist Reformation in Scotland 1542: Queen Catherine Howard executed; Mary, Queen of Scots, at six days of age 1543: Henry VIII marries Catherine Parr 1545: Prince Edward educated by Protestant leaders	1545: Truce between Charles V, Ferdinand and Suleiman I	1541: Calvin returns to Geneva, establishes theocratic regime
1546-1550	1546: Civil war between Charles V & Schmalkaldic League; Luther dies 1547: Charles V defeats Schmalkaldic League	1546: Michelangelo designs the dome of St. Peter's, and works to complete construction 1549: Xavier sets up Jesuit mission in Japan 1550: Pope Julius III	1547: Henry VIII dies, Edward VI king of England		

done because Portugal desired exclusive control over the spice trade. As is so often seen throughout history, breaking spiritual laws for monetary gain does not lead to blessing. Portugal never obtained supremacy of the Indian Ocean as the expanse was much too large for its small fleet, and it was never able to wield exclusive control of the trade. The distance, the difficulties, and the desire of individual sailors to get rich at the Crown's expense meant that far less profit arrived in Portugal than was expected. And, as we'll see in the next Unit, Portugal would soon be swallowed up by Philip II of Spain.

Spain did not get to the spices. It was not deterred by that loss, however, once gold was rumored to have been found somewhere in the yet-unnamed new world in the 1510s. The same desire for profit shown by the Portuguese also fueled the Spanish conquistadors, once these rumors

Spain/Portugal	France	Ottomans	Asia/Africa
1538: "America" and "North America" used for the first time on maps 1540: Spanish discover Grand Canyon	1536: War between Francis I & Charles V resumes	1540: Peace treaty signed between Venice and Ottomans at Constantinople	1540: Afghan, Sher Shah—not descendant of Babur—captures the throne, becomes Emperor of Delhi
1541: Coronado's expedition across New Mexico; de Soto discovers Mississippi River; Spanish explore Amazon River 1543: First Protestants martyred by Inquisition; Portuguese reach Japan 1544: Silver mines discovered in Peru		1541: Ottomans annex Austria 1545: Truce between Charles V, Ferdinand, & Suleiman I	1542: Jesuit missionaries in Goa, India 1543: First Europeans enter Japan—shipwrecked Portuguese sailors
1548: Silver mines in Mexico mined by Spanish 1549: Jesuit missionaries in South America 1550: Spain at peak of political & economic power	1547: Francis I dies, Henry II king of France	1548: Ottomans occupy Tabriz, Persia	1549: Jesuit missionaries begin work in Japan

surfaced. And the native people of this fertile land were often subjected to the same kind of violence, treachery, and cruelty by the Christian Spaniards that the Hindus and Muslims of India had experienced at the hands of the Portuguese. The desire for gold, spices, and wealth proved a deadly temptation which overrode any religious background these soldiers and sailors might have had. *Author's note: Though some might lay the blame for these atrocities on deficiencies in the Catholic faith of the Spanish & Portuguese, later in history, as we shall see, Protestants failed as fully as Catholics when greed was involved. Difficult as this is for Christians to comprehend, it is, nevertheless, the truth. We need to reflect on this and in utter sincerity pray, "Search me, O God, and know my heart, try me and know my anxieties, and see if there is any wicked way in me, and lead me in the way everlasting!" (Psalm 139:23–24).*

The Reformation

However, before Spanish conquistadors actually found the gold of the Aztec (1519) and Inca (1532), significant developments continued unfolding in the Old World. In 1513 Giovanni de Medici, the second son of Lorenzo de Medici, was elected Pope Leo X. Raised in the glittering, pre-Savonarola court of Florence, with the best education money could buy, Giovanni was very much a product of the High Renaissance. With his ascendancy to the papacy, Leo X set out to enjoy it. In many ways, the adage "like father, like son" held true. He lavishly spent money (both the Church's and his own) to finish the construction of St. Peter's Basilica, to fill the Vatican Library, and to support the artists and architects of the Renaissance. He was also kept busy protecting Italy from the power-hungry armies of France and Spain. This became very trying when, in 1519, the young king of Spain became the new Holy Roman Emperor: historically, the Emperor had certain proprietary rights (or, at least, claimed them) to Italy. As the newly created Spanish strength was bound to the might of the Holy Roman Empire in nineteen year old Charles V, this new sovereign became a power to be reckoned with.

As it turned out, Charles V was not the greatest of Leo X's troubles. Two years prior to the election of Emperor Charles, Martin Luther,

The Sistine Chapel by Michelangelo, Vatican City

a German Augustinian monk and professor, took the momentous step of arguing against the practice of selling indulgences. According to the local Dominican salesman Johann Tetzel, indulgences actually provided forgiveness of sins—if one had the money to pay for it. Studying the newly released Greek New Testament Erasmus had compiled, Luther had become convinced doctrinally and experientially that sins were forgiven based on what Jesus did on the cross, and that Christians were to live by faith in Him. This reliance on Jesus contrasted completely with the medieval system that relied on man to relieve himself of the penalty of his own choices through good works, through indulgences, through pilgrimage, or any of the other means to be justified. The significance of this small action was exponentially magnified through the publication and wide distribution of Luther's arguments in Germany and Europe. The annoying actions of an unimportant monk in an out-of-the-way town suddenly blossomed into a full-scale threat to the papacy and the Catholic Church.

In the same year that Martin Luther posted his 95 Theses to the Wittenberg cathedral door, the Ottoman ruler Selim I defeated the Egyptian and Syrian Mamluks. This completed his subjugation of the Middle East, placing Egypt, Syria, Palestine, and Arabia under his control. When the keys to the city of Mecca were presented to Selim I, it made the Ottoman sultan, for the first time, the acknowledged leader of the Muslim world. With a united Islam, the threat to a divided Europe increased significantly.

In what ways was Europe divided at this time? Consider the chart on the previous pages. See the numerous personalities and events in the cataclysmic changes ushered in by the Reformation, both within the Church and also in the political realm. Additionally, notice the approach of the Muslim Ottomans to Christian Europe, the activities of the Spanish in the Americas, the Jesuits, and the Counter Reformation of the Catholic Church.

In 1550, as the chart shows, Spain was at its height of power due to the extraordinary riches of the New World—gold and silver—pouring into the treasury. Protestantism did not gain a foothold in Spain, and the king was also the Holy Roman Emperor. Charles V saw, in the year 1554, his greatest dreams of universal dominion come within the grasp of his family when his son Philip married Queen Mary of England. The English Parliament, however, did not cooperate with Charles V's vision. They steadfastly refused to give Philip the right to govern England in any way, regardless of his marriage to their queen. With no forthcoming crown nor heir, Philip took leave of his wife and sailed away, never to return. Charles V, after one more fruitless attack against France, abdicated his throne. He gave the Holy Roman Empire to his brother, Ferdinand, and then handed over the Spanish Empire (including Spain, its colonies, and the Netherlands) to his son. This son became known to the world as Philip II, Catholic leader of the fight against Protestantism, wooer of the Protestant hand of Queen Elizabeth, and the architect of the fated Spanish Armada—all of which we will see in the next Unit!◀

Phase 1

▶ Listen to This

What in the World? VOL. 2

DISC THREE:

» The Renaissance (track 9)

DISC FOUR:

» Exploration & Politics (track 1)

» The Reformation & its Consequences (track 2)

True Tales VOL. 2

DISC THREE:

» Cortez (track 1)

Digging Deeper VOL. 2

DISC THREE: THE REFORMING CHURCH

» Introduction through Counter-Reformation & Thirty Years' War (tracks 1–6)

▶ Read For Your Life

The Holy Bible

» **Luther's enlightenment:** Habbakuk 2:4, Romans 1:17

» **Contrast with medieval system of indulgences:** Romans 5:1–11; Romans 8:2; Galatians 2:16

» **God's gifts of righteousness and grace bestowed on us:** Ephesians 2:8–10; Philippians 3:8–11; 2 Corinthians 5:21; 2 Timothy 1:9

» **Authority and power of Scripture:** 2 Timothy 3:15–17, Hebrews 4:12

» **Living faith:** James 2:14–26

» **Scripture neglected during Reformation:** 1 John 4:7–5:3

► Talk Together

Opinion Column

» Who was the most interesting or controversial person you encountered in your introduction to the Renaissance and Reformation?

» Leonardo da Vinci was considered to have been a true Renaissance man because of his studies in so many areas, including painting, sculpture, anatomy, architecture, mathematics, philosophy and engineering. What words would you use to describe da Vinci? What subjects of interest do you have in common with him?

» Some people consider Columbus a hero, while others consider him a villain. Why do you think there are such different opinions about the same person? What do you think about him?

» Pope Alexander VI drew up the "Line of Demarcation" in the New World, which gave Portugal all non-Christian territories east of the line and Spain all non-Christian territories west of the line. If you were English, what do you think your attitude would be about this line?

» Pope Leo X was the son of Lorenzo de Medici, one of the foremost patrons of Renaissance art. Knowing his background, what do you suppose Pope Leo meant when he said, "God has given us the papacy, let us enjoy it!"?

» Imagine you were among the students studying theology in Wittenberg. What do you think your reaction would have been when you attended church on All Saints Day in 1517 and saw what Martin Luther had posted on the door—his 95 theses against indulgences?

Critical Puzzling

» Charles V was one of the most important and powerful political figures of his time. He governed Spain, the Netherlands, the Holy Roman Empire, and parts of Italy. He was involved in Luther's trial, Henry VIII's request for annulment, and battles with France. From what you have read and heard thus far, how would you evaluate his reign in terms of his influence and activities?

Key People (World)

Lorenzo de Medici
Patron of the arts

Ferdinand & Isabella
Completed Reconquista

Christopher Columbus
Opened route to New World

Leonardo da Vinci
Epitomized Renaissance

Vasco da Gama
Sea route to India

Copernicus
Heliocentric theory

Ferdinand Magellan
First to circumnavigate

Cortez
Conquered Aztecs

Henry VIII
Pivotal English king

Charles V
Hapsburg Emperor

Mary I
English queen

Ivan IV
First Russian tsar

Philip II
Powerful Spanish king

» *"Power corrupts, and absolute power corrupts absolutely."* In what ways does this statement apply to the reign of Pope Alexander VI, perhaps the most notorious clergyman in history?

» Consider the view held by humanists during the Renaissance which begins with Man, ends with Man, and centers on Man. In what ways does this differ from the biblical view—which begins with God, ends with God, and centers on our relationship to God—in relation to politics, art, culture, literature, families, or ethics?

» Ferdinand and Isabella forced the Jews to convert or leave Spain (without their treasures) even after the Jews had helped to support Ferdinand and Isabella's war against the Moors. What do you think of the concept of creating a Christian nation by ejecting everyone who does not profess Christianity? Support your ideas from Scripture.

» When Copernicus published his book describing his heliocentric theories (the planets revolve around the sun), it shocked many people. In what ways might this theory, as opposed to the Greek/medieval concept that the planets and sun revolve around the earth, impact people's religious beliefs?

» The conquistadors of Spain made many statements about going in the name of Christ and for the glory of God as they conquered and colonized the New World. They also made many statements about gold and personal glory as they enslaved and even destroyed the native inhabitants in the process. Do you think their actions reflected or hindered the Gospel? Explain your reasoning.

▶ Resources for Digging Deeper

Choose a few books that look interesting, or find your own.

THE RENAISSANCE

The Renaissance

Mary Quigley • An overview of the culture and lifestyle of the Renaissance, written in an engaging manner for younger students. **E+**

Rats, Bulls, and Flying Machines A
HISTORY OF THE RENAISSANCE AND REFORMATION

Deborah Mazzotta Prum • This is a fascinating description of events, people, and ideas in this pivotal time period. Highly recommended! **UE+**

The Renaissance and The New World

Giovanni Caselli • Different cultures experienced this time period in various ways. Take a quick trip through these differences, from 1400–1780, in this thoughtfully conceived book. **UE+**

The Story of the Renaissance

Suzanne Strauss Art • An excellent look at the Renaissance, Reformation, and the conquest of the New World. **MS+**

Renaissance

Alison Cole • This gorgeous, full-color book is packed with paintings, statues, architecture, and descriptions. (Note: this book reflects the artistic appreciation for the human form during the Renaissance.) **MS+**

A Renaissance Town

Jacqueline Morley & Mark Peppe • Rather than taking a brief look at many countries as does the title listed above, this book focuses on one place in the Renaissance, the city of Florence. Fascinating! **UE+**

Famous Men of the Renaissance & Reformation

Rob Shearer • This is a wonderful introduction to the people of this time period, with descriptions of such people as Lorenzo de Medici, Michelangelo, John Wycliffe, Martin Luther, and many more. **UE+**

ARTISTS OF THE RENAISSANCE

Leonardo da Vinci

Diane Stanley • Diane Stanley's books are a treasure to see as well as read, and this one is no exception. Be introduced to da Vinci and his art through this wonderful book. **E+**

Michelangelo

Diane Stanley • Another great introduction to a famous Renaissance artist. **E+**

Leonardo da Vinci A HORIZON CARAVEL BOOK

Jay Williams • A detailed and wonderful look at this "Renaissance Man"—the painter, engineer, scientist, and inventor. **UE+**

The Apprentice

Pilar Molina Llorente • Discover the realities of life for a boy apprenticed to an artist in Renaissance Florence through this fascinating historical fiction book. **UE+**

HISTORICAL FICTION

The Dove in the Eagle's Nest

Charlotte M. Yonge • This wonderfully written book gives one a taste of the life of the robber barons of Germany, along with one family's redemption. Set in the late 1400s and early 1500s. **UE+**

The Black Arrow

Robert Louis Stevenson • A classic in literature, this novel tells a story set in the time of the War of the Roses and Richard III. It is interesting to see that Stevenson's depiction of Richard III is exactly the opposite of that described in *The Daughter of Time*. **MS+**

The Daughter of Time

Josephine Tey • Not your normal historical fiction, this is a detective story set in our day, looking back to the time of Richard III. He has been accused throughout history of murdering his two nephews and of being an evil monster in English history. This fascinating story approaches the "historical gossip" with a policeman's nose for truth. Absolutely riveting! **HS+**

The Trumpeter of Krakow

Eric P. Kelly • Based on a true story, this book is set in 1400's Poland. It will give the reader a better understanding of the cost of duty. **MS+**

DVD/VIDEOS

The Agony and the Ecstasy

Irving Stone • This is a movie about the painting of the Sistine Chapel ceiling. It is a fascinating look at Michelangelo, the painting of frescoes, and some of the political aspects of the Renaissance papacy. (Caution: There are two brief scenes where you may want to fast forward.) **UE+**

How Should We Then Live?

Francis A. Schaeffer • If you are not familiar with these videos, this would be a wonderful time to view them since many of Dr. Schaeffer's comments concern the Renaissance and the Reformation. **UE+**

IMPORTANT RULERS

World Leaders Past and Present:

Books from this series are often available in libraries. If you can locate these titles, they are very insightful and well-researched. **MS+**

Ferdinand & Isabella Paul Stevens

Henry of Navarre Albert C. Gross

Henry VIII Frank Dwyer

Martin Luther Sally Stepanek

John Calvin Sally Stepanek

CONQUISTADORS & EXPLORERS

The World of Columbus & Sons

Genevieve Foster • A fascinating look at the relationship between Spain and England, France and Germany, India and Portugal, explorers and monarchs, and much more. Highly recommended. **UE+**

Explorers Who Got Lost

Diane Sansevere-Dreher • From the intriguing title through the informative biographies on Dias, Columbus, Cabot, Magellan, and others, this is a book well worth reading. **UE+**

Christopher Columbus

Struan Reid • This book gives background information as well as the major events of Columbus's life. **UE+**

By Right of Conquest, Or With Cortez in Mexico

G. A. Henty • Follow Cortez into the Aztec capital, and watch in suspense as the hair-raising events unfold. Written as historical fiction, Henty's books are, nonetheless, an excellent introduction to history. **UE+**

Hernàn Cortés

Brendan January • A balanced view of the controversial accomplishments of the conqueror of Mexico. **UE+**

Ferdinand Magellan

Struan Reid • Similar to the title listed above, this biography focuses on Magellan and his voyage around the world. (Remember, Magellan did not survive the trip, but eighteen of his sailors did.) **UE+**

Francisco Pizarro

Ruth Manning • A biography of the conquistador who conquered the Incas. **UE+**

Eternity in Their Hearts

Don Richardson • The author of *Peace Child*, Don Richardson provides a startling look at the redemptive witness God has provided to various cultures throughout history. His story of the Incas before Pizarro (in chapter one) should be read by every Christian. Highly recommended! **MS+**

MESOAMERICAN & ANDEAN CIVILIZATIONS

The Aztec News

Philip Steele • Written in the style of a newspaper, this fascinating book helps students to understand life at the time of the Spanish conquistadors—from the Aztec point of view! **UE+**

Aztec, Inca & Maya A DK EYEWITNESS BOOK

Elizabeth Baquedano • Filled with photographs and information, this book will provide a basic overview of the beliefs, rituals, and culture of these three New World civilizations. **MS+**

Aztecs & Incas: A Guide to the Pre-Colonized Americas in 1504

Sue Nicholson • This delightful book gives you all of the tips and information you'll need for a trip back in time. **UE+**

THE REFORMATION

Spy for the Night Riders MARTIN LUTHER

Dave & Neta Jackson · This Trailblazer book provides an introduction for elementary students to Martin Luther through spine-tingling historical fiction. **E+**

The Queen's Smuggler WILLIAM TYNDALE

Dave & Neta Jackson · This Trailblazer title is the exciting story of "God's Smuggler" during the 1500s. William Tyndale, who was an English martyr, had a tremendous impact on the Church in England. . **E+**

The Hawk That Dare Not Hunt by Day

Scott O'Dell · The story of William Tyndale, whose calling was to provide the Word of God in English to the people of England. **UE+**

The Betrayer's Fortune MENNO SIMONS

Dave & Neta Jackson · A story of the Anabaptists during the mid-1500s, this is a wonderful book. **E+**

The Man Who Laid the Egg

Louise A. Vernon · This is the story of Erasmus, the man of whom the monks said, "Erasmus laid the egg that Luther hatched." Written as historical fiction for younger children. **E+**

Luther and His World

Graham Tomlin · This is a well-balanced account of Luther and the tremendous revolution unleashed by his actions. **MS+**

Luther: Biography of a Reformer

Frederick Nohl · Engaging and easy to read, this is a good introduction for younger students to the life of Martin Luther. **UE+**

Here I Stand A LIFE OF MARTIN LUTHER

Roland H. Bainton · This is the definitive biography of Martin Luther, yet it is very readable and filled with fascinating insights into his life. **MS+**

What books did you like best?

_____

_____

_____

_____

The Internet also contains a wealth of information about the Renaissance & the Reformation.

What sites were the most helpful?

_____

_____

_____

For more books, use these Dewey Decimal numbers in your library:

Renaissance: #940

Reformation: #270

Conquistadors; Mesoamerican & Andean Civilizations: #972

Ferdinand & Isabella: #946.03

Henry of Navarre: #944.03

Henry VIII: #942.05

Martin Luther & John Calvin: #284

▶ # Student Self-Evaluation UNIT 7, PHASE 1

Dates and hours:_____

Key Concepts

Rephrase the five Key Concepts of this Unit and confirm your understanding of each:

- The Renaissance:

  _____

- The Reformation:

  _____

- The Age of Exploration:

  _____

- The New World:

  _____

- The Scientific Revolution:

  _____

Tools for Self-Evaulation

Evaluate your personal participation in the discussions of this Phase. Bearing in mind that a good participant in a discussion is not always the most vocal participant, ask yourself these questions: Were you an active participant? Did you ask perceptive questions? Were you willing to listen to other participants of the discussion and draw out their opinions? Record your observations and how you would like to improve your participation in the future:

_____

_____

Every time period is too complex to be understood in one Phase of study. Evaluate your current knowledge of the Renaissance & the Reformation. What have you focused on so far? What are your weakest areas of knowledge?

_____

Based on the evaluation of this introduction, project ahead what you would like to study more of in the following Phases:

_____

_____

Phase 2

▶ Research & Reporting

Explore one or more of these areas to discover something significant!

The Renaissance

Learn more about this time period. When was the term "Renaissance" first used, and what does it mean? When, where and what was the Renaissance? Who were the most significant people of the Renaissance? How were cultures affected and changed by the Renaissance?

Artists of the Renaissance

Investigate the lives and works of the master artists of the Renaissance such as Leonardo da Vinci, Michelangelo, Raphael, Titian, or Botticelli. How did their work reflect the ideas of the Renaissance?

The Reformation

The Protestant Reformation was not a reforming of the Catholic Church, but, instead, the birth of a separate, non-Catholic Church. Investigate and report on this phenomenon. Where did the Reformation take place? In what locations did it take lasting root? How did the plea "Sola Scriptura" change the medieval understanding of the Church? How were cultures affected and changed by the Reformation?

The Reformers

Choose one or all of these names to research: Martin Luther, John Calvin, Ulrich Zwingli, Menno Simons, Thomas Cranmer, William Tyndale, John Knox. In your report, be sure to include information about relations between Church and State in their countries, their unique personalities and character traits, their followers, the effects of their ministries, and the personal cost of their commitments.

Protestant Denominations

Research and report on the historical beginnings of your own church. Ask your pastor for a good source for understanding the history of your denomination. Show where it fits within the reform movements of the 1500s, or, if it does not fit within that context, show when it developed. If you attend a non-denominational church, what are the basic beliefs about Church-State relations, baptism, pacifism, communion, and other defining doctrines? Using what you have learned about the different groups of churches, to what stream of the Reformation would your church be most closely related?

Erasmus

Though Erasmus "laid the egg that Luther hatched," he disagreed with the Protestant Reformation and remained a loyal Catholic. Learn more about this scholastic who befriended kings and queens, ridiculed Church practices, printed the first Greek New Testament for Europeans, and rejected Luther's theology.

Copernicus

Research and report on Copernicus and his heliocentric theory of the solar system. What was his background and training, and what occupation did he hold? How did this new theory break with previous models? What impact did the heliocentric theory have on this moment in history?

Mesoamerica

Discover more about the pre-Columbian kingdoms and empires of Mexico and Central America, including the Maya, the Aztec, and the Olmec. Investigate their technology, their scientific and mathematical achievements, and their culture— all prior to their first contact with Europeans.

Ferdinand & Isabella

Discover more about these sovereigns, the rulers

of Spain. Describe the political impact of their marriage; their wars to unite Spain and to free it from the Islamic Moors; their sponsorship of Columbus and of the Spanish Inquisition; their banishment of the Jews from Spain; and some of the political positions obtained by their descendants.

The Conquistadors

Choose one or all of these names to research: Christopher Columbus, Cortés, Balboa, Pizzaro, Coronado, Ponce de León, de Soto. Try to discover their motivations for conquest; how successful they were in terms of conquest and finding treasure; the way they treated the native people; and the use of the Spanish Inquisition in the New World. How did the riches discovered in the New World impact the country of Spain? Report your findings.

Explorers

Consider these European explorers: Magellan, da Gama, Vespucci, Cabot, Cartier. How were these explorers different from the conquistadors? Discover their motivations, the results of their explorations, and the way native people were treated who came in contact with them. How was trade affected by these explorations?

Bartolomé de Las Casas

Research and report on this Dominican missionary to the New World who first documented and reported the abuse against the native people by European conquerors and colonizers. What impact did his writings and activities have? With whom was his message most and least received in Europe? –in the New World? You might consider a comparison of his life to that of William Wilberforce.

Francis Xavier

Francis Xavier was a Jesuit priest who went to Japan and China and had a tremendous impact in these two countries. Research and report on his methods of introducing Christianity to different cultures. How were these methods different from those used by the Spanish conquistadors? What was the result of his labors?

The War of the Roses

Learn more about this English civil war which erupted at the close of the Hundred Years' War. Describe the causes and results of this war. Who were the leaders and what did they do? Who came to power at the end of the war, and how was the war finally resolved?

Henry VIII

Discover and describe the state of England during the reign of Henry VIII, his son Edward VI, and his daughter Mary. What was the Reformation Parliament and what was its purpose? Describe Thomas Cranmer and his contribution to the Anglican Church. As you consider the events in England, be sure to correlate with the events taking place in Europe. How were these related?

Charles V

Charles V, the grandson of Ferdinand and Isabella, was king of Spain, archduke of Austria, and Holy Roman Emperor. He tried Luther for heresy, threatened the pope, fought the Turks and the French, and abdicated the throne of his empire. Learn more about this fascinating man who ruled during a pivotal moment of history.

► Brain Stretchers

Russia

Research and report on the Russian overthrow of the Golden Horde. Examine the lives of the early Russian tsars, especially Ivan the Terrible. Describe the political and religious atmosphere in Russia during this time. How did the rest of Europe view Russia? Compare and contrast this with the current view of Russia held by Europe and the United States.

Renaissance Popes

The Renaissance popes were known for their extravagance and ambitions. Research and report on Pope Julius II, Leo X, and Alexander VI. Compare and contrast their lives with Pope Gregory the Great. What was the response of Europe to these men? How did the Catholic Church respond at the Council of Trent to the types of excesses committed by these men?

Two Florentines

Research and report on Lorenzo de Medici and Savonarola. Both of these men were leaders in Florence for a time. Compare and contrast their lives and the impact of their rule. How did each man affect the city? Were there any long lasting

results from either of their lives? Describe the conditions of the city under each man.

The Reformation in England

Discover the differences between the Reformation in England and the Reformation in other parts of Europe. In what ways does the Church of England reflect the Catholic Church? In what ways does it break from the Catholic Church? How is it unique among other Protestant churches?

The Counter Reformation

Learn about the Council of Trent and the Counter Reformation of the Catholic Church. What issues were addressed in the Council of Trent? How did this council respond to the need for reform in the Catholic Church? What was the council's findings on Luther and the Reformation?

Create Your Own Research Topic

_____

_____

_____

▶ Timeline

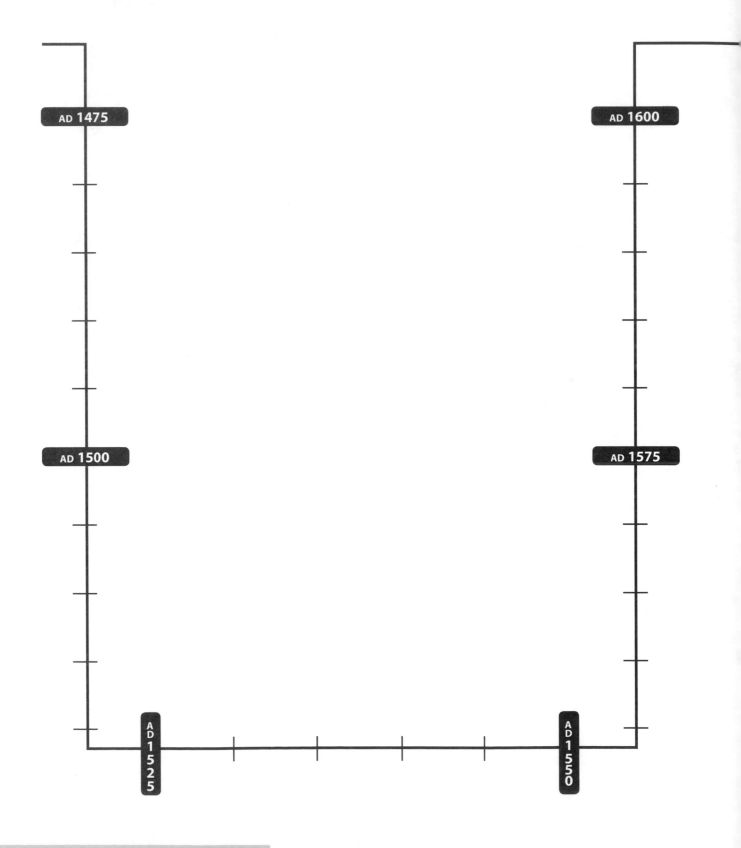

AD 1475

AD 1600

AD 1500

AD 1575

AD 1525

AD 1550

Consider this for your timeline

This time period witnesses titanic collisions between the old and the new: between the Catholic Church and the emerging Protestant churches; between medieval thinking and the ideas of the Renaissance; between the Old and New Worlds. It is also the time of new discoveries: the Age of Exploration and the Scientific Revolution. Some of the most daunting, diverse, and astonishing personalities in world history emerge: Columbus, Martin Luther, Henry VIII, Cortez, Montezuma, Francis Xavier, and Magellan. All in all, it is a fascinating and momentous time.

Key Events

Columbus's first voyage to the New World

Cortez conquers the Aztecs

The Council of Trent

Luther's 95 Theses on the Wittenberg door

Henry VIII, Church of England

The Jesuits

Magellan's voyage around the world

Russia under the tsars

CONSIDER:

There were many new plants, new foods, and new experiences in the New World. Our vocabulary and our menu have been greatly enriched because of it. Here is a partial list of what the Indians of the Americas gave to the world:

potato

rubber

American cotton

corn

wild rice

chocolate

chiles

maple syrup

tomato

peanut

pecan

cashew

avocado

passion fruit

zucchini

green bean

clams

lima bean

turkey

pumpkin

▶ # Words to Watch

Remember—The easiest way to learn a subject is to master its terms:

papal bull	repudiate	reformation	renaissance
Protestant	justification	merit	indulgences
Anabaptist	Mennonite	Calvinist	congregational
sovereignty	annulment	patron	astrolabe
compass	circumnavigate	demarcation	conquistadors
dynasty	vanities	heliocentric	thesis

Other words you need to look up:

_____

_____

_____

_____

_____

▶ **Student Self-Evaluation** UNIT 7, PHASE 2

Dates and hours:_____

Research Project

- Summarize your research question:

  _____

  _____

- List your most useful sources by author, title and page number or URL where applicable (continue list in margin if necessary):

  _____

  _____

  _____

- Now take a moment to evaluate the sources you just listed. Do they provide a balanced view of your research question? Should you have sought an additional opinion? Are your sources credible (if you found them on your own)? Record your observations:

  _____

  _____

- Evaluate your research project in its final presentation. What are its strengths? If you had time to revisit this project, what would you change? Consider giving yourself a letter grade based on your project's merits and weaknesses.

  _____

  _____

- Letter grade: _____

- You have just completed an area of specific research in the time of the Renaissance & the Reformation. Now what would you like to explore in the upcoming Phases? Set some objectives for yourself:

  _____

Phase 3

▶ Maps & Mapping

Physical Terrain

» Locate and label Spain, the jumping-off place for Spanish explorers. Locate and label Portugal, the jumping-off place for Portuguese explorers. Shade Spain one color and Portugal a second color.

» Locate and label the Caribbean islands, the point of first contact between the Old World and the New, and locate and label Mexico, the site of Cortèz's conquest of the Aztecs. Shade both of these with Spain's color.

» Locate and label Indonesia, home of the Spice Islands, and India, the site of Portugal's trade route headquarters. Shade the area from India to Japan (known as the Indies) with Portugal's color.

» Locate and label Brazil, which Portugal claimed in the New World. Shade Brazil with Portugal's color.

» Locate and label Italy, the major center of the Renaissance, and Germany, the birthplace of the Reformation.

Geopolitical

» Draw the route Vasco da Gama took from Portugal to the Indies. Label the Cape of Good Hope in Africa and Goa in India (a former Portuguese colony).

» Draw the Line of Demarcation which the pope officially sanctioned in order to determine whether lands discovered in exploration belonged to the Spanish or the Portuguese. Shade the areas of Spanish conquest, and with a different color, shade the areas of Portuguese conquest.

» Draw the route Ferdinand Magellan's ships took from Spain, crossing the Atlantic and the Pacific oceans in the process of circumnavigating the earth. Label the Straits of Magellan and the countries he visited.

» Locate and label the geographical area of the highly advanced civilizations in the New World: Mesoamerica and the Andes.

Explore

» *Christian Outreach:* What is the status of evangelical outreach today in Indonesia, land of the Spice Islands? What opportunities and what difficulties face those who share the gospel in these areas?

» *Gold & Conquest:* After Columbus's initial voyage, conquistadors, colonists and clergy poured into the New World, mostly in search of gold and glory. Investigate the geographical locations of the Mesoamerican and Andean civilizations, of the Spanish conquests, and of the exploration for and discovery of gold.

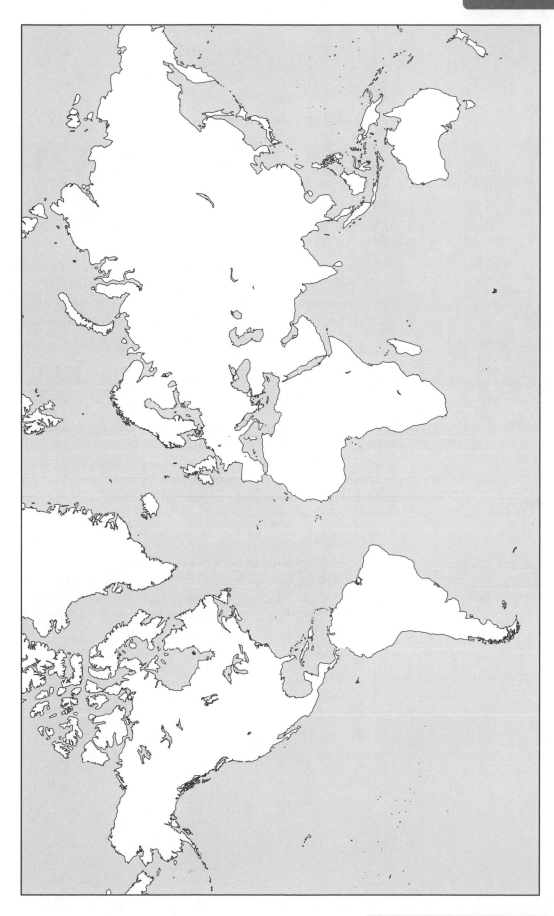

▶ Art Appreciation

Pietà by Michelangelo, 1498–1499
St. Peter's Basilica, Rome

In his own lifetime, Michelangelo was considered to be the greatest artist living, a rare occurrence for any artist. His paintings on the ceiling of the Sistine Chapel in Rome are probably the most famous artistic works he created, but he thought of himself as a sculptor rather than a painter. In fact, Pope Julius II seems to have had to coerce Michelangelo to stop sculpting and come paint the ceiling!

» Locate a photo, or series of photos, of this marble sculpture. How would you describe the figure of Mary? Of Jesus? Michelangelo saw himself as "liberating" three-dimensional bodies from the marble which encased them. How well do you think he succeeded with this *Pietà*?

The School of Athens by Raphael, 1510–1511
Vatican Palace, Rome

Raphael studied for a time in Florence under Leonardo da Vinci and Michelangelo. When he later came to Rome, he won such approval for his work that he was called, "the prince of painters." H. W. Janson, the renowned art historian, wrote of Raphael, "…he is the central painter of the High Renaissance; our conception of the entire style rests more on his work than on any other master's."

» Look for a photo of *The School of Athens*, which was Raphael's most famous painting. The two figures in the center are Plato and Aristotle, surrounded by other philosophers. Remembering that this is the time of the Renaissance, a time of idealizing ancient Rome and Greece, what do you think Raphael may have been trying to communicate? How would you describe this painting? How does the architectural setting contribute to or detract from the painting?

► Architecture

St. Peter's Basilica, begun 1506

Pope Julius II conceived the idea of replacing the old basilica of St. Peter with a church so magnificent that it would outshine all the monuments of ancient Rome. He hired Donato Bramante as the architect, the one considered to be the creator of High Renaissance architecture.

> » Locate photos of St. Peter's Basilica in Rome. Bramante reportedly stated that his aim was to "place the Pantheon on top of the Basilica of Constantine." In what ways do you think this structure fulfilled his ambition? What words can you use to describe this monumental building?

► Arts in Action

Select one or more, and let your artistic juices flow!

Portraiture

Look at some portraits done by Hans Holbein, court painter for Henry VIII. Then try your hand at creating a portrait in the style of the sixteenth century. Possibilities could include painting, drawing, or photography.

Drawing with perspective

Discover the use of "perspective" in drawing, such as that utilized by the architect Brunelleschi, and by the painter Masaccio. Try drawing a line of telephone poles receding into the distance in order to understand a little of what is necessary to paint with perspective. There are excellent books on perspective—look for them at your library or online.

Realistic drawing

Renaissance artists painted nature scenes in such realistic ways that many of the paintings seem to be a window onto a scene. Try your hand at drawing realistically, either an animal or a scene in nature, such as a waterfall or mountain. There are excellent books in the library and online to help you learn to draw horses, cats, and more.

▶ Science

The scientific theory of Copernicus, that the earth was not the center of the universe, was cataclysmic to the people of his time. However, it made sense of what Copernicus observed in the heavens. The science of astronomy allowed people to understand a bit of God's marvels in the heavens.

"When I consider Your heavens, the work of Your fingers,
The moon and the stars, which You have ordained,
What is man that You are mindful of him?" Psalm 8:3–4

The Solar System

» Learn more about the solar system. If you have access to a telescope, find as many planets as you can. An eye-opening project is to hang representative sun and planets from your ceiling in their appropriate ratio of distances from the sun and from each other.

At the same time that Copernicus was gazing heavenward and Christopher Columbus was sailing on his historic voyage, a Nuremberg geographer was working to make the first terrestrial globe ever designed!

Papier Maché Globe

» Try your hand at making a papier maché globe. Blow up a round balloon, and then put six or seven layers of papier maché on the balloon. When it dries, draw the continents. Paint the ocean and the continents. You may wish to label the major mountain ranges and major cities with a fine tip marker. Include the equator, the poles, the Tropic of Cancer, and the Tropic of Capricorn.

▶ Music

Music within the Church changed drastically at the time of the Reformation. Martin Luther replaced Latin liturgical hymns sung by choirs with joyous, rousing hymns sung by enthusiastic worshippers in their native languages. This invigorated the music of the Church to such a degree that, since the Reformation, there has been a veritable avalanche of hymns written to praise God!

Discover

A Mighty Fortress is Our God

Martin Luther (1483–1546) • Written during the tumultuous struggle with the Catholic Church, it expressed for Luther that the Protestants had only one helper—God.

Try This

With the idea that this hymn was a battle cry of the Protestants, try singing this song while marching together as soldiers. What effect does this have on your mind, your heart and your spirit? Try singing the hymn, "I Sing the Mighty Power of God," while marching. Does it have the same effect?

Listen

All Glory, Laud, & Honor MUSIC CD

All People that on Earth Do Dwell
tune attributed to Louis Bourgeois (1510–1561)

The words of this hymn are based on Psalm 100. The tune, which should be very familiar (it is the tune of the Doxology) was written by Louis Bourgeois. He was choirmaster at two churches in Geneva and worked closely with John Calvin.

> **CONSIDER:**
>
> When you are struggling or overwhelmed, remember to sing of God's power and might!

▶ Cooking

To celebrate the nailing of the 95 Thesis on the Wittenberg door, let's have some good German mustard! This is a fantastic recipe to have on hand.

Spiced German Mustard

⅓ cup white mustard seed
½ cup cold water
1 small onion, chopped
1 tsp salt
½ tsp ground cinnamon
⅛ tsp turmeric

¼ cup dry mustard
1 cup cider vinegar
2 tbsp brown sugar
2 cloves garlic, minced
¼ tsp each ground allspice, dill seeds, tarragon (dried)

Combine the seed, mustard, and water; let stand for 3 hours. In a 2-quart non-corrosive pan, combine the other ingredients, and simmer uncovered over medium heat for 10–15 minutes or until reduced by half. Strain liquid into mustard seed mixture and blend in a blender until smooth. Pour into double boiler and cook over simmering water until thick as very heavy cream (be sure to stir often). This will probably take 10 to 15 minutes. Let cool, mixture will thicken slightly. Cover and refrigerate for up to 2 years! Makes about 1 cup.

Now cook up bratwurst and sauerkraut for a real German feast!

▶ **Student Self-Evaluation** UNIT 7, PHASE 3

Dates and hours:_____

Evaluate your projects

- List which of the activities listed in this Phase you did:

  _____

  _____

- Rate your enthusiasm: _____

  Explain: _____

  _____

- Rate the precision of your approach:_____

  Explain: _____

  _____

- Rate your effort towards the completion of the project: _____

  Explain: _____

  _____

- Ask yourself what worked and what did not. What would you do differently in the future, and what would you repeat?

  _____

  _____

- How specifically did these hands-on activities enhance your knowledge of the Renaissance & the Reformation? What made them worthwhile?

  _____

  _____

- In the first three Phases of this Unit, what aspect of the time period has most captured your imagination? What would you like to creatively pursue to conclude your study?

  _____

  _____

Phase 4

▶ In Your Own Way . . .

We have seen a rebirth of Greco-Roman ideas, art, and architecture in Europe; a dramatic break in the Western Church, which led to the formation of an entirely separate group of Christians—the Protestants; the discovery of a vast new world previously unknown to Europeans and inhabited by diverse people groups misnamed "Indians;" an earthshaking revolution in the realm of science which has continued to this day; and the first known circumnavigation of the world. The world has become both smaller and infinitely more complex during this time. Now, choose a selection of these activities, or create your own, which will best express what you have learned from this Unit.

LINGUISTICS

Journalism

The editor of *The Spanish World* smells a good story in the making. He assigns you to accompany Christopher Columbus on his voyage to Asia in 1492. Write your report in the most interesting and fast-paced way you can.

You are the court reporter at the Diet of Worms. Charles V has asked you to make a copy of the proceedings from your notes for his private records. He has encouraged you to add any local "color" that might help others understand what is taking place.

Interview Leonardo da Vinci for the television series "Arts About Town." Ask him to explain his role in helping Cesare Borgia, whether Mona Lisa was smiling or not, and where he got the confidence to design his flying machine.

Playing with Words

Finish this limerick:

There once was a large king in Britain
Who married with whom he was smitten . . .

Prose

Imagine you are Katharine von Bora, Martin Luther's wife. Write a series of letters to your friends about your life. Remember, you are married to a celebrity, so people will want to know what he's really like. And since Luther wrote, *"There is no more lovely, friendly, and charming relationship, communion, or company than a good marriage,"* this is also your chance to affirm the truth of that statement.

Write a book for children about Michelangelo's amazing life. Include stories of his sculptures, his paintings, his architecture, and how his contemporaries viewed him. Most importantly, tell children how Michelangelo's Christian faith impacted his life and work.

ART

Painting/Drawing

Create a collage of the Renaissance, including the people, art, and architecture, that will give viewers a distilled essence of this time period.

Paint a scene from the Age of Exploration, whether the voyage of Magellan, the oceanic discovery of Balboa, the journey of Columbus, or of any of the other epic explorers.

Cartooning

Create a political cartoon showing John Tetzel selling indulgences. (Note: There were actually caricatures of Tetzel drawn at the time of the Reformation!)

Graphic Design

Francis Xavier has pioneered missions among the pearl divers in India, the headhunters in the Spice Islands, and the highly cultured residents of Japan. Now, design a two-page, full-color magazine advertisement to help him recruit volunteers to join this exciting work.

Mary I of England (formidably known as "Bloody Mary" for her attempts at curtailing Protestantism) has hired your advertising firm to improve her ratings at the polls. Use whatever means you can devise to bolster Mary's public image.

MUSIC

Performance Practice

With your teacher's help, select an appropriate piece of music which expresses some particular aspect studied in this Unit, whether it comes from the Old World or the New World, from the Renaissance or the Reformation. Prepare and perform the piece for an audience. Communicate with your audience the reason for your selection either in the program notes or in a short speech.

DRAMA

Comedy

Create a comedic skit about Copernicus's heliocentric theory—how different it was than the contemporary theory—and his concern over the probable reaction of others.

Philip II of Spain married Mary I of England, but her country would not crown him king. Create a comedy routine showing her royal demands, his royal frustration, and the unyielding hostility of Parliament toward this foreign husband.

Drama

Create a short drama showing the lifestyles and values of the two Florentine leaders, Lorenzo de Medici and Savonarola, and their intertwining in the city of Florence. Remember, Savonarola was called to the deathbed of Lorenzo.

Puppetry

With puppets, show the different flavors of the Reformation in the different countries of Europe. Be sure to include Martin Luther, John Calvin, Menno Simons, and William Tyndale.

Prop Needs

_____

_____

Costume Ideas

_____

_____

Role/Player

_____

_____

Set Suggestions

_____

_____

MOVEMENT

Dance

Choreograph a dance to depict Pope Leo X, patron of the arts and protagonist of the Reformation. His expressed attitude was, *"God has given us the papacy, let us enjoy it!"*

Action

Reenact the Night of Sorrows in Tenochtitlan, when the Spanish conquistadors tried to flee the city weighted down with immense quantities of gold, and the Aztec sought to prevent them.

Pantomime

Pantomime the life and work of Ivan IV of Russia. Be sure to show the fact that he reorganized the Russian government, the military, and aspects of the Russian Orthodox Church, as well as showing his belief that God had given him the right and the power to rule as the Caesar, or "tsar," of Russia.

CONCEPTUAL DESIGN

Game of Discovery

Create a board game in which the people of the Americas discover Europe—and choose to exploit the wealth and the workers. Use the historical experience of Europeans flooding the New World for your model of the New World conquering the Old. You may choose to have several different groups exploring and conquering, or focus on one group only (such as the Aztec or Inca). Show the impact on both the Old World and the New World countries. (Remember, the native people did not use gold for money but for decoration.)

CREATE YOUR OWN EXPRESSION

_____

_____

_____

_____

_____

▶ **Student Self-Evaluation** UNIT 7, PHASE 4

Dates and hours:_____

Evaluate your projects

*   What creative project did you choose:

    _____

*   What did you expect from your project, and how does the final project compare to your initial expectations?

    _____

*   What do you like about your project? What would you change?

    _____

In Conclusion

Revisit the five Key Concepts from the beginning of this Unit. Explain how your understanding of and appreciation for each has grown over the course of your study.

*   _____

    _____

*   _____

    _____

*   _____

    _____

*   _____

    _____

*   _____

Record your concluding thoughts on the Renaissance & the Reformation:

_____

_____

Puritans, Pietists, & the Divine Right of Kings

Statue of Louis XIV in Versailles, France

Brother Against Brother . . .

Though Germany had suffered violent convulsions in the birth of the Reformation and would soon experience the life-draining trauma of the Thirty Years' War, it was, in the year 1572, quietly waiting backstage for its next cue. That year was, however, anything but quiet for other European nations like France, England, Spain, and the Netherlands. As political and religious enmity between Catholics and Protestants was stirring up strife and violence in these countries, Europe continued to take significant steps away from the medieval conception of a united Christendom. In order to better understand how the political dynamics unleashed at the time of the Reformation were continuing to impact the world, let us begin our study in the mid-1500s.

French wars of religion

In 1559 France was ruled by a teenage boy and his teenage queen. This was Francis II (the son of Henri II and Catherine de Medici), who the year prior had married Mary, Queen of Scots. A weak leader often provides power mongers with an open door for inciting strife in their realm, and it was certainly the case with the frail French king who reigned during this tumultuous time. The Reformation was taking hold of powerful nobles in France, as well as many artisans and craftsmen. Those in power who remained loyal Catholics were dismayed at these developments, and sought to influence the young king and queen to suppress what they saw as the Protestant heresy. The mother of Mary, Queen of Scots was related to the House of Guise, the fierce agitators leading the Catholic faction. The French Protestants, or *Huguenots*, believed this family influence would be harmful to their precarious position amid the staunchly Catholic country, so in March of 1560 they attempted unsuccessfully to kidnap the boy king in what is known as the Conspiracy of Amboise. Francis II was not long under the influence of the Guises, as he died in December of that year from an ear infection that led to a brain abscess.

> *Make no mistake: this was war, with both sides—Catholic and Huguenot—armed, active, and ready to kill.*

While Francis's widow returned to Scotland, married and bore a son—the future King James I of England—Francis's ten-year-old brother Charles came to the throne under the regency of Catherine de Medici. Catherine sought to bring the country back to stability and so proclaimed a limited toleration of the Huguenots. Her hope was that, if they had certain places for their worship and certain rights in their country, the religious and political unrest would end. Unfortunately, this was not to be. When one large group of Huguenots assembled for worship, a Catholic nobleman believed them to be outside the legal bounds and sent his fighting men against them in the Massacre of Vassy. Dozens of people were slain in this incident, which unleashed the French Wars of Religion.

Make no mistake: this was war, with both sides—Catholic and Huguenot—armed, active, and ready to kill. When the Duke of Guise was assassinated by Huguenots, it set in motion a thirst for revenge, culminating in the horrendous St. Bartholomew's Day Massacre of 1572.

Elizabeth I

Meanwhile, returning to mid-century, Elizabeth I had inherited the English throne on the death of her sister Mary I, Queen of England. While much of England rejoiced mightily at the Protestant leanings of Queen Elizabeth, Catholics in Europe declared her monarchy invalid—thanks to her royal father's clumsy divorce and remarriage. However, one Catholic monarch seemed willing to overlook this fault in parentage: Philip II of Spain. For several months after Elizabeth's accession to the throne, he sought her hand in marriage. These two, who would eventually become mortal enemies in politics and religion, were, at this point, on diplomatically friendly terms. Elizabeth had no intention or desire to marry Philip, however. Actually, she seems to have had no intention nor desire to marry anyone. As she informed her Parliament when they earnestly begged her to marry, "Now that the public care of governing the Kingdom is laid upon me, to draw upon me also the cares of marriage may seem a point of inconsiderate folly. Yea, to satisfy you, I have already joined myself in marriage to an husband, namely, the Kingdom of England."

Beyond merely their sixteenth-century belief that every woman should marry, these Protestant leaders in Parliament were also extremely concerned that Elizabeth's death without heirs would place the very Catholic Mary, Queen of Scots squarely upon the English throne. Only Elizabeth's fruitful marriage could prevent this. And, during this time when England was militarily and economically weakened by the churning religious struggles, Elizabeth's marriage to a strong Protestant ruler would have provided much needed support. Two such Protestants presented themselves as willing and able suitors: the King of Sweden and a Scottish earl. But Elizabeth I, for better or worse, had no desire to share her power or her realm with anyone.

This sovereignty manifested itself early in her reign concerning the English church. One of the Queen's tasks, with the aid and support of Parliament, was to constitutionally structure the laws of England as a Protestant country. Though Elizabeth I was not interested in formulating strict theological doctrines and enforcing them on her people, she thought it important to have everyone practice a unified form of worship. In other words, you could believe whatever you wished—as long as you attended the Anglican Church service. The Act of Uniformity was passed during Parliament's 1559 session requiring, among other things, that preachers wear *priestly vestments* (attire hearkening back to medieval times) during church services. When Elizabeth resolutely required that all preachers in England obey this Act, a fierce controversy arose between those who would conform and those who refused. Their refusal was based on the principle that vestments were Catholic tradition and had no place in a Protestant land. It was this controversy that gave rise to the Puritan movement, which would grow in power to eventually, though temporarily, overthrow the English monarchy.

While these agitations were whirling around the country, an even greater agitation was being planned beyond its borders: the assassination of a monarch. In 1570 Pope Pius V excommunicated Elizabeth I, releasing her Catholic subjects from obedience to her rule. This was in effect an invitation, to all those who would, to topple her from her throne. Conspirators began hatching plots to assassinate

Elizabeth I, for better or worse, had no desire to share her power or her realm with anyone.

Elizabeth and make her cousin Mary, Queen of Scots the new Queen of England (though she was currently held captive in one of Elizabeth's castles). Though unsuccessful, these conspiracies continued for nearly twenty years, certainly contributing to the growing hostility between Protestant England and the Catholic countries where these assassination plots were so often devised.

> *Conspirators began hatching plots to assassinate Elizabeth.*

Philip II

Back at mid-century again, the mightiest of all Catholic countries, indeed of all European countries at this point in history, was Spain. Spanish colonies in South America and the expanding Spanish Empire throughout the world brought Spain enormous income and a powerful navy. Standing at the head of this empire was King Philip II. He seems to have been undismayed by Elizabeth's rejection of him, because within just a few months after this slight, he married a French princess. This diplomatic marriage brought a much-needed peace between Spain and France and was evidently a welcome relief to him personally, since Philip had much bigger enemies in sight. First were the Ottoman Turks, under the leadership of Sulieman the Magnificent. Their strength in the Mediterranean had become such a menace to Catholic Europe that Spain was determined to actively do something about it. And they did, capturing cities in Morocco and lifting the siege of Malta. The ongoing threat posed by the Ottomans had loomed foremost in the strategies (and had done its part to empty the treasuries) of the Hapsburg rulers of both Spain and the Holy Roman Empire for many years. Only slightly behind the Ottomans was the secondary and closer threat of the Protestants in their realms.

Queen Elizabeth I by George Gower, 1588

Part of the land bequeathed to Philip II was the Netherlands. The Protestant Reformation had taken hold in the northern Netherlands, much to the annoyance and frustration of its Catholic overlord. When Calvinists began to riot in 1566, Philip sent his most terrifying general, the Duke of Alba, to quell the disturbances. Alba unleashed a reign of terror against the Protestants, but it did not accomplish the purpose of stamping out Protestantism in the Netherlands. Instead, it led to an eighty-year war between Spain and the Northern Netherlands (or The Dutch Republic) known as the Dutch War of Independence.

Philip II, in his continuing quest for power and Catholic dominion, took Portugal by force when its king died without heirs. This left the far-flung overseas Portuguese trading colonies open to exploitation by a more powerful country, which the Dutch would soon prove to be. Gaining Portugal and fighting the Dutch Republic was not enough for Philip, however. With the violent French wars of religion taking place in his neighboring country, Philip decided to enter in there as well and to support the Catholic cause with money and troops.

In England, Elizabeth countered Philip's moves by quietly supporting the Huguenots of France and by more openly supporting the Dutch quest for independence with the Treaty of Nonsuch in 1585. One of her knighted subjects, Sir Francis Drake, added his fuel to the Spanish fire by successfully raiding Spanish commerce in the Caribbean. Philip's sense of outrage at England's audacity reached the boiling point, however, when Elizabeth dared to sign the death warrant for Mary, Queen of Scots after it was proved that Mary had foolishly been part of a conspiracy to assassinate Elizabeth and establish herself as queen. In 1588 Philip ordered his invincible Spanish Armada to sail against England and Elizabeth, seeking to clear the English channel in order for Spain's army to cross from the Netherlands and invade England. If they had been successful, not only would England have been defeated but the Protestant Dutch, standing utterly alone against the most powerful empire in the world, would have surely lost their struggle. As it was, the mighty Spanish Armada was defeated by the underpowered English navy and by the weather.

Philip II, though unsuccessful in his plan to attack England, in 1589 formulated a plan for gaining France and holding Protestantism at bay. France's Catholic king Henry III had been assassinated and the next person in line for the French throne was a Protestant: Henry of Navarre. Philip was not about to let another Protestant become king. Instead, he claimed the French throne for his own daughter (born to the French princess) despite the French law, which prevents a woman from ruling in her own right. Henry of Navarre was able to outwit Philip's designs, however, by converting to Catholicism. Henry, who became Henry IV, was crowned King of France in 1594 and promptly declared war on Spain. When a treaty was finally signed, Henry's lawful right to the French throne was acknowledged by the Spanish king. It no doubt caused Philip II pain to do so because Henry IV had recently provided the Protestant Huguenots of France tremendous protection and freedom under the law in his historic Edict of Nantes, though he personally remained within the Catholic Church.

Gaining Portugal and fighting the Dutch Republic was not enough for Philip, however.

Colonization of North America

With France experiencing the reign of a competent and judicious king, and free from internal and external wars, it found time to begin setting up the colonies, which would become New France in North America. (This was about the same time that England was establishing permanent colonies on that continent.) In 1608 Samuel de Champlain started the fur trading post at Quebec, which would eventually become the capital of New France. When Henry IV was assassinated in 1610, however, the resulting religious turmoil in France was quickly mirrored in New France, when Huguenot officials were confronted with newly arrived Jesuit missionaries coming to evangelize the Native Americans. In the same year that Henry IV died, the French established the settlement at Port Royal in Nova Scotia. Three years later, this settlement would be destroyed by a group of English colonists from Virginia—the opening shots in a one-hundred-fifty-year war between England and France in the new world.

Before things developed to that point, however, in 1603 James I (son of Mary, Queen of Scots) had come to the English throne upon Elizabeth's death. Within a short time, he had established peace with Spain and signed a commercial treaty with France. This left England free to concentrate on potential colonies, thereby challenging the waning power of Spain and Portugal to hold onto their own lucrative colonies. In 1607 the first permanent English settlement in America was established at Jamestown, Virginia. (*Note: Virginia was named after the Virgin Queen, Elizabeth I.*) It was here the English learned that the lucrative wealth of Spain's South American mines was not to be had in North America. Instead, other sources of income had to be found and exploited. As it turned out, a plant native to the Americas, tobacco, was to be the mother lode for Virginia—worth its weight in silver.

Henry, who became Henry IV, was crowned King of France in 1594 and promptly declared war on Spain.

As in New France, the English colonies of America reflected the religious struggles of the mother country. Those who upheld the Church of England, with its bishops and ceremonies, were content with moderate changes from Catholicism and with the separation from Rome. Others, who had come to be known as Puritans, sought a second Reformation, a purification of the English Church from all "*popish*" (papal, Roman Catholic) traditions. Within this second group there was a further division. Moderate Puritans wanted to see this purification process take place within the ecclesiastical structure of the Church of England. Radical Puritans, or *Separatists*, believed that each church should operate independently, apart from the State (and not subject to its control). In 1620 one of these Separatist groups, known as the Pilgrims, left England after a decade-long stay in the tolerant atmosphere of the Dutch Republic to establish a home in *New England*, in the wilderness of North America. It would not be long before a group of moderate Puritans would come to set up their own version of an English Puritan colony not far from the Pilgrims. And, before it was over, Catholics would find their own haven in the British colonies, as would English dissenters from Puritanism AND the Church of England.

The Dutch and Spanish established a twelve-year truce in the midst of their brutal eighty-year war, beginning in 1609. Due to the religious climate in the Dutch Republic, after experiencing years of immense suffering and war with Spain over religious issues, it became a haven of safety for others whose religious beliefs were not accepted in their own countries, such as the English Separatists and French Huguenots. Far beyond just welcoming refugees, however, the Dutch Republic used this twelve year break from war to dramatically expand its shipping, fishing, and trade throughout the world. In fact, this truce is the beginning of what is known as the "Golden Age" for the Dutch, a time of extraordinary wealth for this indomitable merchant republic. They, too, were interested in establishing colonies throughout the world, including the Dutch colony of New Amsterdam on Manhattan Island in the mid-1620s.

Thirty Years' War

The focus of England, France, and The Dutch Republic—looking beyond the borders of Europe for ways to diversify their income and influence—contrasted starkly with the Holy Roman Empire seeking to enforce religious uniformity within its boundaries. Previous Catholic emperors had reluctantly tolerated Protestantism in their subjects, but when a champion of the Counter-Reformation became King of Bohemia just prior to becoming emperor, a new, tumultuous wind began to blow through the Holy Roman Empire. Ferdinand II, on his accession to the throne of Bohemia in 1617, immediately began to institute a policy requiring everyone in the country to worship as Roman Catholics. Bohemians, who were largely Protestant by this time, revolted against his high-handed ways. The resulting Thirty Years' War, which began in 1618, eventually drew several nations into the fray as Protestant rulers warred against the Catholic Hapsburg emperors. Because the religious issues between Catholic and Protestant were woven intricately into the fabric of national identity by this time, this long and costly war eventually changed the balance of political power in Europe. When the war ended in 1648, France was the most powerful country in the West; the Dutch Republic was recognized as an independent nation; the Holy Roman Empire was composed of a loose confederation of approximately three hundred independent principalities and more than a thousand semi-independent states; Spain no longer owned the Netherlands and was no longer a significant player in European politics; and the medieval concept of a Roman Catholic Empire ruled by a Christian Emperor and Pope lay in ashes, buried permanently in the German battlefields where the Thirty Years' War had been fought.

Radical Puritans, or Separatists, believed that each church should operate independently, apart from the State.

The Puritan revolution

England, though not a participant in the Thirty Years' War, had been embroiled in a vicious civil war between the Puritans who were running Parliament and the Royalists who were defending the king. This led to a hitherto unthinkable result: regicide. Parliament brought King Charles I to trial in 1649, found him guilty of wrongdoing, and executed him. Not only was the action shocking, but to the reigning monarchs throughout Europe, the concept was deeply disturbing.

Among the radical (or *independent*) Puritans of England however, the idea of government without kings was quite attractive. There was a problem, though, since the centuries-old structure of English government did not function effectively without a king at the head. Oliver Cromwell, head of the Puritan army which toppled Charles I, though unwilling to become king, was nonetheless amenable to becoming *Lord Protector* of the Commonwealth of England. Beyond invading Ireland to dismantle the Catholic/Royalist coalition (which was seen to be a great threat to the Commonwealth), and invading Scotland (which had dared to recognize Charles II as King of the Scots), Cromwell set his sights on restoring England to a place of health and prosperity in politics and in religion.

Something that deterred financial prosperity was the Dutch Republic. Its fleet of ships was the envy of all of Europe and the source of great wealth to these Dutch merchants, through their eastern spice trade, their Baltic trade, and their fishing fleets. With this vast fleet they dominated international trade throughout the world in the 17th century. This was not the least of

> *The medieval concept of a Roman Catholic Empire ruled by a Christian Emperor and Pope lay in ashes.*

their crimes, as far as the English were concerned, however. Somehow, the Dutch had managed, to the great consternation and hostility of English businessmen, to become the shipping agents transporting merchandise between English colonies in North America and the mother country. This system apparently had been established during the chaos of the English Civil War. So, the Commonwealth passed the Navigation Act of 1651 in order to wrest English colonial business away from their Dutch competitors. This led, in 1652, to the first Anglo-Dutch war.

The Anglo-Dutch wars of the mid-1600s to the latter-1700s illustrate the changing reasons for war. In the previous century, European wars had been focused on Catholic versus Protestant issues. Now, if you can imagine, two countries, both republics at this point and both Puritan in doctrine, went to war over business competition! Oliver Cromwell found this war utterly distasteful for these very reasons, and welcomed a treaty of peace in 1654, ending the first Anglo-Dutch War.

Things changed, however, when Cromwell died and Charles II returned to England as king. Though Charles II had a soft spot in his heart for the Dutch because they had helped fund his father's efforts in the late civil war, there were others close to the throne who were eager for a war, which might improve English commerce, including capturing lucrative Dutch colonies. In 1664 the English successfully snatched New Amsterdam from the Dutch, renaming it New York (after the king's brother, the Duke of York, who would later become King James II). This act, along with other international incidents, led to the Second Anglo-Dutch War. One of the interesting sidelights of this particular conflict was the addition of the nation of France as an ally to the Dutch. In order to understand how wars make for strange alliances, not to mention *changing* alliances, let's take a brief look at the international plottings of Louis XIV, the Sun King of France.

Louis XIV

Louis XIV was married in 1659 to the royal princess of Spain, Maria Teresa, the daughter of Philip IV. It was a marriage of State rather than of love, and Louis seemed determined to profit fully from this Spanish connection, since Maria Teresa's dowry had never been paid. So, when Philip IV died, the question of who would rule the Spanish Netherlands caused Louis XIV to invoke the ancient law of *devolution*. This law in the Netherlands stated that the daughter of a first marriage would inherit land before the son of a second marriage. Louis XIV used this to support his claim to the Spanish Netherlands, since it was, as this law asserted, his wife's rightful inheritance. This greatly concerned the Dutch, whose lands bordered the Spanish Netherlands. For them, despite the fact that France had been an important ally during previous wars, it was a far healthier strategy to have a weak Spain as the overlord of their neighboring Netherlands than a strong France. England was of the same mind as the Dutch. If France, their traditional enemy, gained territory in the Netherlands, it would make them a far more formidable foe. Thus, the Dutch and English banded together, along with Sweden, in the Triple Alliance against France in the war known as the War of Devolution. In the face of overwhelming pressure by the Dutch, France was forced to back down. Though Louis XIV submitted to this humiliation in 1668, he determined then and there to defeat the Dutch, who were now his sworn enemies.

Four year later, with various countries jockeying for position, Europe saw the astonishing spectacle of a complete change of alliance as Louis XIV plunged France into war once again. This time, however, England was allied with the French (indeed, one section of the Franco-Dutch War is called the Third Anglo-Dutch War!), at least until 1674, when the English signed a treaty of peace with the Dutch. Meantime, in the Dutch Republic, French military forces quickly captured three of the seven provinces. In the face of France's overwhelming battlefield superiority, the leader of the weak and ill-prepared Dutch army (William III, prince of Orange—who would eventually become king of England), opened the dikes and flooded a large portion of low-lying land while the army rallied around him at this water-line. This defense was quite successful, much to the chagrin of Louis XIV. Coming belatedly to the rescue of the Dutch was an alliance of the Spanish king, the Holy Roman Emperor, and the Elector of Brandenburg. Together, they were able to force the French out of the Dutch Republic. What Philip II might have

Two countries, both republics at this point and both Puritan in doctrine, went to war over business competition!

thought of Spain rescuing the Dutch, his Achilles heel, gives one pause. It certainly shows how much the world was changing during this time.

Though France was not able to conquer the Dutch Republic, it did capture territory in the Spanish Netherlands (a goal from the previous war), thereby winning Louis XIV's second war of conquest, which ended in 1678. France, by this time, was flexing very strong muscles indeed. Its colonial territory in North America reached from Quebec all the way to the mouth of the Mississippi River, while Paris was considered to be the cultural center of Europe. The French army was the strongest in Europe, its navy was larger than the navies of both England and the Dutch Republic combined. It was a heady time for the king and the country.

Louis XIV determined then and there to defeat the Dutch, who were now his sworn enemies.

Events in England in the year 1688 proved to be a fly in France's ointment, however. When the Catholic Duke of York was crowned James II, king of England in 1685, it meant that a fellow Catholic had become sovereign—an acceptable concept to Louis XIV but a tremendous concern to the Protestant country of England. Three years after the experiment of allowing an English Catholic to reign had begun, James II's new Catholic wife gave birth to a son. The nation recoiled, rather than rejoiced, because now the succession included a son who would certainly be raised Catholic. Things had deteriorated to such an extent between the king and his subjects that seven leading Englishmen wrote to William III of Orange—hero of the Dutch Republic, arch-enemy of Louis XIV and the acknowledged political leader of the Protestant world—to ask him to bring an army to England. His wife Mary was the daughter of James II and the Protestant heir to the throne, while William III was himself the grandson of Charles I. His claim to the throne was good, but the fact that another king still sat there meant war was on the horizon. Louis XIV offered assistance to his fellow sovereign, but James II was confident that his forces could repel the Dutch invasion. He was mistaken, largely due to his miscalculation of the loyalty of Protestant army officers when they had a chance to fight for a Protestant ruler. His will to rule was shattered when his other daughter Anne (who would become Queen Anne) went over to the enemy.

In 1689 Parliament formally declared that James II had abdicated, and offered the throne to William and Mary. This is known as the "Glorious Revolution" in England, but was anything but glorious to Louis XIV, who now saw his greatest foe on the throne of his greatest enemy. This enmity between France and England would continue on into the eighteenth century, even beyond the venerable lifetime of Louis XIV, and would be fought not only in Europe but on American and Asian soil. That story, fascinating, intricate, and wholly amazing, will be told in the next and final Unit. ◄

Phase 1

▶ Listen to This

What in the World? VOL. 2

DISC FOUR:

» England Defeats the Spanish Armada (track 3)

» The Thirty Years' War (track 4)

» Religion & the Divine Right of Kings (track 5)

True Tales VOL. 2

DISC THREE:

» Sir Isaac Newton (track 3)

Digging Deeper VOL. 2

DISC THREE: THE REFORMING CHURCH

» Counter-Reformation & Thirty Years' War (track 6)

» 1600s to Wesley (track 7)

▶ Read For Your Life

The Holy Bible

» **Personal relationship to God as opposed to outward religious form (Pietism):** Psalm 16, Jude 3–4

» **God as Judge (Thirty Years' War):** Psalm 50:1–6

» **Equipping for ministry (Puritans & Congregationalists):** Romans 12:3–8, Ephesians 4:11–16

Key People (Church)

Matteo Ricci
Missionary to China, Catholic

John Smyth
Founded English Baptists

John Robinson
Pilgrims' pastor

Richelieu
Powerful French cardinal

John Comenius
Founded modern education

John Bunyan
Wrote Pilgrim's Progress

George Fox
Founded Quakers

Philipp Spener
German Pietist

August Francke
Educational reformer, Pietist

Key People (World)

Elizabeth I
Ruler of the Elizabethan Age

Henry IV
Reunified France

Shakespeare
Bard of Avon

Galileo
Pioneered telescope in astronomy

Oliver Cromwell
Lord Protector of England

Rembrandt
Storyteller in art

Blaise Pascal
Christian mathematician

Louis XIV
Absolute monarchy

Isaac Newton
Calculus & gravity theories

Peter the Great
Reformer of Russia

▶ Talk Together

Opinion Column

» What did you find to be the most interesting aspect, or the most fascinating person, you encountered in your introduction to the Puritans, the Pietists, and the powerful kings who were absolute monarchs?

» Imagine you had accompanied Francis Drake on a voyage to the Spanish Main. Talk about your thoughts on piracy, loyalty to your own Good Queen Bess, the Spanish Inquisition, and the Spaniard Philip II.

» If you had been living in Holland at the time of the Dutch Revolt against Spain, what do you think your attitude would be concerning defending your town against the Spanish?

» Imagine you were living on the coast of England in 1588. The whole country is agitated, waiting for the Spanish Armada to arrive. What do you think will be in store for the English people if the Spaniards are able to land their troops?

» King James I of England was both ruler of Scotland (as James VI) and England. For what reasons do you suppose the Puritans and Separatists were happy to see the Scottish king come to the throne? In what ways do you think they were later surprised?

» Sir Isaac Newton was not only the man who discovered calculus AND the law of universal gravitation, but he was also a Bible scholar. What do you think Newton's reaction would be to the total secularization of science in today's world?

Critical Puzzling

» Henry of Navarre converted to Catholicism in order to become the king of France. As legend has it, he remarked, "Paris is worth a mass." History records that he was among the most popular kings France ever had, subduing the wars of religion and ushering in an era of peace and prosperity. His Edict of Nantes was a powerful aid and support to the French Protestants. What do you think of his reasons for converting? How would you characterize King Henry's religious convictions?

» In what ways do you think the English colonies in North America differed from the Spanish colonies in Central and South America? How were English attitudes toward the native people similar to the Spanish? How were they different?

» Louis XIV, the Sun King, was an absolute monarch in the fullest sense of the word, ruling France with an unyielding belief in the Divine Right of Kings. How do you view this perspective? How do you think this belief system would have affected the people of France—the nobility, the merchants, and the peasants? Why do you think he reversed the Edict of Nantes?

» The Defenestration of Prague began the incredibly complex Thirty Years' War, which ravaged Germany. What are some of the factors that caused this war to continue for so long?

» Galileo was a Catholic scientist living in Italy. When he began to observe and experiment in the area of astronomy, his discoveries contradicted the ancient Greek philosopher, Aristotle. Unfortunately, Aristotle's theories were held to be biblically true by the Roman Catholic Church at this time, while Copernicus's heliocentric theory was proclaimed heresy. When Galileo published a book based on his own observations, which upheld the heliocentric theory, he was sent to the Inquisition and sentenced to life imprisonment. In what specific ways do you think Galileo's writings might have been seen as undermining the truth of Scripture? (See www.answersingenesis.org/go/galielo for more information.)

» The Pietist movement in Germany took place many years after the devastation of the Thirty Years War. Why do you think the church in Germany might have become cold and formal at this point? In what ways do you think Pietism appealed to the common people? What are some areas in which you see that Pietism still influences us today?

» Why do you think Oliver Cromwell refused to be king, choosing to be "Lord Protector" of England instead? What do you think of the Puritans in the Rump Parliament sentencing Charles I to death? Do you think they accomplished their aims?

▶ Resources for Digging Deeper

Choose a few books that look interesting, or find your own.

PURITANS & THE PURITAN REVOLUTION

The English Puritans: The Rise and Fall of the Puritan Movement

John Brown · This blow-by-blow account of the rise and fall of Puritanism through the reigns of Elizabeth I, James I, Charles I, and Oliver Cromwell shows the rationale behind the monarch-defying stance of the Puritans against the Divine Right of Kings. **HS+**

Church History in Plain Language

Bruce L. Shelley · Dr. Shelley gives a clear understanding of the Puritan movement and the Puritan revolution, as well as the seventeenth century beginnings of, and reasons for, the Age of Reason (or the Enlightenment). He also sets the Pietists and Blaise Pascal into their historical context. Highly recommended! **MS+**

A History of the English Speaking Peoples: The New World

Winston Churchill · In this very readable book, Sir Winston Churchill provides a fascinating look at Queen Elizabeth, the Spanish Armada, King James I, King Charles I, the Puritan Revolution, and Oliver Cromwell among others. **MS+**

The Flight and Adventures of Charles II WORLD LANDMARK BOOKS

Charles Norman · This is the story of the young prince who regained the British throne after his father was executed during the Puritan Revolution. Fascinating story! **UE+**

PIETISM

The Pietists SELECTED WRITINGS

Foreword by Phyllis Tickle • This book allows you to read the actual words of Philipp Spener and August Francke, as well as later Pietists. Francke's autobiography, one of the selections, is a fascinating story. **MS+**

Understanding Pietism

Dale W. Brown • Pietism was a historic movement within the Lutheran Church in Germany, though its influence can be felt throughout Protestant and Catholic churches, even today. Learn more about its historic roots and theological beliefs in this excellent book. **HS+**

ELIZABETHAN AGE

Elizabeth I & Tudor England LIFE AND TIMES

Stephen White-Thomson • Great book about Queen Elizabeth and the Elizabethan Age. **E+**

Queen Elizabeth and the Spanish Armada WORLD LANDMARK BOOKS

Francis Winwar • A well-researched introduction to the story of the Spanish Armada. **UE+**

Mary, Queen of Scots

WORLD LANDMARK BOOKS

Emily Hahn • Read about the woman who had everything and then lost it—even her life. Appropriate for the whole family. **UE+**

The Spanish Armada

A HORIZON CARAVEL BOOK

Jay Williams • A fascinating look at one of the great naval battles of all time. It not only gives information about the countries involved, but also describes the various personalities in "living color." **UE+**

Under Drake's Flag

G. A. Henty • Though Henty wrote historical fiction, he knew the facts of history, and included them liberally in his stories. This particular book is the adventure of a boy sailing with Drake along the Spanish Main in the Americas. **UE+**

Francis Drake THE WORLD'S GREAT EXPLORERS

Roberta Bard • This is a fascinating account of the life of one of the most interesting adventurers the world has ever known. **UE+**

Sir Francis Drake GROUNDBREAKERS

Neil Champion • How long did it take Francis Drake to sail around the world? Why was Drake knighted? How did Drake "singe the King of Spain's beard"? **UE+**

Walter Raleigh: Man of Two Worlds WORLD LANDMARK BOOKS

Henrietta Buckmaster • Read about the man who influenced both England and the New World. Fascinating! **UE+**

Will Shakespeare and the Globe Theater WORLD LANDMARK BOOKS

Anne Terry White • Discover more about the Bard of England in this engaging book for all ages. **UE+**

The Shakespeare Stealer

Gary Blackwood • Historical fiction, this is the story of a young boy sent to the Globe Theatre to steal the script for "Hamlet." Well written and engaging. **UE+**

Shakespeare's England A
HORIZON CARAVEL BOOK

Louis B. Wright • This book includes historical information, biographical details, art from the time period, architecture, and more. Learn the background of many of Shakespeare's plays, and the influence of the British monarchs on Shakespeare. **UE+**

Shakespeare EYEWITNESS BOOKS

Peter Chrisp • Crammed with photos of replicas and actual items from Shakespeare's time, this oversized volume shares with readers everything they ever wanted to know (and some things they probably didn't want to know) about the Bard of England. **UE+**

IMPORTANT RULERS

World Leaders Past and Present:
Books from this series are often available in libraries. If you can locate these titles, they are very insightful and well-researched. **MS+**

Elizabeth I Catherine Bush
Mary, Queen of Scots Sally Stepanek
King Louis XIV Pierre Horn
Peter the Great Kathleen McDermott
Oliver Cromwell Lawrence Kaplan

RELIGIOUS WARS IN EUROPE

St. Bartholomew's Eve
A TALE OF THE HUGUENOT WARS

G. A. Henty • Meet Henry of Navarre, a Protestant ruler, whose marriage to the French King's sister provided the opportunity for the massacre of thousands of French Huguenots. **UE+**

How They Kept the Faith
Grace Raymond • Set in the time of Louis XIV, this is a fictional story of the the reversal of the Edict of Nantes and its effect upon the Huguenots in France. **MS+**

By Pike and Dike
G. A. Henty • This is Henty's version of how Protestant Netherlands broke away from Catholic Spain. It is filled with battles, sieges, slaughter, and suspense, much like the real-life history of the time. **UE+**

Gustavus Adolphus
A HERO OF THE REFORMATION

C. A. LaCroix • Learn about the Swedish king who turned the course of the Thirty Years' War, giving his life for the cause. **UE+**

BRITISH COLONIES

Jamestown, First English Colony
AMERICAN HERITAGE JUNIOR LIBRARY

Marshall William Fishwick • Isn't it fascinating to consider that the settlement of Jamestown took place during the reign of King James 1, the king who allowed the King James Bible to be translated and printed? This book is filled with details of the historic settlement. **UE+**

Surviving Jamestown
Gail Karwoski • Historical fiction, this riveting tale about a boy apprenticed to Captain John Smith is a good introduction to the first English settlement in the New World. **UE+**

William Penn LIBERTY AND JUSTICE FOR ALL
Janet & Geoff Benge • Discover the story of one English Quaker's efforts to provide a place of religious freedom. **UE+**

The World of Captain John Smith
Genevieve Foster • This book give readers an interesting overview of the time period from 1580 to 1631. **UE+**

Of Plymouth Plantation
William Bradford • Read the first-hand account of the early years of the Plymouth settlement by the man who became their leader. Excellent! **HS+**

RUSSIA

Russia Under the Czars
A HORIZON CARAVEL BOOK

Henry Moscow • This is an introduction to the history of Russia for students. The chapter dealing with Peter the Great is fascinating! Did you know that Peter the Great was nearly seven feet tall? Or that he learned to build a ship with his own hands? It's worth the search. **UE+**

Peter the Great

Diane Stanley • Well written and beautifully illustrated, this is a wonderful introduction to the man who tried singlehandedly to pull Russia into the modern world. **E+**

MATHEMATICIANS & SCIENTISTS IN THE 1600S

A Piece of the Mountain THE
STORY OF BLAISE PASCAL

Joyce McPherson • A very interesting story about the French mathematician and Christian apologist. This is the man who gave us "Pascal's Wager," and spoke of the God-shaped vacuum in people. **E+**

The Universe of Galileo and
Newton A HORIZON CARAVEL BOOK

William Bixby • The author shows the profound relationship between the scientific discoveries of Galileo and the scientific proofs of Isaac Newton. Also deals briefly with Copernicus, Brahe, Kepler, and Halley. Ties science together with history in a readable format. **UE+**

The Ocean of Truth
THE STORY OF SIR ISAAC NEWTON

Joyce McPherson • An intriguing look at the man who is known as one of the greatest scientists and mathematicians of all time, but who was also a Bible-believing Christian. Well written and enjoyable. **UE+**

Johannes Kepler THE SOWER SERIES

John Hudson Tiner • Kepler lived during the time of the Thirty Years' War in Germany. This book gives a very good account of the time in which Kepler lived. **UE+**

Along Came Galileo

Jeanne Bendick • A good introduction to one of the most significant scientists of this age. **E+**

Robert Boyle THE SOWER SERIES

John Hudson Tiner • Robert Boyle is considered to be the Father of Modern Chemistry. This book includes interesting details of his life and faith. **UE+**

Isaac Newton THE SOWER SERIES

John Hudson Tiner • Read about the Christian beliefs of this giant of science—it will be eye-opening! **UE+**

Isaac Newton GROUNDBREAKERS

Tony Allan • Interesting biography of physicist Isaac Newton with many insights into his life. **UE+**

HISTORICAL FICTION

The Three Musketeers

Alexandre Dumas • Classic historical fiction, this is a rousing adventure of the French swordsmen who were sworn to protect King Louis XIII. It is filled with intrigue, chivalry, bad guys, and lots of action. (Abbreviated version would be preferable for younger students.) **HS+**

The Pilgrim's Progress

John Bunyan • One of the most-loved, best-selling classics in Christian literature, this is the allegory of Christian, who makes his way from the City of Destruction to the Celestial City. John Bunyan, a simple preacher, wrote this enduring tale while he was in jail for his faith. Great read-aloud. **UE+**

What books did you like best?

_____

_____

_____

_____

_____

_____

The Internet also contains a wealth of information about the Puritans, Pietists, and the Divine Right of Kings.

What sites were the most helpful?

_____

_____

_____

_____

_____

_____

For more books, use these Dewey Decimal numbers in your library:

Puritans & the Puritan Revolution: #941

Elizabethan Age: #942

Pietism: #273

Elizabeth I: #942.055

Mary, Queen of Scots: #941

King Louis XIV: #944

Peter the Great: #947

Oliver Cromwell: #942

Religious Wars in Europe: #940

British Colonies: #973

Russia: #947

Mathematicians & Scientist in the 1600s: #520

▶ **Student Self-Evaluation** UNIT 8, PHASE 1

Dates and hours:_____

Key Concepts

Rephrase the five Key Concepts of this Unit and confirm your understanding of each:

- Europe's Thirty Years' War:

  _____

- British colonization of New World:

  _____

- Galileo & Newton:

  _____

- The Puritan revolution:

  _____

- Pietism:

  _____

Tools for Self-Evaulation

Evaluate your personal participation in the discussions of this Phase. Bearing in mind that a good participant in a discussion is not always the most vocal participant, ask yourself these questions: Were you an active participant? Did you ask perceptive questions? Were you willing to listen to other participants of the discussion and draw out their opinions? Record your observations and how you would like to improve your participation in the future:

_____

_____

Every time period is too complex to be understood in one Phase of study. Evaluate your current knowledge of Puritans, Pietists, & the Divine Right of Kings. What have you focused on so far? What are your weakest areas of knowledge?

_____

Based on the evaluation of this introduction, project ahead what you would like to study more of in the following Phases:

_____

_____

Phase 2

▶ Research & Reporting

Explore one or more of these areas to discover something significant!

The Puritans

Learn more about this branch of Christianity, which developed in England. How were they different in their beliefs and in their actions from those who fully supported the State church (the Church of England)? Who were some of the prominent Puritans during the 1600s? Who were the Separatists and how did they differ from the Puritans? Why did one group of Puritans move to the New World rather than remain in England?

Pietism

Study the Pietist movement in Germany. Report on the lives of Spener and Francke—the two most influential Pietists of the 1600s. What were the defining characteristics of this movement? (Be sure to include information on the missionaries to India sent from the Pietists at Halle.)

Dutch Struggle for Independence

Research and report on the Dutch war for independence from Spain. Include the causes and results of this war; how long it lasted; truces; which areas were in revolt and which were in submission to Spain; the defenses available to the Dutch.

Queen Elizabeth

Research and report on the long reign of Queen Elizabeth. What type of ruler was she? What was her position on war and on the activities of the British in the Spanish Main? What were the results of her rule? How did she impact the Church of England?

Henry IV of France

Henry IV, or Henry of Navarre, was one of the most important kings to ever rule France. Investigate his life: his marriage celebration, how he came to the throne, the Edict of Nantes, his style of rule, his policies, the impact of his reign. How and why did he die?

Divine Right of Kings

Discover more about this political/religious philosophy, where kings receive their authority directly from God and are, therefore, not subject or accountable to anyone on earth. King Louis XIV of France and King James I of England are the prime examples in the 1600s. How did this philosophy affect the government and the people of France and England under these two rulers? What was the impact on the Church?

The Thirty Years' War

Study more about this complex religious conflict. What were its causes? Describe the different personalities and leaders involved, the military strategies used by each side, and the impact of the Treaty of Westphalia. How was Germany impacted by the war? What were the results of this war in other European countries? Who profited the most from this war? Who profited the least?

The Spanish Armada

Study the Spanish Armada. Compare and contrast the military strategies of the Spanish and the English. How did the English Channel, the Atlantic, and the weather all play a part in the outcome? How did the English prepare themselves for the Spanish Armada? What were the goals and plans of the Spanish? How well were these goals met? What was the impact of the Spanish Armada in Spain? In England?

The Puritan Revolution of 1640 & The Restoration

Research and report on King Charles I, Oliver Cromwell, the Puritan Revolution, and Charles II. How did the Irish Revolt impact the Puritan Revolution? How did the religious/political beliefs of the rulers influence this revolution? How did the Puritans change the government of England? What were the results in Parliament? In the everyday lives of the people? In the Church of England? What caused the Restoration of the Monarchy?

European Settlements in North America

Learn more about British, Dutch, French or Spanish colonies in North America. What kind of relationship did the colony have with the home country? What defined their relations with the native people? How did they acquire their land? Was religious unity required or was religious freedom preferred for the colony?

Louis XIV

This absolute monarch—the Sun King—was a tremendously powerful and influential ruler. Learn more about his reign in France. What was his style of government? Why were the nobility required to live at court? Why and how did he fight his "glorious wars"? How was this government funded?

Peter the Great

Investigate this fascinating tzar of the 1600s. What kind of ruler was Peter the Great? How did he implement his changes in Russia? In what fashion did he tour Europe? What did Europeans think of the Russians? How were Estonia and Livonia brought into his realm? Describe the building of the city of St. Petersburg.

English Scientists

Discover the fascinating lives of Isaac Newton and Robert Boyle. Each of these Englishmen were remarkable in their contributions to science, as well as their study of the Scriptures. Describe their achievements.

Trade in the 1600s

Learn more about trade in the East and in the West. What was the East India Company? What was the Dutch East India Company? What companies were created for trade in the West? Was biblical justice and righteousness the norm for the European countries involved in trade? How did they impact the regions in which they traded? What were the major items sought in trade? Where were these items found?

Christian Missions in China

Research and report on Matteo Ricci, a Jesuit missionary to China in the late 1500s. How did his view of missions affect the Chinese? How was his mission philosophy viewed by Europeans? How is his mission philosophy viewed today?

The Telescope

Research and report on the development of the telescope. Who first invented it? How did Galileo create a telescope, and what did he use it for? What improvements were made in later years? Who made these improvements? What were some subsequent discoveries which the telescope allowed?

Shakespeare

Learn more about the Bard of Avon. What is known of his life? Describe English life during the time of Shakespeare. What types of plays did he write? How influential is his work today? If you encounter the question of whether Shakespeare actually wrote all of his plays, decide whether this controversy is based in reality.

▶ Brain Stretchers

The Hapsburgs

Research and report on the Hapsburg dynasty who ruled much of Europe as Holy Roman Emperors and as Spanish kings. When did they come to power? How was power consolidated? When were they finally overthrown? What kind of rulers did this family provide? What religion did the Hapsburgs profess?

Richelieu

Cardinal Richelieu was one of the most powerful men to ever hold the reins of political power in France. Learn more about his life, his work, his attitude towards the Huguenots, and how he influenced 17th century France.

Jansenism

Research and report on the Jansenists in France. Be sure to include Blaise Pascal in your report. What did this reform movement in Catholicism want to change? How effective were they? What happened to the movement?

John Comenius

Comenius is considered by many to be the "Father of Modern Education." Learn more about this man who gained a biblical understanding of education by studying God's Word and the natural world.

Religion in the American Colonies

Discover how the colonies handled the Catholic/Protestant issue. Investigate the various branches of Protestantism and Catholicism, and where they were welcomed in the colonies. Compare and contrast the colonies with the European governments in their handling of religious differences among their citizens.

The Quakers

Learn more about the Quakers. How did their views conflict with other Protestants? How did they live out their belief system? William Penn's Quaker beliefs greatly affected his approach to founding an American colony. How was Pennsylvania different from the other colonies in theory and in practice?

Create Your Own Research Topic

_____

_____

_____

▶ **Timeline**

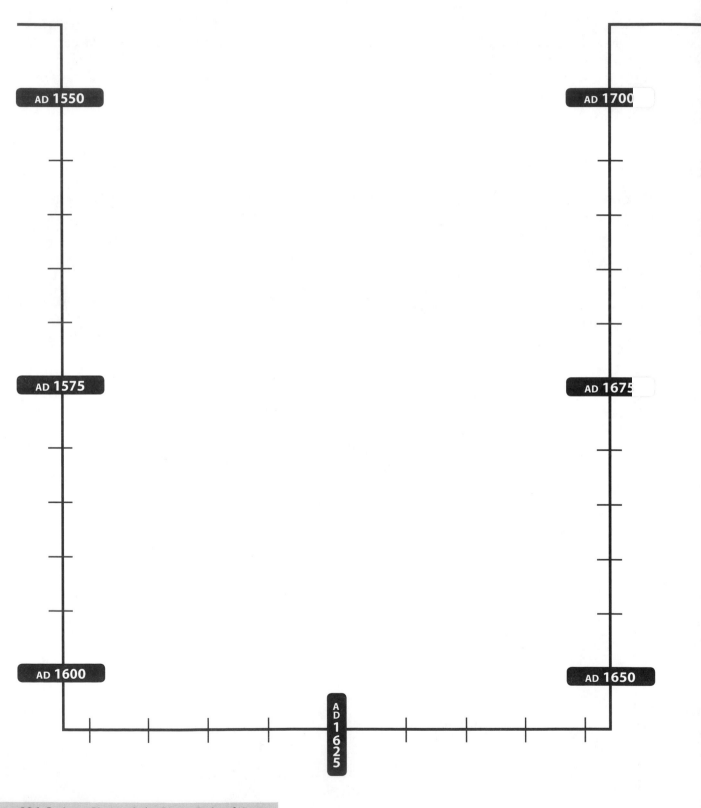

AD 1550

AD 1700

AD 1575

AD 1675

AD 1600

AD 1650

AD 1625

Consider this for your timeline

This time period witnesses the continuing ferocity of struggle between Protestants and Catholics in Europe, between the might of Spain in her Armada and the doughtiness of England in her navy, between American Indians and European colonizers in North America, and between the Divine Right of Kings and the rights of freedom for people in France and England. It is a time of deep-thinking Christians, such as Blaise Pascal, and profoundly Christian scientists, such as Sir Isaac Newton. It is the first time when a crowned monarch of a Christian country is executed by some of its leading Christian citizens—which horrifies the world. It is a complex, riveting, disastrous, and profoundly moving time in history.

Key Events

The Edict of Nantes and its later revocation

Defenestration of Prague

The Thirty Years' War

The Spanish Armada

St. Bartholomew's Day Massacre

Dutch Revolt

The Puritan Revolution

The Pietist movement

The American Colonies established

CONSIDER:

This is the time period in which great advances were made in astronomy, physics, and chemistry. Here are some great vocabulary words, which come from these scientific disciplines, courtesy of Dr. Jay Wile:

acceleration

comet

compound

condensation

distillation

element

force

friction

galaxy

ion

meteor

molecule

perihelion

planet

refraction

speed

transpiration

velocity

▶ # Words to Watch

Remember—The easiest way to learn a subject is to master its terms:

revolt	defenestration	independence	resistance
republic	baroque	gravity	telescope
expedition	truce	parliament	protectorate
commonwealth	divine right	Puritan	Pietist
Jansenist	Separatist	regicide	

Other words you need to look up:

_____

_____

_____

_____

_____

► # Student Self-Evaluation UNIT 8, PHASE 2

Dates and hours:_____

Research Project

- Summarize your research question:

  _____

  _____

- List your most useful sources by author, title, and page number or URL where applicable (continue list in margin if necessary):

  _____

  _____

- Now take a moment to evaluate the sources you just listed. Do they provide a balanced view of your research question? Should you have sought an additional opinion? Are your sources credible (if you found them on your own)? Record your observations:

  _____

  _____

- Evaluate your research project in its final presentation. What are its strengths? If you had time to revisit this project, what would you change? Consider giving yourself a letter grade based on your project's merits and weaknesses.

  _____

  _____

Letter grade _____

You have just completed an area of specific research in the time of the Puritans, Pietists, & the Divine Right of Kings. Now what would you like to explore in the upcoming Phases? Set some objectives for yourself:

_____

Phase 3

► Maps & Mapping

Physical Terrain

» Locate and label Great Britain along with the British colonies in North America, along with Newfoundland in Canada. Shade these with one color.

» Locate and label France along with the French colonies in North America—Nova Scotia (or Acadia) in Canada and Louisiana. Also locate and label Senegal in West Africa. Shade these with a second color.

» Locate and label Spain along with the Spanish colonies in Florida, Central America, and South America (the map provided does not include all of South America). Shade these with a third color.

» Locate and label Holland along with the trading post areas held by the Dutch in the Americas: New Amsterdam (North America) and Guyana (South America). Shade these with a fourth color.

» Locate and label the area in which the Thirty Years' War took place.

Geopolitical

» Locate and color the Spanish Main, from which the Spanish gathered and shipped the gold of the New World to Spain, labeling the major port cities. You might wish to learn more about international piracy along the Spanish Main as you do this exercise—the Spanish treasure fleets drew pirates like flowers draw bees!

» Some colonies/cities were traded by European countries as part of a treaty, while others changed ownership after a successful attack. Locate as many of these changeable colonies as you can find and label them showing to whom they belonged (both past and present).

» Draw the route of the Spanish Armada, showing what happened to it.

» With the end of the Thirty Years' War, label and shade the areas of Catholic Europe and, with a separate color, label and shade the areas of Protestant Europe.

Explore

» *Christian Outreach:* What is the status of evangelical outreach today among Native Americans? What opportunities and what difficulties face those who share the gospel in these areas?

» *Slavery:* With the decimation of the native people in the Americas, due largely to newly introduced European diseases such as smallpox, colonists looked more and more to Africa for slaves to work in the mines and fields. Investigate the geographical locations of the African slave trade to the Americas, beginning in the early 1500s.

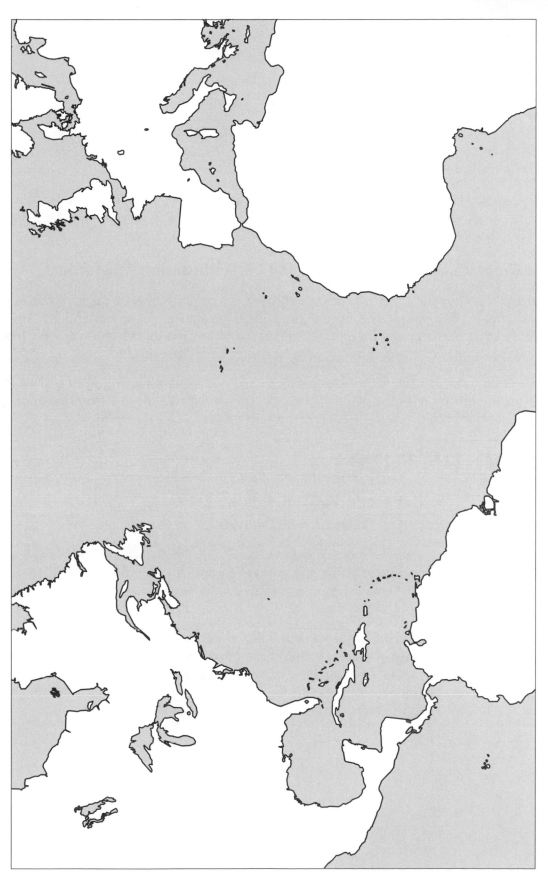

► Art Appreciation

Calling of Saint Matthew by Caravaggio, 1599–1600 Contarelli Chapel, Rome

Michelangelo Merisi, known as Caravaggio (after his birthplace), was the most notable painter of the 17th century in Italy. His unconventional approach to religious art—showing sacred stories through common scenes—revolutionized art.

> » Locate a photo of this painting. How would you describe the figures in the painting? What setting did the artist use for this biblical story? Why do you think this painting was shocking to many of his contemporaries?

The Night Watch by Rembrandt, 1642 Rijksmuseum, Amsterdam

Rembrandt, one of the great geniuses in art history, was commissioned to paint a group portrait of The Company of Captain Frans Banning Cocq and Lieutenant Willem van Ruytenburch. The result was one of his masterpieces, though with the shadowed and indistinct features of some members of the company, his commissions for portraits seem to have dropped off!

> » How would you describe this painting to someone who was not viewing it? What impression does the painting give of the night watch? How did Rembrandt use light and shadow to create mystery?

► Architecture

Cathedra Petri, St. Peter's, Vatican, Rome, architect Gianlorenzo Bernini, 1657–1666

Bernini was the quintessential sculptor and architect of the High Baroque in Rome, and one of the most influential artists of the seventeenth century in Europe. When his friend, Cardinal Barberini, became Pope Urban VIII, Bernini was given so many commissions for St. Peter's in Rome, that he spent much of his life completing them!

> » Locate photos of the Cathedra Petri. This architectural wonder was a reliquary, built to house what was believed to be the chair of Peter. How many different materials can you identify in this structure? How would you describe it? What is the focus point? Why do you think he included the figures of Augustine, Ambrose, Athanasius and John Chrysostom in this structure at the heart of the Vatican?

CONSIDER:

This time period, beginning around AD 1600 is known as the Baroque. It signaled a change from the earlier Renaissance art and architecture, and was fueled by three very significant factors:

The first was that the Counter-Reformation of the Catholic Church used art as one of the means of returning Protestants to the fold, as it was intended to make worship more inviting.

The second factor had to do with a changing understanding of the universe and man's place in it, both from Copernicus's theory and the discovery of the New World. This brought a change to the way artists painted portraits, nature, and everyday life.

The third factor of this time period was the development of absolute monarchies after the tumultuous wars of religion. Kings, such as Louis XIV with his palace of Versailles, wanted appropriately splendid palaces for their dwellings to display on earth the Divine Right of Kings.

▶ Arts in Action

Select one or more, and let your artistic juices flow!

Landscapes

Landscape paintings were popular during the Baroque. They contained a sense of infinitude, of a flatter landscape, a more distant view, and a lowered horizon. Sometimes they included people, and sometimes they did not. (One outstanding example of a Baroque landscape artist is Claude Lorrain.)

Try your hand at drawing or painting a landscape in the Baroque style. You may choose to include people and buildings, or you may focus on nature itself.

Trompe-l'oeil Painting

Another technique used in the Baroque was trompe-l'oeil, which is pronounced "tromp loy," and literally means "to deceive the eye." It was used to create an illusion through the use of perspective. These paintings gave a false perspective, which enabled the artist to

make it seem as if the walls and ceilings were actually extending far beyond their true positions. (The best example is Andrea Pozzo's painted ceiling, "Missionary Work of the Jesuits," in Sant Ignazio, Rome.) See if you can create a bit of trompe-l'oeil:

One suggestion is to take a sheet of poster board and make a window scene. Using perspective, draw or paint the window frame, window sill, and the outdoor scene of your choice. When finished, it should "deceive the eye," and look as if it is a real window! (What a great gift for a shut-in…)

Another suggestion is to take poster board and create a door (in perspective) that fills the entire board. Now put it on a wall in your room. Does it look as if you can open the door and walk into another room?

Trompe-l'oeil ideas courtesy of Sharon Jeffus, Visual Manna.

▶ Science

In 1599 Ulissi Aldrovandi, an Italian naturalist, published his studies in ornithology, the study of birds. Have you ever watched birds and tried to learn more about them? Have you ever listened to a bird song and tried to identify it from its sound? Then you may be a budding ornithologist.

Birds

» Learn more about birds using a good bird book that identifies different types of birds in your region. (Check with your library.) To bring the birds to you, set up a bird feeder outside one of your windows. Make sure to keep the bird feeder full as the birds might come to depend upon it for a food source. Keep a bird journal, notating what kinds of birds come to dine at your feeder, how many, and, perhaps, a sketch of each kind. If you continue the journal through the year, notice the different types of birds that come in different seasons.

According to legend, Galileo sat in church one day and noticed the swinging of a lantern. He observed that, regardless of how long or how short was the sweep of the lantern, each sweep took the same amount of time. This discovery was what allowed pendulum clocks to be invented, which were very accurate in their timekeeping.

Timing the Pendulum

» Try your hand at creating a pendulum. With a stopwatch and a designated timer, go to a local swing set. Time ten sweeps of the swing for each sampling, and then divide by ten. (This will provide better accuracy.) Try going high and fast, low and slow, youngest to oldest. Now shorten the swing and try it again. What did you observe?

Robert Boyle is known as the Father of Modern Chemistry. One of his chemical discoveries involved salting ice to lower the temperature of the contents of a container in the ice. Sound familiar?

Chemistry

» Try this chemistry experiment: Make homemade ice cream! Check what happens when you add salt to the crushed ice. What happens if you add more salt to the ice than is called for in the recipe? What happens if you do not add as much salt to the ice as the recipe suggests?

► Music

The Pietist movement in Germany brought forth hymns that were designed to be sung by every person; therefore they were very simple in composition.

Discover

Jesus, Priceless Treasure

Johann Franck (1618–1677) • This hymn was considered by some Lutherans to be too emotional for congregational use. It is said that Peter the Great had a Russian version made of this hymn in 1724!

Listen

All Glory, Laud, & Honor MUSIC CD

Jesus, Priceless Treasure by Johann Franck (1618–1677)

Baroque music is the beginning of what many term "classical music," though classical is actually a style of its own, which developed soon after the baroque. This is the time period where such masters of music as Vivaldi, Bach, and Handel were composing. The style of music is exuberant and dynamic, and from it were defined the forms and types of music such as the suite, the sonata, the concerto, the opera, and the cantata.

Discover

The Four Seasons   Vivaldi (1678-1741)

Did you know that Vivaldi wrote more than four hundred concertos for the orphan girls at the Conservatory of the Opsedale della Pietà in Venice? He was the head of the conservatory, and performances by these girls were given every Sunday and on all holidays! Listen to a recording of Vivaldi's *The Four Seasons*. Would you describe his music as lively? Do you think students at the conservatory would have enjoyed playing his music?

▶ Cooking

Since we are studying Queen Elizabeth, King James I, and the Puritan Revolution in England, it seems highly appropriate to sample some delightful English foods. This wonderful cake is named for the pastry cook who created it—Sally Lunn, proprietress of a refreshment house in Bath around 1680.

Sally Lunn Bread

½ cup warm water

1 cup milk

⅓ cup sugar

3 eggs

3 *more* cups all-purpose flour

1 pkg. active dry yeast

½ cup cold butter, cut into small pieces

1 tsp salt

3 cups all-purpose flour

Pour the water into a large, warm bowl. Sprinkle on yeast and let stand until bubbly (5–12 minutes). In a small pan, combine milk, butter, sugar, and salt; heat to about 110º (butter need not melt completely). Add to dissolved yeast, then stir in eggs and 3 cups of the flour. Beat until smooth. Add 2½ cups to 3 cups more flour, or enough to make a stiff dough that's too sticky to knead. Cover and let rise in a warm place until doubled (about 1½ hours). Generously grease a 10" tube pan (sides, center tube and bottom) with a removable bottom. Stir down dough, then turn into prepared pan, pushing and punching dough to cover pan bottom evenly. Cover and let rise in a warm place until level with pan top (about 1 hour). Meanwhile, preheat oven to 375º. Bake for about 35 minutes or until well browned. Run a long spatula around pan sides, lift out tube and bread. Loosen bottom of bread with spatula; invert bread and gently twist out tube. Place bread upright on a wire rack; let cool completely. Cut into thin wedges to serve. Makes one large loaf.

► # Student Self-Evaluation UNIT 8, PHASE 3

Dates and hours:_____

Evaluate your projects

List which of the activities listed in this Phase you did:

_____

_____

• Rate your enthusiasm: _____

  Explain: _____

  _____

• Rate the precision of your approach:_____

  Explain: _____

  _____

• Rate your effort towards the completion of the project: _____

  Explain: _____

  _____

• Ask yourself what worked and what did not. What would you do differently in the future, and what would you repeat?

  _____

  _____

• How specifically did these hands-on activities enhance your knowledge of Puritans, Pietists, & the Divine Right of Kings? What made them worthwhile?

  _____

  _____

• In the first three Phases of this Unit, what aspect of the time period has most captured your imagination? What would you like to creatively pursue to conclude your study?

  _____

  _____

Phase 4

▶ In Your Own Way...

We have seen the Spanish Armada defeated, a revolution in England, the Sun King in France, North America colonized, the Thirty Years' War in Germany, the scientific achievements of Galileo and Newton, the Pietist influence in Protestantism, and the birth of the Baroque. Now, choose a selection of these activities, or create your own, which will best express what you have learned from this Unit.

LINGUISTICS

Journalism

You are a staff reporter for The *Puritan Paper*. You have been assigned to accompany the Puritan leaders who will speak to King James I just after he is crowned King of England. Write the news of his views. Include any items you consider pertinent.

The Dutch have just won their independence from Spain! Interview the "man on the street" in Holland for his views on this triumph. Next, interview the "man on the street" in Spain for his views on this disaster.

You have been assigned the intriguing story of interviewing Peter the Great as he tours around Europe. There's just one problem: he wants to remain incognito and is, therefore, in disguise. Your mission is to figure out how to interview him while he plays all of his different characters.

Prose

Imagine you were an orphan being cared for by the Pietists of Halle. Write your story, including they way they have instructed you in the faith.

Write a book for children about the Pilgrims going to North America, their native neighbors, and the blessed help of the Pilgrims' unexpected teacher, Squanto.

Playing with Words

Finish this limerick:

King Philip sent out an Armada
Which didn't go quite where it oughta . . .

ART

Painting/Drawing

Create a painting that expresses the heart of Pietism. You may wish to do this as a collage, as an abstract, symbolically, or as a set scene.

Paint a Baroque-style landscape of North America's Eastern seaboard, either just prior to the first British settlements or at the beginning of these colonies. You may choose to include people and buildings in your painting, or focus on the beauties of God's hand in nature.

Cartooning

Create a political cartoon showing the European powers struggling with each other to capture the trade routes in the East. Among the contenders are the British East India Company, the Dutch East India Company, the French East India Company, and the Portuguese and Spanish.

Graphic Design

Cardinal Richelieu has hired you to create an enlistment poster which will help him gain recruits for the army as well as selling the idea to the people of France that Catholic France is taking up arms in the Thirty Years' War on the side of the Protestants! Good luck—you're going to need it.

Sir Isaac Newton's fan club has requested matching T-shirts that graphically demonstrate the genius of their hero. Remember, a picture is worth a thousand words.

MUSIC

Performance Practice

With your teacher's help, select an appropriate piece of Baroque music. Prepare and perform the piece for an audience. Communicate with your audience the reason for your selection either in the program notes or in a short speech.

DRAMA

Comedy

Create a skit with the title, "If it ain't Baroque, don't fix it!" Within the framework of this comic skit, enlighten your audience—help them learn about Baroque art, music, architecture, and a few significant people of the time. REMEMBER, humor is memorable, and boredom is forgettable.

Choose a scene from one of Shakespeare's comedies, such as *The Comedy of Errors* or *As You Like It,* and act it out. Provide your audience with program notes so they understand the setting of what they are about to see.

Drama

Reenact the major events during the struggle of the Puritan Revolution of 1640 in England. You may choose to uphold Oliver Cromwell as the hero, or, instead, choose to make Charles I a tragic martyr. Both views were held by various sides.

Choose a scene from one of Shakespeare's tragedies, such as *Hamlet* or *Romeo & Juliet,* and act it out. As noted above, provide your audience with program notes.

Puppetry

Create the puppets' version of the Spanish Armada for children: ships, roaring waves, and all. Children may enjoy having the opportunity to "boo" at the bad guys!

Prop Needs:

_____

_____

Costume Ideas:

_____

_____

Role/Player:

_____

_____

Set Suggestions:

_____

_____

MOVEMENT

Pantomime

Pantomime the story of John Bunyan's *Pilgrim's Progress*. It might be helpful to have a narrator read occasional and appropriate selections from the book during the performance of the mime.

Dance:

Choreograph a dance that shows Matteo Ricci's mission to the Chinese, and their response to the gospel. Appropriate music and costume will greatly enhance this performance!

Action

With a group of four, create a stylized action of the most important events of Henry IV's rule of France, including how he came to the throne. Either provide program notes or brief narrations so that the audience will understand what they are watching.

CONCEPTUAL DESIGN

Outshine the Sun . . . King

Texans say "Everything's bigger in Texas." Therefore, with a Texas-sized attitude, your assignment is to outdo—on paper—some visual aspect of life at Versailles. You may choose to outdo the furniture, the architecture, the hair-dos, the clothing, the art, the horse-drawn coaches, etc. Whatever you choose, though, must be designed even more ornately and outrageously than the Baroque style favored by King Louis XIV.

CREATE YOUR OWN EXPRESSION

_____

_____

_____

_____

▶ Student Self-Evaluation UNIT 8, PHASE 4

Dates and hours:_____

Evaluate your projects

- What creative project did you choose?

  _____

- What did you expect from your project, and how does the final project compare to your initial expectations?

  _____

- What do you like about your project? What would you change?

  _____

In Conclusion

Revisit the five Key Concepts from the beginning of this Unit. Explain how your understanding of and appreciation for each has grown over the course of your study.

- _____

  _____

- _____

  _____

- _____

  _____

- _____

  _____

- _____

  _____

Record your concluding thoughts on the Puritans, Pietists, & the Divine Right of Kings:

_____

_____

_____

Revivals & Revolutions

Key Concepts

- The Enlightenment

- The Great Awakening & beginning of abolition

- The Seven Years' War

- Revolutions in France & America

- Cook's voyages

Oil painting by Johann Valentin Haidt (1700-1780) depicting Count von Zinzendorf preaching to the nations of the world

Winds of change begin to blow . . .

As the eighteenth century dawned, the struggle for mastery in commerce, world trade, and international power continued between France and England, causing unrest to ripple across Europe and the overseas colonies. One measure of this rivalry was displayed at the French court of Louis XIV when he welcomed with open arms the deposed king of England, James II. Not only were he and his family welcomed, they were treated royally. In fact, James II set up a court in exile, known as the *Jacobite* court (from the Latin form of James: *Jacobus*). At the death of James II in 1701, his son was recognized by France, Spain, and the pope as James III, King of England, though the title was hollow since he did not have the throne to go with it. From their French exile, just across the water from England, the Jacobites plotted and attempted many times to gain that throne.

Power stuggles in Europe

Just prior to the death of James II, Charles II, king of Spain and last of the Spanish Hapsburg kings, died without heirs. Though Spain was no longer a major military power, it still retained much of its wealthy overseas holdings, making the empty throne a significant and alarming political event in Europe. For several years, various proposals had been suggested for the successor, but in the end, Charles II formally named Duke Philip, the grandson of Louis XIV, to be the next king of Spain.

Louis XIV was not concerned with balance, however.

As you might imagine, this was not well received in the rest of Europe. The startling concept of uniting the massively powerful nation of France with the Spanish Empire was utterly abhorrent to other European rulers, great and small. Instead of Duke Philip, most preferred Archduke Charles, an Austrian Hapsburg and brother of the Holy Roman Emperor, in order to maintain the fragile political balance of power in Europe.

Louis XIV was not concerned with balance, however. As soon as Charles II died, he embarked on his fourth and final war of aggression, which is known as the War of the Spanish Succession. His invasion of the Spanish Netherlands (yet again) caused England, the Dutch Republic, and Austria to sign an alliance and go to war against him. This was not to be a successful war for Louis. Facing superior military opponents, he was unable to withstand his enemies on the battlefields in Europe or in the North American colonies. This prompted his earnest desire to come to peaceful terms with his opponents. However, they were not interested UNLESS Louis agreed to assist them with money and soldiers in forcibly removing his grandson from the Spanish throne. Negotiations broke down, understandably, at this point.

Then, in a startling and unexpected development, Archduke Charles succeeded his deceased brother as the new Holy Roman Emperor. Under his new title, Charles VI, he controlled the vast lands of the Austrian Hapsburg territory, which comprised much of Central Europe. His allies in the War of Spanish Succession were now confronted with an even more unpleasant scenario: a return to the days when the Hapsburg emperor also held the reigns of the Spanish Empire. That had been the envious position of the powerful Charles V (the king/emperor who tried Martin Luther), and they were unwilling to help in any way to make this possible. So, lacking motivation for continuing this war, they willingly negotiated with Louis XIV to end it, and Philip remained the Spanish king.

The treaty in 1714, which ended the war, known as the Treaty of Utrecht, accomplished more than just the cessation of hostilities. It raised a new nation to a place of dominance through acquisition of territory and trade. The treaty took some of France's possessions and gave them to Britain:

Newfoundland and Acadia (which became known as Nova Scotia) in North America, and Gibraltar and Minorca in the Mediterranean. Spain also had to bow to British superiority by awarding to the British South Sea Company the *asiento*—the much coveted privilege to supply African slaves to the Spanish colonies (a privilege that was nonetheless vile and horrendous in terms of human life). This *asiento* promised to be a lucrative venture that would yield the English new trading opportunities, as well as a chance to legally gain some of the gold and silver bullion flowing from the Spanish Main, without having to steal it. Britain emerged from this war as the clear winner, the new global powerhouse.

Ministry in North America

There is more at stake in this world, though, than power and profit. The Creator of all is working out His plans and purposes for redemption. This can be seen in the early stirrings of an extraordinary move of God known as the *Great Awakening*. It began in 1700, when a humble country clergyman was sent to the colony of Maryland by the bishop of London. Maryland, which had been a haven of refuge for Catholics, was now largely under the authority of the Church of England. With its many parishes scattered throughout the colony, demand grew for a priest who could superintend the entire area. Thomas Bray, the Anglican parish priest sent to meet this need, was deeply concerned with the lack of books and resources available to those ministering in the colony. Recognizing this problem even before his departure, Bray organized the Society for Promoting Christian Knowledge

This was not a mere intellectual exercise in academics.

(S.P.C.K.), to fund the establishment of libraries in the colonies and in England. This was not a mere intellectual exercise in academics. Thomas Bray had a deep desire to make the rich heritage of Christianity available to clergy and laity alike, that they might be rooted and built up in Christ and established in the faith (Colossians 2.7). Even more, Bray yearned for the spread of the good news of Jesus beyond the colonists to the Native Americans and the African slaves. He believed that the contribution of these other people groups would add great richness and diversity to the Body of Christ. His vision led, in 1701, to the Society for the Propagation of the Gospel in Foreign Parts (S.P.G.), which continues to this day under the name *United Society for the Propagation of the Gospel*.

Beginning of modern missions

The founding of the S.P.G. had an unanticipated consequence, which would become the source of tremendous Christian ministry to India. When the king of Denmark, Frederick IV, learned that the English had formed an organization for taking the gospel to non-Europeans in the West, he determined in 1705 that he would do something to promote Christianity in the East. According to Dr. W. F. Stevenson in his book *Dawn of the Modern Mission*, the Danish king realized, "for ninety years there had been a Danish East India Company; for ninety years Danish ships had sailed to Tranquebar (on the southern coast of India); Danish merchants had traded and grown rich in the settlement, Danish governors had ruled it, Danish soldiers had protected it; but no ship had ever carried a Danish missionary to preach the gospel." It was for this reason that missionaries from the German Pietists (the Danish-Halle mission) were sent out by the Danish king to minister to the Tamil people—arguably the first missionary venture of the Protestant Church in history. The most famous of these missionaries was Bartholomaeus Ziegenbalg, who ministered at Tranquebar from 1706 until his death in 1719, despite the objections and opposition of the Danish colonial rulers. In that short time, Ziegenbalg translated the New Testament and part of the Old Testament into the Tamil language, saw 355 Tamil people convert to Christianity, established schools, and wrote a Tamil dictionary and grammar. Having learned the language, studied the literature, and conversed directly with the people (since he had no need of interpreters), Ziegenbalg proved to also be instrumental in educating Europeans about the people and culture of India.

> In this same year, Queen Anne of England, the last daughter of the deposed King James II, died without heirs.

In 1714 Frederick IV took a more permanent step for missions when he established the Royal College for Advancing the Cause of the Gospel. This college, closely connected with the German Pietists of Halle, sent out dozens of missionaries to India to touch the lives of those who had previously been seen merely as a source of trade and wealth.

British House of Hanover

In this same year, Queen Anne of England, the last daughter of the deposed King James II, died without heirs. Some years earlier, Parliament had passed the Act of Settlement, which stated that her successor must be Protestant. This meant that the next king would not be the remaining Catholic son of James II, but the Protestant great grandson of James I.

Reigning as the Elector of Hanover, this distantly related, German-born, French-speaking, disagreeable man would now become George I, king of England. His succession to the throne, while a son of James II still lived, was a very unpopular move among many people in the British Isles, resulting in riots in England when he came to power. The discontent in Scotland was even greater than in England, leading, in 1715, to the First Jacobite Rising. This was a short-lived attempt to bring James Edward (known to his friends as James III, and to his opponents as *The Pretender*) to the throne.

With many people becoming increasingly disillusioned with the immoral lifestyle of George I, another attempt was made in 1719, this time with the aid of Spain. It failed even more miserably than its predecessor. As history has shown, the House of Hanover was there to stay.

The Moravians

In 1727, the same year that George II of England ascended to the throne, the Holy Spirit was moving powerfully among a group of persecuted Protestant believers. They had been living together as refugees on an estate in Saxony, in what is now Germany, but it had been neither peaceful nor joyous. In fact, there were bitter rivalries, unkind accusations and disagreements over theological differences. This all changed, however, when Count von Zinzendorf, on whose land they had been living, called them to a time of prayer, repentance, and reconciliation. As they began to unite in prayer, God brought revival, radically changing hearts and lives. These believers, known to us as the *Moravians*, now filled to overflowing with God's love, began to joyfully and courageously take the gospel throughout the world. Some went to the West Indies to work among the African slaves, while others journeyed to America to share with Native Americans. Still others went out to Greenland, Suriname, West and South Africa, Estonia, Labrador, and even to the remote islands of Nicobar off the coast of India. This was not a good idea, conceived by nice people. It was a God idea, fulfilled by obedient people.

As they began to unite in prayer, God brought revival, radically changing hearts and lives.

One of the more famous stories of the Moravians comes from the journey of John Wesley to the colony of Georgia in America. Georgia (named for King George II) had been founded by James Ogelthorpe in 1732 as a place where the poor and destitute in England might find a new life and where those who had been persecuted for their Protestant faith might find a haven. He took a group of settlers to this new colony in 1733, and a group of German refugees who had been expelled from their homes in Salzburg followed the next year. In 1735 the Anglican minister John Wesley, at the request of General Ogelthorpe, sailed to Georgia to serve the needs of the widely diverse, growing community. It was on this four-month voyage to America that he saw the solid and unshakeable faith of the Moravians in action, during a storm that was so vicious and terrifying that it actually broke the ship's mast. While everyone else was panicking and crying out in fear, the Moravians, with utmost peace and calmness, sang hymns and prayed—a startling contrast, which caused John Wesley to question the reality of his own faith. He would come to that same peace and trust in God in 1738, but not until after first failing miserably in his attempts to serve the Georgia colony (he was actually put on trial there!) and his subsequent return to England.

The Great Awakening

To those hungry to see the reality of God expressed through His Church, it was obvious that this was, indeed, a divine stirring sent from above.

Prior to Wesley's departure, he wrote his colleague, George Whitefield, to request that he also come serve in Georgia. Whitefield arrived in the colony too late to see his friend, but his three month sojourn there gave him an opportunity to start an orphanage for boys and to lay the foundation for ongoing ministry, which would last for decades throughout the American colonies. George Whitefield's preaching, and people's response to it, was part of the powerful revival known as the *Great Awakening*, which took place simultaneously in England and in America. It is interesting to note that it was these two friends who were among the best known preachers of the 1700s, and, in certain circles, the most controversial. John Wesley's main place of ministry during the Great Awakening was in Britain while George Whitefield ministered throughout America and the British Isles.

The third noted preacher of the Great Awakening was the American Jonathan Edwards. His book *A Faithful Narrative of the Surprising Work of God*, on the 1734–35 revival of Northampton in the Massachusetts colony, provided Christians on both sides of the Atlantic insight into God's mysterious move among lethargic and lukewarm church-goers. To those hungry to see the reality of God expressed through His Church, it was obvious that this was, indeed, a divine stirring sent from above.

Though many people in England and America were turning their hearts and thoughts to God, others remained solidly fixed on the kingdoms of this earth. This was demonstrated in 1739 when Parliament and the nation of England were roused to fury against the Spanish to the point of war. Not coincidentally, this was just as the *asiento* given by Spain to the English was about to expire. The cause for this fury?—the display of a severed ear, reportedly belonging to the British sea captain Robert Jenkins. He dramatically told the story of Spanish coast guards who, under the privileges of the *asiento*, had boarded his ship and then tortured him. The ensuing war between Spain and England, appropriately known as the War of Jenkin's Ear, was the opening prelude to a much larger and more encompassing conflict, known as the War of Austrian Succession.

War of Austrian Succession

The reasons for a war over succession in Austria are similar to what we have already seen in the Spanish succession. And remarkably, one of the central figures of the earlier war, Archduke Charles, is central to the beginning of this new war. Charles, who had become Emperor Charles VI, did not have a living son to succeed him. So he spent the last decades of his reign convincing other European rulers to agree to his Pragmatic Sanction, which stated that all of the Austrian Hapsburg lands would descend, in their entirety, to his daughter, Maria Theresa. Though all said a diplomatic "Yes" to his proposition, two changed their minds after Charles died.

The most aggressive and audacious of these two was Frederick II of Prussia. Casting a covetous eye on one province belonging to Maria Theresa, Frederick marched his unopposed and very powerful army into that rich land of Silesia before anyone realized what was happening. Frederick had hoped that Maria Theresa, with her poor finances and insufficient army, would recognize his superiority and gracefully relinquish all rights to Silesia—even believing that she would welcome him as an ally against her other enemies. His hopes were unfounded.

From 1740 until 1748, much of Europe was embroiled in the struggle between Prussia and Austria. France, Spain, and Bavaria joined forces with Prussia, hoping to win some of the spoils of war, while Austria had only one ally on its side, the seagoing nation of Britain. The contest raged back and forth for years, with Austria gaining in strength and power, until France tried a different ploy. When the French promised armed support to Bonnie Prince Charlie (the Catholic son of the Old Pretender) in the next chapter of the Jacobite Rebellion, England quickly took its soldiers from the field and brought them home to protect the throne of Hanover from the Jacobites. With Austria fighting alone, Maria Theresa was forced to surrender most of Silesia to Frederick II in the 1748 treaty ending this war.

The contest raged back and forth for years, with Austria gaining in strength and power, until France tried a different ploy.

While nations battled on the European continent, the colonies of France and England faced each other on the American continent in what was known to the colonists as King George's War. It really was an escalation of the Anglo-Spanish War of Jenkin's Ear, which had been fought in the Caribbean and in Georgia. Now, the war was being fought in the northernmost North American colonies, with British colonists and their native allies on one side and the French with their natives allies on the other. Many border skirmishes took place between 1744 and 1748, but the only major victory was when the English captured Louisburg at the mouth of the St. Lawrence river, a strategic French fortress. The English returned it to the French, however, at the signing of the treaty, which ended the War of Austrian Succession. The reason? They preferred the British colony of Madras in India (which had been captured by the French during this conflict), and were willing to trade for it.

Though a much greater armed conflict would soon erupt in India as part of the global Seven Years' War, the War of Austrian Succession did, for a time, pit the French East India Company against the British East India Company. Each of these companies existed for the purpose of commercial trade, though the British East India Company was far more profitable. The French were the undisputed winners of this brief contest, though, at the end of the war, they actually returned everything they had conquered to the British in order to regain their North American fortress of Louisburg. It looked, to the unsuspecting eye, that things had returned to status quo in India, but such was not the case.

It looked, to the unsuspecting eye, that things had returned to status quo in India.

In order to better understand the tension between these two trading companies, let us consider the situation of India in the 1700s. With the rulership of the Mogul dynasty (a branch of Tamerlane's Mongol horde), northern India had experienced an unusual political stability for about two hundred years. The Mogul emperors, though Muslim, had been able to remain in power over their native subjects for centuries, partly due to their tolerance of Hinduism, the religion of India, and partly due to their extraordinary effectiveness as administrators. This began to change toward the end of the 1600s, when the Mogul emperor Aurangzeb changed this policy of religious tolerance. His successors found themselves ruling an empire in decline, and by the 1740s, there were several political and religious factions working at cross purposes. Not the least of these were the political connections made by various Indian rulers with both the French and British East India companies. The conclusion, at least as far as the colonial conflict between these two countries, was just beyond the horizon.

Seven Years' War

In 1754 the final conflict in a century and a half of hostility between the colonial aspirations of France and England began not in India, but in North America. The resulting war was known in America as the French and Indian War (1754–1763) and as the Seven Years' War (1756–63) after it spread to Europe. It was titled by English contemporaries, "The Great War for Empire," because the result was Britain's acquisition of massive amounts of colonial territory, comprising most of France's holdings in North America and the East.

Why did this war begin in North America? At issue was the foundational question of whether the British or French owned the vast wilderness between the Allegheny Mountains and the Mississippi River. The ever-expanding number of British colonists were hungry for land, while the French traders were eager to protect their sources and profits by keeping native lands free of settlers. Working at cross-purposes, fueled by strong religious differences, and bitterly hostile to each other by virtue of the age-old French/English rivalry, these colonists did not sit down at the negotiating table to work out their differences. When the French sent an explorer through the Ohio River valley in 1749, the British quickly sent a surveyor to the same land in 1750. The French then built a string of forts along the Allegheny River in Pennsylvania, to clearly delineate and separate New France from British lands. This was like throwing down the gauntlet for the British. The colonial governor of Virginia sent George Washington to the French to protest against their actions, but the fortified French were not about to leave. So, in 1754, a fateful decision was reached: to send Washington and a group of colonial troops to forcibly remove the French. Though they were unsuccessful in this first battle of the French and Indian War, the British colonists continued to struggle against the better trained and more numerous French forces. The tide turned when the English statesman, William Pitt, took charge of the war effort. He correctly saw that England's greatest need was to fully support the war effort in the colonies, and thus committed a large number of British regulars to assist the colonists. This was the first time Britain had taken such an active role in the colonial wars, and, though it accomplished the desired victory, eventually it also had the revolutionary and wholly undesirable effect of setting the British colonies of North America against their homeland. We'll learn more about that shortly.

With the capture of Quebec in 1759, England became the virtual master of North America. The treaty which ended the war gave almost all of New France—which we now call Canada—and the territory east of the Mississippi to England. The British also were granted the Spanish holdings in Florida, while Spain received in compensation the Isle of Orleans (including the city of New Orleans) and all of the French lands west of the Mississippi River.

The tide turned when the English statesman, William Pitt, took charge of the war effort.

On the European continent, the Seven Years' War pitted Prussia (with its new ally, England) against Austria, who had allied itself with France and Russia. Since England was focusing its efforts on the colonial side of the war, the undersized Prussia was left to battle against major nations who had a seemingly endless supply of soldiers. Though Frederick was by far the best military general in this war, as the years and battles continued in this life and death struggle, he had finally come to the point where defeat was standing right outside his door. It was at this moment that an extraordinary turn of events changed his ashes to glory. The Russian Empress, who was Frederick's implacable foe, died, leaving her empire to Peter III. The new emperor, as it turns out, was a devoted admirer of Frederick II! He quickly ended his part of the war with Prussia and formed an alliance with Frederick II. This shocking act, highly unpopular with the Russian nation, which had successfully captured Frederick's capital city of Berlin in the war, was one of but a few taken by Tsar Peter III—he was assassinated shortly afterwards. It did the trick for Frederick, however, since Maria Theresa realized that facing a Russian-Prussian alliance was certain to spell failure for her. The war ended in 1763, with Prussia keeping Silesia, and England winning both prestige and territory—the vast colonial lands formerly belonging to France in North America and India.

The British victory came with an enormous price tag. The cost for military expenditures more than doubled Britain's yearly budget, which required huge increases in taxes. With the acquisition of Canada at the end of the war, the cost of defending their vastly expanded North American colonies suddenly added an immense strain to the already burdensome British debt load. It seemed perfectly reasonable to the British Parliament that those who had benefited by the terrific amount of money expended should share the burden, especially given the fact that the colonies were quite wealthy.

It was at this moment that an extraordinary turn of events changed his ashes to glory.

Stirrings of the American Revolution

The colonists saw it quite differently. They had been protecting their own borders for years, and had worked diligently to gain the wealth they now possessed. Though they were grateful for the recent assistance, they did not believe it gave England the right to take what was rightfully theirs, and saw Parliament as unlawfully seeking to violate their rights as Englishmen.

The Great Awakening played a part in this argument. Under the American preaching tours of George Whitefield, the colonies had their first taste of a nationwide event, with him as their first cultural hero. No longer divided and separate colonies, the revived colonists began to see themselves as united in Christ. A growing sense of national unity was the result.

Also, the religious fires lit by the revival changed the values of many people. Their day-to-day lives now included a heightened awareness of the Kingdom of God, and because of this, they sought to put Him first in their actions and attitudes. It was no longer business as usual.

As time went on, many began to see America, with its religious liberty, as central to God's end-time purposes. Later, as the revival cooled, some began to equate the biblical definition of freedom (free from sin) with political freedom. This meant that civil oppression, which was their perspective of England's increasing tax demands on the colonies, was now the archenemy of the liberty God intended people to have. Since they had the example of Christians, during the French wars of religion, claiming the right to go to war against religious oppression, this was probably a logical step for the time.

Instead of submitting to political injustice, many colonial Americans believed that the answer lay in forming an entirely new style of government— one based upon the biblical idea of a covenant. Rather than allowing an oppressive monarchy to

Statue of Captain James Cook, London, England

reign over them, colonists began to dialogue with one another about what should be done. Some held the position that justice and liberty would be better achieved by formulating a new framework for civil government, and, with this new framework as a guide, to allow citizens an active voice in choosing who would rule over them. This was the seed of the American vision of republic.

Not every colonist, and certainly not every Christian, agreed with this idea. To achieve it would require a rebellion and necessitate taking up arms against the lawful ruler. Among the American colonists, there were numerous groups, such as the Quakers, the Mennonites, and the Moravians, who believed the proper approach to tyranny was pacifism. On the other side of the Atlantic, John Wesley—called the Father of the Great Awakening in England—believed that materialism had choked the good fruit of revival in the colonies and was, in fact, the real source of rebellion.

Regardless of the actual motivation of the colonists, the British Parliament and the newly crowned King George III regarded the actions of the dissenting colonists, such as the Boston Tea Party, as treason and, in 1775 they took strong measures to shut them down. This unleashed the American Revolution, which lasted from 1775 to 1783. The war presented quite a picture to interested bystanders. On one side was the most powerful empire in the world and its formidable navy, and on the other side, a struggling collection of colonies who could barely host an army of men on the field, much less pay their salaries. Very little hope and even less help were offered to the Americans by the watching Europeans—apart from the heroic efforts of the French aristocrat Lafayette—until a much-needed American victory at Saratoga in 1777 showed they had a fighting chance.

The colonists saw it quite differently.

France, under its new king and ever ready to take up a battle against its long-term foe England, joined the Americans as allies in 1778, sending their naval fleet and troops to fight the British in America. Spain and the Netherlands also joined with the Americans in their struggle, making this an international war rather than an inhouse colonial revolt. Almost unbelievably, the Americans and their allies were able to bring the war to a triumphant conclusion with the surrender of Britain's General Cornwallis at Yorktown in 1781. Negotiations for formally ending the war dragged on for two years, but at last a treaty was signed in which Britain recognized the independence of the United States.

Stirrings of the French Revolution

Four years prior to France's American alliance, a new French king, Louis XVI, had come to power. At his accession to the throne, France still claimed the distinction of being the most powerful and wealthy nation in the world, though Britain would have disputed this title most earnestly. Despite the fact that they had lost most of their empire at the end of the Seven Years' War and had been the losers in several expensive wars, the French still had one of the highest standards of living in the world.

However, by the 1780s, the problem of taxation without representation, which initially raised the flag of revolt in the American colonies was now causing problems in France. The enormous burden of taxation was falling squarely on the shoulders of the bourgeois and the peasants, who could least afford it, while the nobility and clergy remained exempt from taxation. Discontented rumblings were being heard throughout the cities and villages, voicing the need to address this perceived injustice.

The war presented quite a picture to interested bystanders.

At the same time, Louis XVI found that his government was facing a wall of insurmountable debt. It was time to ask the aristocracy to help out, to bear their share of the load by paying taxes. Unfortunately, they refused. There was no where else to turn, so in 1789, he summoned the Estates-General (the French version of the British Parliament), which had not met for more than one hundred and fifty years. The country erupted with excitement, as people throughout the nation began to see the possibility of at last gaining a voice in the government. The excitement turned to furor, however, when the king attempted to use force to shut down the Estates-General for not obeying his commands. And once the furor began, it could not be quenched. The French Revolution (1789–99) and its revolutionary army turned not only France but much of Europe upside down.

Without the leavening action of the Great Awakening, the revolution of France had little in common with the American Revolution beyond the use of weapons and words. Where the Americans had cried out to God to aid them in their struggle, the French enthroned an actress on the altar of Notre Dame Cathedral in Paris as the goddess of Reason. Where the Americans had been able to draw other nations to their cause, France was left isolated and alone, as other European nations viewed the terror of their revolution (including the massive number of executions) with horror. Where America's colonies united in the struggle against their common enemy, France found itself a house divided, as more than two-thirds of its departments (districts) rose up in rebellion—against the revolution!

What they needed was a savior. What they found was a military genius. His name? Napoleon Bonaparte. Discover his story, what he learned about the Savior of the world, and what happened next in the final volume of History Revealed: *World Empires, World Missions, World Wars.*◄

Phase 1

▶ Listen to This

What in the World? VOL. 2

DISC FOUR:

» The Enlightenment (track 6)

» The Church's Response (track 7)

» The Seven Years' War (track 8)

» Revolutions (track 9)

True Tales VOL. 2

DISC THREE:

» The Moravians (track 2)

» Captain Cook (track 4)

Digging Deeper VOL. 2

DISC THREE: THE REFORMING CHURCH

» Great Awakening in America (track 8)

▶ Read For Your Life

The Holy Bible

» **The place of man's intellect in the Enlightenment:** Proverbs 14:12

» **The Great Awakening's invitation to the poor and down-trodden:** Luke 14:16–24

» **The Church's answer to the Enlightenment (consider the emptiness & futility of Rousseau's philosophy):** Romans 1:16–23

» **The Great Awakening's impact on Christians:** Romans 12:1-2; Ephesians 3:14–21

» **Wesley's discipleship of others & Methodism's beginning:** 2 Timothy 2:2–5, 4:2; Titus 2:11–15, 2 Corinthians 2:14–17; Colossians 4:6; 1 Peter 3:15

Key People (Church)

Isaac Watts
English hymn writer

Count von Zinzendorf
Moravian Church leader

Jonathan Edwards
Colonial theologian

John Wesley
Cofounder of Methodist Church

Charles Wesley
Cofounder & hymn writer

George Whitefield
Evangelist of Great Awakening

John Newton
Slaver turned preacher

Robert Raikes
Founded Sunday Schools

Phillis Wheatley
First published African-American woman poet

Key People
(World)

Voltaire
Influential French writer

Benjamin Franklin
American scientist & diplomat

Rousseau
French political theorist

Frederick the Great
Prussia's Enlightenment king

Captain Cook
Famous explorer

Catherine the Great
Empress of Russia

George Washington
First U.S. President

Louis XVI
King prior to revolution

Mozart
Musical genius

Lafayette
Aristocrat/revolutionary

▶ # Talk Together

Opinion Column

» What did you find to be the most interesting aspect, or the most fascinating person, you encountered in your introduction to the Great Awakening, the Enlightenment, the American Revolution, and the French Revolution?

» Imagine you had the opportunity to travel with Captain Cook on his voyages. Do you think you would want to accompany him? Why or why not? For what reasons do you think people of his own time might have wanted to accompany him?

» John Wesley, after an incident when he was saved out of a burning house, described himself as "a brand plucked from the fire," a biblical metaphor from Zechariah 3:2. Have you had any experiences in your life that helped you to know that God had a plan for you? What happened? Do you have a Scripture to describe it, as Wesley did?

» Imagine you are a British colonist living in America. There is a rumor that King George III may be planning to appoint English Anglican bishops over all of the colonial churches. What is your response? What might be the response of your neighbors?

» George Whitefield's voice was so strong that he could preach to as many as 30,000 people without the use of a microphone, and his preaching caused a stir wherever he went. Knowing this, do you think you would have liked traveling with him? Why do you suppose people came to listen to him? What do you think motivated the "unchurched" miners in England to stand after a long day's work to listen to Whitefield preach?

» Why do you think the abolition of the slave trade came to a head in the 1700s? Why was it not pursued before that time?

» The Declaration of Independence speaks of all men being created equal, and being endowed by their Creator with certain unalienable rights including life, liberty, and the pursuit of happiness. The slogan of the French Revolution was: "Liberty, Equality, Fraternity." In your opinion, did the American Revolution fulfill the goals of the Declaration of Independence? In what ways? Did the French Revolution fulfill its goals? In what ways?

Critical Puzzling

» Charles Wesley, John's brother, was one of the most prolific hymn writers in history, writing more than 7,000 hymns and gospel songs! Why do you think he spent so much time writing hymns? What effect do you think music, especially music to worship God, has on people?

» Consider the philosophy of the Enlightenment. What do you think it means to be "man-centered"? How does this differ from biblical Christianity? What might be the results of this different way of thinking?

» What happens when a society removes God and God's laws from their thoughts and standards? In the French Revolution, how did the leaders show their disregard of the Catholic Church and of God? Do you think that the persecution and exile of the Huguenots during the 1600s made a difference in this moment of history? Why or why not?

» What do you think it means to be methodical? How did this describe John Wesley's approach to serving God? Do you think the term "Methodists" is appropriate for an organization founded by John Wesley? What are some other terms that could be used to describe Wesley's ministry?

» The American Revolution, in some ways, looked back to the Puritan Revolution of 1640. Why do you think this was the case? How were the Puritans in England related in philosophy and thinking to the colonists of America? How did their views impact the way Americans sought their independence?

» Jonathan Edwards was an American pastor in Northampton, Massachusetts, when revival broke out in his church. This revival changed not only the people in the church, but the town as well. Consider some of the changes true revival might bring in people's lives. How would it affect a church? A community? A nation?

» In what ways do you think the French and Indian War in the American colonies helped to bring Europe into the Seven Years' War? How were the events related? What might the impact to Europe have been if the French/Austrian/Russian/Swedish side had won the war? How would it have affected North America? How was Canada affected by the Seven Years' War?

» Catherine the Great of Russia was greatly influenced by the Enlightenment. However, as the reigning monarch of Russia she was utterly horrified when the Reign of Terror began in France. She immediately concluded that the Reign of Terror was a direct result of the Enlightenment. In your opinion, what reasons would there be to connect the two?

▶ Resources for Digging Deeper

Choose a few books that look interesting, or find your own.

BEGINNING OF ABOLITION

The Life of Olaudah Equiano

Olaudah Equiano · This is the autobiography of an Ibo prince from Africa who was captured and enslaved, and lived to write about it. Though his writings were a source of controversy, his book had a significant impact on England in the 1700s—during the time William Wilberforce launched his crusade to eradicate the slave trade from the British Empire. **MS+**

The Runaway's Revenge JOHN NEWTON

Dave & Neta Jackson · Have you ever sung the hymn, "Amazing Grace"? It was written by an ex-slave trader named John Newton, and this is his story, told for children. **E+**

THE ENLIGHTENMENT

How Should We Then Live?

Francis A. Schaeffer · Dr. Schaeffer provides a very discerning explanation of the role that the Enlightenment and Rousseau's philosophy had on the French Revolution. I would suggest for older students that this is a "must read." **HS+**

Church History in Plain Language

Bruce Shelley · The author's explanation of the Age of Reason is very helpful in understanding how revolutionary this movement was in world history. **MS+**

The Story of Christianity

Michael Collins & Matthew A. Price · Weaving the threads together between Pietism and Methodism, from England to America, the authors show the development of thought in the Church as well as the Enlightenment—and some of the impact on the world. **UE+**

SEVEN YEARS' WAR

The Old Regime and the Revolution
THE CAMBRIDGE INTRODUCTION TO HISTORY

Trevor Cairns · From Louis XIV to Napoleon, this is a tremendous book for showing what is happening throughout Europe during the Age of Revolution. If you have ever wanted to understand where Prussia came from, why Russia developed the way it did, and what the Enlightenment was about this is the book for you! **UE+**

Frederick the Great
WORLD LEADERS PAST AND PRESENT

Mary Kittredge · Frederick the Great helped to make Prussia a strong nation. This book does an excellent job of showing how this important ruler of the 1700s accomplished what he did. **MS+**

With Frederick the Great
A TALE OF THE SEVEN YEARS' WAR

G. A. Henty · The hero of this story is a young Scottish man who volunteers to serve in Frederick the Great's Prussian army. Not only do you learn how Prussia survived a vastly greater opposing army, but how it managed to win this war, which Winston Churchill coined, "The First World War." **UE+**

The Age of Revolutions VOLUME 3: A
HISTORY OF THE ENGLISH-SPEAKING PEOPLE

Winston Churchill · Learn more about the British perspective on the Seven Years' War, the American Revolution, and the French Revolution in Churchill's own inimitable style. **HS+**

THE GREAT AWAKENING

Revival Fire

Wesley Duewel · Though the pertinent revivals under Edwards, Whitefield, and Wesley are only a part of the book, it will give you a better understanding of the impact true revival makes upon a culture and upon history. One cannot truly understand the American Revolution apart from the Great Awakening, nor can one understand why the French Revolution was so different than the American without seeing the impact of revival. **UE+**

Jonathan Edwards on Revival

Jonathan Edwards · Originally published in 1736, this book includes Edwards's account of the revival of religion in Northampton from 1740 to 1742 (making it an original source document). **MS+**

George Whitefield, Clergyman and Scholar

Susan Martins Miller · An excellent introduction for younger students to the life of one of the most powerful preachers in history, whose ministry ranged to both sides of the Atlantic. **E+**

The Chimney Sweep's Ransom JOHN WESLEY

Dave & Neta Jackson · This story concerns a boy in the 1700s who works in the mines of England. He is helped by John Wesley, one of the significant preachers during the Great Awakening. **E+**

John Wesley

Basil Miller · This is a challenging look at a man used mightily by God during the 1700s revival in England. **MS+**

Susanna Wesley

Charles Ludwig · A biography of the mother of John & Charles Wesley, this book reveals a woman who had tremendous impact upon the Church. **UE+**

Count Zinzendorf

John R. Weinlick · Published by the Moravian Church in America, this is a fascinating account of the leader of the Moravians in the 1700s. **MS+**

AMERICAN REVOLUTION

Author's note: Though there are countless books on the American Revolution, only a selected few—which illuminate the international connections between America, England, and France—are listed below.

George Washington's World

Genevieve Foster · This intriguing, well-written book looks at tumultuous events in the world from 1740 to 1799, during the Age of Revolutions. **UE+**

George Washington:
A PHOTOGRAPHIC STORY OF A LIFE

Lenny Hort · Learn the story of George Washington's life and accomplishments in this biography, which includes photographs, artwork, and fascinating sidebars. **UE+**

Why Not, Lafayette?

Jean Fritz · The Marquis de Lafayette was the French hero of the American Revolution, and a stalwart defender of liberty during the French Revolution. Learn more about him in this fascinating biography. **UE+**

Lafayette: French Freedom Fighter

JoAnn A. Grote · This book is an excellent introduction for younger students to the life of Lafayette. **E+**

CAPTAIN COOK'S VOYAGES

Captain Cook

Rebecca Levene • This Usborne book presents the adventures of the first European to map Newfoundland, circumnavigate New Zealand, sail along the eastern side of Australia, and land in Hawaii. **E+**

You Wouldn't Want to Travel With Captain Cook! A VOYAGE YOU'D RATHER NOT MAKE

Mark Bergin • Discover, in a humorous style, what life would be like for a sailor on Cook's expeditions. **E+**

Captain Cook and the South Pacific HORIZON CARAVEL BOOK

Oliver Warner • This book provides a well-written, play-by-play explanation of Cook's life and travels, which are among the most adventurous tales that history has ever produced! **UE+**

Captain Cook: Far Voyager

Jean Lee Latham • This is the story of James Cook, told in an engaging, well-researched manner. **UE+**

FRENCH REVOLUTION

The French Revolution

Sean Connolly • As a brief introduction to this cataclysmic event, Connolly's book is excellent. It includes short, firsthand accounts of the events including an excerpt from a letter by Marie Antoinette. **UE+**

The Marquis de Lafayette, Bright Sword for Freedom

Hodding Carter • This is the story of Lafayette and his part in the French Revolution—a remarkably different experience in the experiment of liberty than what he went through during the American Revolution. **UE+**

In the Reign of Terror

G. A. Henty • Follow the adventures of a British boy in Paris during the violent throes of the French Revolution. As always, Henty tells a rousing good tale, and teaches us a lot of history in the process! **MS+**

Marie Antoinette

Bernadine Kielty • This is a biography of the tragic queen of France, daughter of Empress Maria Theresa of Austria. Marie Antoinette's execution during the French Revolution shocked the world. **UE+**

RUSSIA

Catherine: The Great Journey

Kristiana Gregory • Written as fictional entries in a diary, this book allows the reader a glimpse into the difficult and demanding challenge of leaving one's entire world behind in order to become Empress of Russia. **UE+**

Catherine the Great

Katharine Scherman • Tthis biography tells the fascinating story of one of the most powerful women in world history—the Empress of Russia. **E+**

HISTORICAL FICTION

A Tale of Two Cities

Charles Dickens • The story takes place during the Reign of Terror in France, and is a classic of literature. Dickens captures the mood of this time period in France, as well as giving us the story of sacrificial love. **MS+**

The Scarlet Pimpernel

Baroness Orczy • This tale from the French Revolution is a fascinating read—a story of courage, wit, and love. **MS+**

Robinson Crusoe

Daniel Defoe • This classic is about the true adventures of a man by the name of Alexander Selkirk. It was written during the time frame of this Unit. Not only is it a rousing adventure story, it is also a wonderful picture of Christian discipleship. Highly recommended! **MS+**

What books did you like best?

_____

_____

_____

_____

_____

The Internet also contains a wealth of information about Revivals and Revolutions.

What sites were the most helpful?

_____

_____

_____

_____

For more books, use these Dewey Decimal numbers in your library:

The Enlightenment: #944

The Seven Years' War: #940

The Great Awakening: #277

Beginning of Abolition: #326

The American Revolution: #973

The French Revolution: #944

Captain Cook: #910

Russia in the 1700s: #947

▶ # Student Self-Evaluation UNIT 9, PHASE 1

Dates and hours:_____

Key Concepts

Rephrase the five Key Concepts of this Unit and confirm your understanding of each:

•   The Enlightenment:

   _____

•   The Great Awakening & beginning of abolition:

   _____

•   The Seven Years' War:

   _____

•   Revolutions in France & America:

   _____

•   Cook's voyages:

   _____

Tools for Self-Evaualation

Evaluate your personal participation in the discussions of this Phase. Bearing in mind that a good participant in a discussion is not always the most vocal participant, ask yourself these questions: Were you an active participant? Did you ask perceptive questions? Were you willing to listen to other participants of the discussion and draw out their opinions? Record your observations and how you would like to improve your participation in the future:

   _____

   _____

Every time period is too complex to be understood in one Phase of study. Evaluate your current knowledge of Revivals & Revolutions. What have you focused on so far? What are your weakest areas of knowledge?

   _____

   _____

Based on the evaluation of this introduction, project ahead what you would like to study more of in the following Phases:

   _____

   _____

Phase 2

▶ Research & Reporting

Explore one or more of these areas to discover something significant!

The 1700s

Research and report on the major events and significant historical figures of the 1700s touching on any of these areas: politics, religion, art, literature, music, science, or economics.

The Rise of Prussia

Study Prussia's history as it rises to a world power, from Frederick I to Frederick William III, who was defeated by Napoleon.

The Enlightenment

Research and report on this shift in thinking, which is also described as the Age of Reason. When and why did it begin? Describe the lives and influence of Diderot and of Voltaire. What countries were significantly impacted by Enlightenment thinking?

The Great Awakening

Discover more about this major revival of the 1700s, which had a powerful effect upon England, Wales, Scotland, and America. Be sure to include information on the major personalities such as Jonathan Edwards, George Whitefield, John Wesley, and Charles Wesley.

Captain Cook

Learn more about Captain James Cook and his epic travels. Describe his time in Canada, the reasons for and route of his first voyage, his second voyage, and his third voyage. What were the attitudes of the native people he met on his journeys?

The Seven Years' War/The French & Indian War

How were these two wars connected? What issues were at stake? What countries did they involve? What were the results (both short term and long term)? Why could this conceivably be termed the First World War?

The Steam Engine

In 1775 James Watt perfected the invention of the steam engine. Research and report on how a steam engine works, and what applications it was used for in the 1700s. How did it change the world?

Spinning Jenny

Discover what a spinning jenny can do. How did it impact the production of fabric? How did this impact the world—economically, materially, politically, socially?

Hot-Air Balloons

Research and report on the development of hot-air balloons. When were they first successfully used? Who developed this technology? Who used hot-air balloons? How far did they go? How reliable were they?

The Moravians

Learn about Count von Zinzendorf and the revival among the diverse people living on his property, which began in 1727. What were conditions like before the revival? What were some of the results of the revival? What countries were impacted by the Moravians?

The American Revolution

Research and report on the events leading up to the American Revolution, both in England and in the colonies. Be sure to include issues of religion, politics, economics, the military, as well as the major personalities involved on both sides of the Atlantic such as George III, George Washington, and Benjamin Franklin. What were the results of this revolt?

The French Revolution

Investigate the French Revolution, examining the conditions in France prior to the revolution—including the country's involvement in the American Revolution. What were the issues of the day in France? Consider philosophy, religion, politics, economics, the military, as well as the major personalities involved on both sides of the issue such as Louis XVI, Marie Antoinette, and Lafayette.

Compare & Contrast

Chart the step by step changes in America from colonies to an independent nation, including the dates of each significant event. Also chart the step by step changes in France as it moved from a monarchy to a dictatorship, including the dates of each significant event. Now compare the two. What are the similarities? What are the differences?

The Beginning of Abolition

Research and report on the state of slavery and the slave trade during the 1700s, and on the beginning stages of the Abolitionist movement in England. Some of the key figures to study are John Newton, William Wilberforce, Olaudah Equiano, Granville Sharp, James Stephens, and Thomas Clarkson, along with the unyielding influence of the many Quakers in England.

Phillis Wheatley

Research and report on the first published African-American woman poet, Phillis Wheatley, who wrote, among other things, a eulogy for George Whitefield and several poems honoring George Washington. Her talent was so immense that many doubted that an African slave could have produced them.

Sunday Schools

Learn more about the beginning of Sunday schools, and Robert Raikes, the one who initiated this movement. What was the purpose of these schools? For whom were they intended? What controversy surrounded Sunday schools in the late 1700s?

Catherine the Great

Learn more about this powerful empress. What was her country of origin and what were her childhood religious beliefs? Why and when did she convert to Orthodoxy? How did she become sole ruler of Russia? What were the internal policies of Russia during her reign? What were the foreign policies during her reign? What kind of impact did Catherine the Great have on Russia, both short and long term?

Wolfgang Amadeus Mozart

Discover the life and works of one of the greatest musical geniuses of all time. When did he begin composing? How did he receive his training? For whom did he perform as a child? How did he support himself as an adult? How many pieces of music did he compose? How long did it take him to compose and write out a piece of music?

▶ Brain Stretchers

The Philosopher King & Voltaire

Discover the connection between Frederick the Great and Voltaire. How did Voltaire's Enlightenment thinking affect Frederick? How did Voltaire treat him over the course of his life? Was this treatment justifiable and acceptable under a humanist philosophy?

The English Succession

Consider the strife caused by the death of Queen Anne for those who had to determine the succession for the throne of England. Research and report on how the English prevented the succession of any more Catholic sovereigns. Ask these questions: Who was James Stuart? Who supported him? Why? Who was Charles Edward? Who supported him? Why? Who was George of Hanover? Who supported him? Why? What was the objection some English people had to George?

The Enlightenment contrasted with Christianity

Compare and contrast the views of the Enlightenment with biblical Christianity. How would a Christian biblically counter the arguments of an Enlightenment thinker such as Voltaire? (Hint: Francis Schaeffer's *How Should We Then Live?* will help you tremendously.)

Create Your Own Research Topic

_____

_____

_____

_____

▶ Timeline

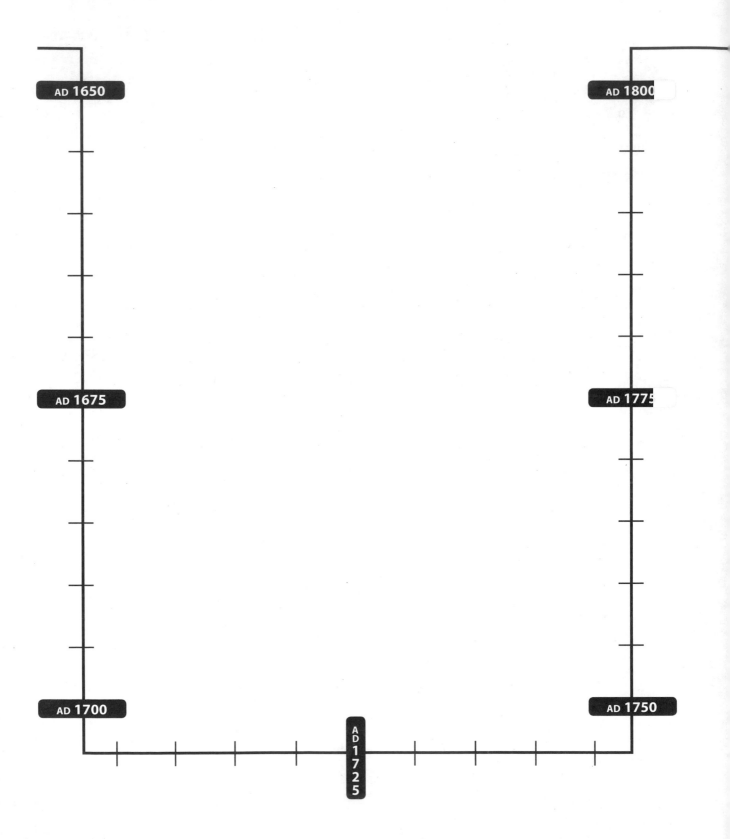

AD 1650

AD 1675

AD 1700

AD 1725

AD 1750

AD 1775

AD 1800

Consider this for your timeline

The Age of Revolutions, which turned the world and many monarchies upside down, began in the 1700s. The steam engine and the spinning jenny, invented during the 1700s, eventually revolutionized economics, trade, families, and society. In the 1700s the Great Awakening showed the power of God to transform people and nations while the Enlightenment praised the power of man's reason. This is a pivotal century!

Key Events

The Enlightenment

The Great Awakening

The Seven Years' War

The American Revolution

The French Revolution

Captain Cook's Journeys

Committee for the Abolition of the Slave Trade

James Watt's Steam Engine

Invention of the Spinning Jenny

CONSIDER:

There are many words which Christians use that nonbelievers do not understand. This is a barrier to communication. On the other hand, the appropriate word can also help us to express exactly what we mean. To solve this dilemma, we need to be able to define our terms—it will allow us to explain clearly and concisely what we mean. Here are a few terms specifically connected to God's work in the Church during times of spiritual awakening:

- revival
- repentance
- renewal
- conversion
- redemption
- transformation
- supernatural
- awesome
- manifestation
- reverential
- outpouring
- awakened

▶ # Words to Watch

Remember—The easiest way to learn a subject is to master its terms:

awakening	enlightenment	reason	reconstruct
Lex Rex	unalienable	liberty	equality
fraternity	tyranny	itinerant	declaration
Bastille	independence	Methodist	abolition

Other words you need to look up:

_____

_____

_____

_____

_____

_____

_____

▶ **Student Self-Evaluation** UNIT 9, PHASE 2

Dates and hours:_____

Research Project

- Summarize your research question:

  _____

  _____

- List your most useful sources by author, title and page number or URL where applicable (continue list in margin if necessary):

  _____

  _____

  _____

- Now take a moment to evaluate the sources you just listed. Do they provide a balanced view of your research question? Should you have sought an additional opinion? Are your sources credible (if you found them on your own)? Record your observations:

  _____

  _____

- Evaluate your research project in its final presentation. What are its strengths? If you had time to revisit this project, what would you change? Consider giving yourself a letter grade based on your project's merits and weaknesses.

  _____

  _____

Letter grade _____

You have just completed an area of specific research in the time of Revivials & Revolutions. Now what would you like to explore in the upcoming Phases? Set some objectives for yourself:

_____

_____

_____

Phase 3

▶ Maps & Mapping

Physical Terrain

» Locate the areas of England, Scotland, Wales, and the eastern coast of the United States. Label these "Great Awakening."

» Locate the territory of New France (in Canada), which was lost to the British at the end of the French and Indian War: from Newfoundland to Lake Superior. Label this to show that, during the 1700s, this vast area at first was claimed by France but was then formally ceded to England, which means it was given to England in a treaty.

» Locate the 1783 boundaries of the newly formed United States of America: the northern boundary being Canada, the eastern boundary being the Atlantic, the southern boundary being Spanish Florida, and the western boundary being the Mississippi river. Label this area "United States."

» Locate and label New Zealand, Australia, and the Sandwich islands (Hawaii), all places to which Captain Cook sailed on his journeys.

Geopolitical

» Locate and label the areas in North America where the French and Indian War was fought.

» Locate and label the area in which the Seven Years' War was fought, coloring Prussia and its allies one color and France, Austria, Russia, and Sweden a second color. At the end of the war, was Prussia any larger or smaller than when it started?

» Draw the journeys of George Whitefield on the map. You might want to indicate how many times, in order to preach the gospel, he crossed the Atlantic. Also, indicate on the map the number of miles John Wesley traveled to preach the gospel in Great Britain.

» Draw lines to indicate and label the three Pacific voyages of Captain Cook. How do the terrain and climate of the lands he saw in the Pacific differ from his homeland?

Explore

» *Christian Outreach:* What is the status of evangelical outreach today in modern Europe? What opportunities and what difficulties face those who share the gospel in these areas?

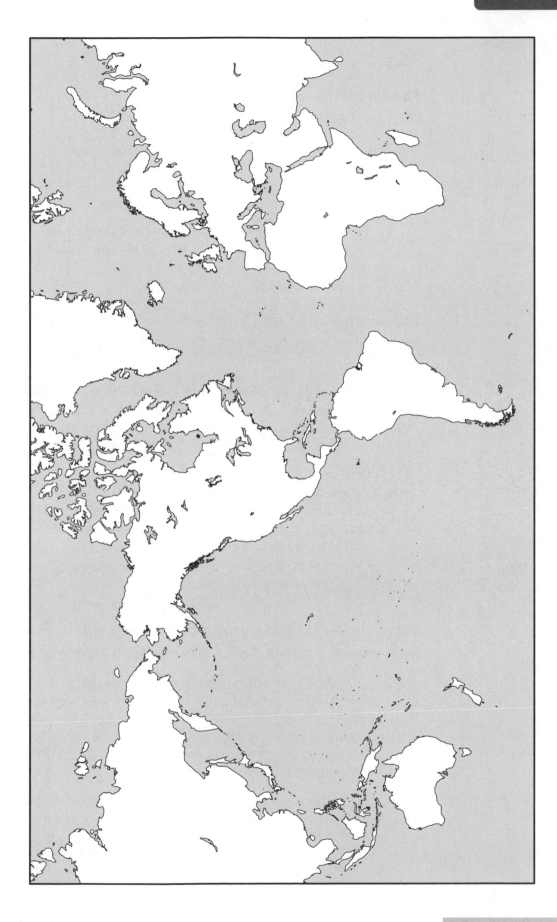

▶ Art Appreciation

The Swing by Jean Fragonard, 1766
Wallace Collection, London

Jean Fragonard's paintings are the epitome of the Rococo style, the style of art popular among the aristocracy just prior to the French Revolution. It is sobering to consider that his patrons were beheaded during the Reign of Terror and he died in obscure poverty.

» Locate a photo of this painting. How would you describe the scene? Why do you think this style of painting might have appealed to the French aristocracy in the court of Louis XVI and Marie Antoinette?

The Embarkation for Cythera
by Antoine Watteau, 1717; Louvre Museum, France

Watteau was unique among all the painters of France in that he was admitted to the prestigious Academy of France without the benefit of friends or fortune—simply on the basis of his talent! In fact, the Academy created a new category specifically for Watteau's paintings: fête galantes (meaning festivals attended by gorgeously-attired gentlemen and ladies in parklike settings).

» Locate a photo of this painting. Watteau is considered to be years ahead of his time in the use of color and technique. How would you contrast his painting with previous artists you have studied? How would you describe this painting?

▶ Architecture

Salon de la Princesse, Hôtel de Soubise, Paris, France
by Germain Boffrand & Charles-Joseph Natoire, 1732

The Rococo style of architecture developed in France about 1720, and spread to many other European countries during the next several years. It was light and delicate, elaborate in its decorations and ornamentation. The emphasis was on overall brightness, lively colors, and asymmetrical decorative forms. In this amazing example of Rococo architecture, one can not tell where the walls end and the ceiling begins!

» Locate photos of the Salon de la Princesse. Notice the windows and mirrors in the room. What effect do you think the mirrors might have had on people walking into the room? How would you describe this room? What colors are used? In what ways does this room reflect a lighthearted and frivolous approach to architecture?

▶ Arts in Action

Let your artistic juices flow!

Mirror

» Create a rococo-style mirror. You will need cardboard, heavy duty aluminum foil, exotic macaroni-style pasta, glue gun, gold and silver paint. Make an oval or other interesting shape on the cardboard. Cut it out. Glue the foil onto the cardboard, wrapping the edges around the back. Find the most interesting macaroni-style pasta at your local grocery store (you might want several different styles). Using a hot glue-gun, glue the pasta around the edge of the "mirror." Once it is dry, paint the pasta with gold and/or silver paint.

▶ Science

Carolus Linnaeus was the scientist in the 1700s who organized plants and animals into their various "kinds," or classifications. According to Henry Morris, in the book *Men of Science, Men of God*, Linnaeus wanted to "delineate the original Genesis kinds. He attempted, in fact, to equate his 'species' category with the 'kind,' believing that variations could occur within the kind, but not from one kind to another kind." (See Genesis 1:11–12, 21–25)

Taxonomy

» Learn more about the classification of animals, which is done by taxonomists. Find out what these classification terms mean: Kingdom, Phylum, Class, Order, Family, Genus, Species. Can you classify a dog in all of these categories? A horse? An earthworm? A crocodile? What is baraminology?

James Watt, the man who perfected the invention of the steam engine in the 1700s, changed the way we do business forever. The machinery powered by steam eventually was used to spin yarn and weave fabric much faster than human workers could. It also powered boats which could move quickly through the water, regardless of the wind. It was the beginning of a different kind of revolution—the Industrial Revolution.

Physics

» Try the amazing experiment of building a steam-powered boat using candle power to create the steam! Online, search for "pop-pop boats" for directions. In the library, look for the *Make It Work!—Machines* book, which has great directions for making a steam-powered balsa boat. (This was a very popular project for Cub Scouts in the mid-1900s!)

▶ Music

There was a veritable explosion of hymn writing which occurred in the 1700s and continues to this day. The Great Awakening on the Continent and in the American colonies produced prolific hymn writers, as well as powerful preachers. Charles Wesley and Isaac Watts are perhaps the best known, though there are many others from this time period.

Discover

Come, We That Love the Lord

Isaac Watts (1664–1748) • Isaac Watts is known as the "Father of English Hymnody." Rather than using only the Psalms of David and the liturgy of the Church, he wrote songs of human composure. He believed that our songs were a human offering of praise to God, so should therefore be composed in our own words.

Jesus, Lover of My Soul

Charles Wesley (1707–1788) • Charles Wesley was called the "sweet singer" of Methodism. He worked with his brother John in the revival in England traveling thousands of miles on horseback. He left us more than 7,000 hymns with which to worship God!

Jesus, Thy Blood and Righteousness

Count von Zinzendorf (1700–1760) • Zinzendorf became the head of the newly reformed Moravian Church, which had its roots in the followers of Jan Hus in the 1400s. He wrote more than 2,000 hymns, though few are still in use today. Fascinatingly, he believed that people should memorize the hymns they sang in order to truly sing it from the heart.

Amazing Grace

John Newton (1725–1807) • This former slave ship owner was gloriously converted, and, through his personal testimony in song, generations since have been blessed.

Listen

All Glory, Laud, & Honor MUSIC CD

Come, We That Love the Lord Isaac Watts
Jesus, Lover of My Soul Charles Wesley
Jesus, Thy Blood and Righteousness Count von Zinzendorf
Amazing Grace John Newton

The most prominent baroque composers in the early 1700s were Johann Sebastian Bach and George Frederick Handel. The baroque style of music, with its ornamentations, improvisations, and focus on the performer, however, gave way to the classical style of music in the 1750s. Classical music solidified the forms in music (such as the sonata, the symphonic form, the concerto), and required the composers to stay strictly within these forms—no improvisation or ornamentation! The main classical composers are Franz Joseph Haydn and Wolfgang Amadeus Mozart. Ludwig von Beethoven's first five symphonies were also written as classical compositions. After this, Beethoven moved toward the style known as "romance" music.

Discover

Toccata and Fugue in D Minor

J. S. Bach (1685–1750) • Bach would sometimes use familiar hymn tunes in his musical compositions. As a true son of the Reformation in Germany, Bach sought above all else to glorify God through his music. Toccata means "to touch," indicating the skill required of the performer on the instrument. Listen to Bach's Toccata and Fugue in D Minor. Why do you think it warrants the name "toccata"?

Messiah

George Frederich Handel (1685–1759) • Handel's glorious masterpiece, *Messiah*, is the most famous oratorio ever written. It was composed in England during the early years of the Great Awakening. Listen to it. In what ways does the music emphasize and clarify the words of Scripture?

Surprise Symphony No. 94

Franz Joseph Haydn (1732–1809) • Audiences of the time were notorious for losing interest in the music, so "Papa" Haydn planned a surprise for them in this famous piece of music. Listen and see if you, too, can discover something that might startle an audience awake!

Eine Kleine Nachtmusik

Wolfgang Amadeus Mozart (1756–1791) • Mozart is one of the world's great musical geniuses, and, uniquely in history, he was able to fluently compose in all of the different musical genres of his time. *Eine Kleine Nachtmusik* ("a little night music") is, perhaps, one of the most familiar pieces he composed. Listen and enjoy. How would you describe this music?

▶ Cooking

From the French came not only Rococo art, but also the king of chocolate treats: Chocolate Truffles!

Chocolate Truffles

4 oz. semisweet chocolate, chopped   2 tbsp whipping cream
2 tbsp ground chocolate or unsweetened cocoa

Place semisweet chocolate and cream in a small pan over low heat (if heat is too high, chocolate will separate). Heat, stirring constantly, until chocolate is melted and well blended with cream. Pour into a small bowl; cover and refrigerate just until mixture is firm enough to hold its shape (about 40 minutes). Meanwhile, spread ground chocolate on a small plate. Using your fingers, quickly shape chocolate-cream mixture into balls, using about 1 tsp. per ball. As each truffle is shaped, roll it in ground chocolate until completely coated. Arrange in a single layer in a shallow container; cover and refrigerate for up to 2 weeks. Let stand at room temperature for 5 to 10 minutes before serving. Makes about one dozen. *C'est merveilleux!*

▶ Student Self-Evaluation UNIT 9, PHASE 3

Dates and hours:_____

Evaluate your projects

- List which of the activities listed in this Phase you did:

  _____

  _____

- Rate your enthusiasm _____

  Explain: _____

  _____

- Rate the precision of your approach_____

  Explain: _____

  _____

- Rate your effort towards the completion of the project _____

  Explain: _____

  _____

- Ask yourself what worked and what did not. What would you do differently in the future, and what would you repeat?

  _____

  _____

- How specifically did these hands-on activities enhance your knowledge of Revivals & Revolutions? What made them worthwhile?

  _____

  _____

- In the first three Phases of this Unit, what aspect of the time period has most captured your imagination? What would you like to creatively pursue to conclude your study?

  _____

  _____

Phase 4

▶ In Your Own Way...

We have seen God move in the Great Awakening, Prussians come to the forefront of Europe in the Seven Years' War, Americans declare independence from England, France give birth to an entirely different kind of revolution, beginnings of the Industrial Revolution, and the epic voyages of Captain Cook. Now, choose a selection of these activities, or create your own, which will best express what you have learned from this Unit.

LINGUISTICS

Journalism

As a staff reporter for the *Anglican Angle*, you have been assigned to interview John Wesley about his outdoor preaching to hooligans. Be sure to discover the reasons for his unusual behavior, especially of preaching on his father's tombstone!

The *Soldiers Illustrated* has asked you to write a feature story on the Prussian Army and its recent rise to stardom in the European theater of operations. What makes these soldiers so good? What kind of training and discipline do they have? Can they share any secrets of soldiering with the rest of the world?

You are the on-the-spot reporter assigned to Russia. News has just leaked about the Reign of Terror in France, and Empress Catherine is unraveling right before your eyes. Do your best to capture on paper the impressions you have of her opinion about this horror, and about its relation to the Enlightenment.

Playing with Words

Create a crossword puzzle with words of the revolutions and revivals.

Finish this poem:

Oh, Cook, now he was a captain,
Adventurous as any might be...

Prose

Write a book for children about George Whitefield, the international evangelist of the Great Awakening. There are so many fascinating stories associated with his life and ministry, including the power of his voice to be heard by up to 30,000 people! Be sure to include the details that would make this book captivating to read.

Write an essay showing the difference between the "rights of man" under the Declaration of Independence and under the French Revolution.

ART

Painting/Drawing

Paint a scene from Captain Cook's travels in the South Pacific. Be sure to show the contrast between the British Navy and the Pacific islanders.

Create a pictorial display of the American Revolution. You might choose to do this as a collage, a series of drawings, or whatever will give the desired effect.

Cartooning

Draw a political cartoon showing the storming of the Bastille on July 14, 1789. Be sure to include the slogan, "Liberty, Equality, Fraternity."

Graphic Design

Thomas Clarkson, an early abolitionist in England, joined forces with William Wilberforce and others in 1787 to form a society for the abolition of the slave trade in the British Empire. Create for this society a poster which will encourage people to join them in their struggle.

Many historians see the direct connection between the Enlightenment writings of Voltaire and Rousseau with the French Revolution and the reign of Terror. With this in mind, create a T-shirt logo for the French clergy which proclaims, "I survived the Enlightenment!"

MUSIC

Performance Practice

With your teacher's help, select an appropriate piece of music which expresses some particular aspect studied in this unit, whether it comes from the music of the Great Awakening, the music of the revolutions, or a piece of classical music. Prepare and perform the piece for an audience. Communicate with your audience the reason for your selection either in the program notes or in a short speech.

Composition

Compose a hymn of revival in the style of Charles Wesley or Isaac Watts. You may choose to write new music for one of their hymn texts, or create an entirely new hymn with words and music.

DRAMA

Comedy

Write and perform a comedic skit of the first Sunday School for the children of Gloucester, England. Remember, they have been running wild in the streets on Sundays before this!

Puppetry

With puppets, show the amazing life story of Lafayette. Remember that he was a hero of both the American and French revolutions.

Drama

Create the dramatic scene in May, 1789, when the French Estates-General met for the first time since 1614. This was what eventually toppled the "*ancien régime.*" Feel free to condense the events in order to present this drama.

Prop Needs

_____

_____

Costume Ideas

_____

_____

Role/Player

_____

_____

Set Suggestions

_____

_____

MOVEMENT

Pantomime

Pantomime the historic scene of the terrible storm at sea, the Moravians' response, and the impression it made upon the terrified Anglican missionary, John Wesley.

Dance

Choreograph a dance to show the inspiring and bittersweet life of Phillis Wheatley, the first African-American woman poet.

Miniature Action

Create a bird's-eye view of the war on all fronts faced by Frederick the Great of Prussia in 1757–58. Show the terrain involved, the various armies opposing Frederick (representing how vastly outnumbered he was), as well as his allies and his enemies.

CONCEPTUAL DESIGN

1700s Revival Tour Book

Design a guide to all of the best Great Awakening spots in Europe and America. Armchair travelers will be interested to know the personalities of the revivalists in each place, transportation and accommodation, sites of interest (historically and scientifically), and the best times to visit.

CREATE YOUR OWN EXPRESSION

_____

_____

_____

_____

▶ Student Self-Evaluation UNIT 9, PHASE 4

Dates and hours:_____

Evaluate your projects

• What creative project did you choose:

_____

• What did you expect from your project, and how does the final project compare to your initial expectations?

_____

• What do you like about your project? What would you change?

_____

In Conclusion

Revisit the five Key Concepts from the beginning of this Unit. Explain how your understanding of and appreciation for each has grown over the course of your study.

• _____

_____

• _____

_____

• _____

_____

• _____

_____

• _____

_____

Record your concluding thoughts on Revivals & Revolutions:

_____

_____

_____

About the Author

Diana Waring has been fascinated by history since she was old enough to discover that World War II had ended ten years prior to her birth in Germany. As a child, she always wanted to understand the chronological march of kings, the connection between momentous events—especially wars—and the international tapestry of fascinating people throughout the ages. The first glimmers of understanding came in a rapid-fire African history course at college, but the full explosion of light dawned when she began teaching world history side by side with the Bible to her three children. It was at that point, with the research required to answer their innumerable questions, that all the pieces began to fall in place. The contagious excitement of discovery led to her speaking and writing about history.

While writing this book, Mrs. Waring lived in a small town in the Black Hills of South Dakota with her husband and dog. She now resides in a small town in Washinton state, when she is not visiting her adult children or traveling around the world to educate teachers and parents on the wonders of learning.